A Practical Guide to

Depreciation under Companies Act, 2013

A Practical Guide to

Depreciation under Companies Act, 2013

CA (Dr) Sanjeev Singhal

CA R. Sankaraiah

Assisted by
Rachita Garg & Aditi Gupta

BLOOMSBURY
NEW DELHI • LONDON • OXFORD • NEW YORK • SYDNEY

First published in India 2017

ISBN 9789386349545

10 9 8 7 6 5 4 3 2 1

Bloomsbury Publishing India Pvt. Ltd
DDA Complex, LSC Building No.4
Second Floor, Pocket C–6 & 7, Vasant Kunj
New Delhi 110070
www.bloomsbury.com

Printed and bound in India by Rajkamal Electric Press, Kundli

With the belssings of
Shri Khatu Shyam Baba and Om Muruga

Dedicated to

Our fathers

Late Sh. M. L. Singhal & Late M Rajagopal Naidu

About the authors

CA (Dr) Sanjeev Singhal

- Sanjeev Singhal did his graduation from Shri Ram College of Commerce and post graduation from Delhi School of Economics. He is a fellow member of ICAI. He has done his PhD in International Finance from Faculty of Management Studies (Delhi).
- He has received the following prestigious awards:
  - Prof. Jai Naraian Vaish Gold Medal at the graduation level for being the topper in B Com (Hons) in the Delhi University
  - Prof. AB Ghosh prize at the post-graduation level for being the topper in Economics Group papers
  - CA Professional Achiever Award 2014 (by ICAI) for excellent contribution to the manufacturing sector and the profession
  - NIRC of ICAI best faculty award
- He has represented India at the World Accounting forum held at Dubai and was invited to address at the Asian Institute of Technology Bangkok. Besides, he was also invited by Ministry of Finance, Bhutan to deliver lecture on IFRS. He has also contributed extensively to the professional development on IFRS in Nepal in the programs organized by Accounting Standards Board of Nepal.
- He has conducted MDPs for Corporate Executives, addressed hundreds of national & international seminars on Accounting Standards, IPSAS, IFRS, XBRL, Companies Act etc organised for leading corporate and professional bodies such as ICAI, ICSI, ICWAI, CII, ASSOCHAM, ONGC, HPCL, BHEL, GAIL, NTPC, HPCL, NHPC etc in India and abroad. He is a renowned trainer and an expert in accounting standards and IFRS.
- He represented CII and FICCI in the interaction with IASB.
- He has published 15 books and over 40 articles on accounting standards, IFRS, Companies Act, etc. His articles have been published in leading print and online journals.
- He has also been part of debate on various issues on Doordarshan, CNN IBN etc. He has also done several live programs on accounting standards at Gyan Darshan Channel for members and students of ICAI.
- He has been a co-opted member/special invitee on the following:
  - Member, NACAS (National Advisory Committee on Accounting Standards) constituted by MCA (Ministry of Corporate Affairs) under the Companies Act, 2013
  - CII representative on Accounting Standards Board of ICAI
  - Member, CII, National Financial Reporting Committee
  - CII representative on Cost Accounting Standards Board
  - Chairman-CII Task Force on Accounting and Auditing Standards
  - Co-opted member/ special invitee on the Accounting Standards Board of ICAI
  - Co-opted member/special invitee on the IFRS implementation Committee of ICAI

  - Special invitee, Research Committee, ICAI for CSR Expenditure
  - CII representative on Auditing and Assurance Standards Board of ICAI
- Dr Singhal has contributed extensively for members and students related activities at ICAI. He has contributed study material for ICAI. He has been the technical co-ordinator for ICAI for certificate course on IFRS at Delhi.
- He has worked as Vice President, Finance & Head, Centre of Excellence for Accounting and Management Assurance function at Jubilant Life Sciences. He has previously worked with Fortis Healthcare, Cyber Media and Religare Enterprises handling various finance function such as Treasury, Financial Reporting, Budgeting, MIS, Financial Planning, Taxation, Investor relations, etc. Currently, he is serving the profession in the field of auditing and accounting advisory.

CA R. Sankaraiah

CA R. Sankaraiah is a Science Graduate and a Fellow Member of ICAI. Presently, he is the Executive Director - Finance, Jubilant Life Sciences Ltd and also the Group Finance Director, Jubilant Bhartia Group.

He is a special invitee on NACAS and has been a member of IFRS Advisory Council of IASB for two terms, SEBI Committee on Disclosures and Accounting Standards (SCODA), CII National Council on Corporate Governance & Regulatory Affairs and CII National Committee on Financial Reporting. He is a member of the CFO working group formed by MCA to look into the issues related to Convergence of IGAAP with IFRS and was also a member of the Coalition on International Taxation, in India. He has also been a Government Nominee on the Central Council of ICSI.

He has extensive experience in the Development and Implementation of Business Strategies, Mergers & Acquisitions, Corporate Planning, Banking and Finance, Forex Management, Direct & Indirect Taxation, Legal, Secretarial and other expertise which has been acquired over 30 years of his career.

He has been conferred with several prestigious awards such as:

- The India CFO Award 2007- Excellence in Finance (Large Corporate) in 2008 by IMA;
- Best performing CFO in the Pharma Sector in 2009 by CNBC TV 18;
- Best CFO (FMCG, Health and Retail Sector), in 2010 by Institute of Chartered Accountants of India; and
- Best CFO in Pharma & Healthcare space in 2011 all Asia Executive Team Survey by Institutional investor;
- Most Influential CFO Award in 2016.

Mr Sankaraiah is a prominent speaker at various professional seminars related to IFRS, Taxation, Mergers & Acquisition, Financial Instruments, etc. He has co-authored several books with Dr Sanjeev Singhal on Accounting Standards, XBRL, Companies Act and several other financial issues. He has also been part of debates on various topics on leading TV channels.

Preface

The Financial reporting landscape in India has been changing very fast in the last few years. Companies Act, 2013, Ind AS converged with IFRS and revision in the accounting standards for companies not covered by Ind AS road map, has been keeping the finance professionals busy all the times.

Since the notification of the Schedule II to the Companies Act,2013, many developments have taken place at frequent intervals, in matters relating to depreciation, such as component accounting, estimation of useful lives, changes in transitional provisions, issuance of AS 10 (revised) on "property, plant and equipment" effective from the current financial year 2016-17. These frequent and far reaching changes have resulted in a lot of queries being raised by professionals. While we have been addressing these queries in a number of seminars, we thought it would be prudent to incorporate the same in our book and, hence, we decided to come out with the revised edition of our book.

To help decrypt the critical nuances and effects of the provisions relating to depreciation under the Companies Act, 2013 and AS 10 (Revised), we have crystallised them into 12 Chapters. We have also incorporated various matters arising from the issuance of AS 10 (Revised) and the guidance given by ICAI in its Guidance Note on Accounting for Depreciation in companies in the context of Schedule II to the Companies Act, 2013. We have also incorporated a large number of practical issues in a separate chapter, besides discussing other relevant practical issues at appropriate places.

The book also has useful annexures that contains the text of Schedule II to the Companies Act, 2013 along with various amendments that have taken place from time to time, text of AS 10 (revised), text of Ind AS 16 etc.

We duly acknowledge the use of all sources be it the Government notifications, ICAI publications or the annual reports of various companies and do not claim copyright on the material taken from those sources.

We acknowledge the guidance of our mentors CA Amarjit Chopra, Dr Girish Ahuja, Dr Ravi Gupta, our teachers and guide. We are also thankful to all our professional colleagues and friends for their continued support.

We admire the support of our family members, Mrs Sandhya Singhal, Mrs Chitra Sankaraiah and the children Viraj and Madhav Singhal and Samyukhta and Sangamitra Sankaraiah who constantly motivate us to contribute to our profession.

We would be failing in our duty if we do not thank our publishers Bloomsbury India particularly our dear friend Toby Thomas and the editor of the book Nikita Jain, for giving us an opportunity to work with their publication house and enable the present work to see the light of the day in such a quick time.

We thank all our readers who have given us the suggestions for improvement in the past. We would urge all our readers to keep writing to us. Suggestions and criticism from all readers would be highly appreciated and acknowledged.

Christmas
December 25, 2016

CA (Dr) Sanjeev Singhal & CA R. Sankaraiah
email us at:
sanjeevsinghalca1997@gmail.com
sankaraiah@jubl.com

Contents at a glance

Table of contents

Chapter 1

Basic principles governing depreciation

This chapter discusses the basic principles governing depreciation. The discussion is based on Schedule II to the Companies Act, 2013, AS 10 relating to 'Property, Plant and Equipment'. We have also discussed the basic principles governing depreciation as per Ind AS 16 on 'Property, Plant and Equipment'.

1.1 WHAT IS DEPRECIATION?

Depreciation is a measure of the wearing out, consumption or other loss of value of a depreciable asset arising from use, effluxion of time or obsolescence through technology and market changes. Depreciation is allocated so as to charge a fair proportion of the depreciable amount in each accounting period during the expected useful life of the asset. Depreciation in common parlance includes amortisation of assets whose useful life is predetermined.

Para 1 of Part A to Schedule II of the Companies Act, 2013 on *'useful lives to compute depreciation'* defines depreciation as the 'systematic allocation of the depreciable amount of an asset over its useful life'.

As per Ind AS 16 on 'Property, Plant and Equipment', depreciation is the systematic allocation of the depreciable amount of an asset over its useful life.

Meaning given in AS 10 (Revised) on 'Property, Plant and Equipment' is similar to Ind AS 16.

Essentially, the definition under Accounting Standard 10 on 'Property, Plant and Equipment, Ind AS 16 on 'Property, Plant and Equipment' and the Companies Act, 2013 are similar.

1.2 WHAT ARE DEPRECIABLE ASSETS?

'Depreciable assets' are items of property, plant and equipment that are subject to depreciation, i.e., the assets which:

(1) are expected to be used during more than one accounting period;

(2) have a limited useful life; and

(3) are held by an enterprise for use in the production or supply of goods and services, for rental to others, or for administrative purposes and not for the purpose of sale in the ordinary course of business.

1.3 WHY DEPRECIATION NEEDS TO BE PROVIDED?

Fixed assets like building, plant, furniture, etc, lose the value over a period of time due to usage and normal wear and tear. Thus, depreciation needs to be provided so as to:

- ensure allocation of original cost of a fixed asset over its useful life;
- ascertaining the true cost of operations;
- providing current valuation of fixed assets in the balance sheet.

1.4 ASSETS ON WHICH AN ENTERPRISE NEEDS TO PROVIDE DEPRECIATION

Depreciation is to be charged only on assets that are subject to depreciation, eg, plant and machinery, furniture and fixtures, vehicles, etc. On the other hand, there are certain assets on which depreciation is not usually required to be provided, eg, land (unless it has a limited useful life).

1.5 ACCOUNTING FOR DEPRECIATION

1.5.1 Key terms

Before we discuss accounting for depreciation, let us discuss some of the key terms that will be used throughout this guide.

(i) **Property, plant and equipment:** Property, plant and equipment are tangible items that:

(a) are held for use in the production or supply of goods or services, for rental to others, or for administrative purposes; and

(b) are expected to be used during more than a period of twelve months. *(Para 6 of AS 10 (Revised), 'Property, Plant and Equipment')*

Meaning given in Ind AS 16 is similar to AS 10 (Revised).

(ii) **Intangible assets:** An intangible asset is an identifiable non-monetary asset, without physical substance, held for use in the production or supply of goods or services, for rental to others, or for administrative purposes. (*Para 6.1 of AS 26, 'Intangible Assets'*)

(iii) **Cost:** Cost is the amount of cash or cash equivalents paid or the fair value of the other consideration given to acquire an asset at the time of its acquisition or construction or, where applicable, the amount attributed to that asset when initially recognised in accordance with the specific requirements of other Accounting Standards. *(Para 6 of AS 10 (Revised) 'Property, Plant and Equipment')*

Meaning given in AS 10 (Revised) on 'Property, Plant and Equipment' is similar to Ind AS 16.

(iv) **Useful life:** Useful life is:

(a) the period over which an asset is expected to be available for use by an enterprise; or

(b) the number of production or similar units expected to be obtained from the asset by an enterprise. *(Para 6 of AS 10 (Revised) 'Property, Plant and Equipment')*

Meaning given in AS 10 (Revised) on 'Property, Plant and Equipment' is similar to Ind AS 16.

There is a similar definition of useful life under the Companies Act, 2013 which states that, 'the useful life of an asset is the period over which an asset is expected to be available for use by an entity, or the number of production or similar units expected to be obtained from the asset by the entity'. (*Para 1 of Part-A to Schedule II of the Companies Act, 2013 on 'useful lives to compute depreciation'*)

(v) **Depreciable amount:** Depreciable amount of an asset is its cost, or other amount substituted for cost, less its residual value. (*Para 6 of AS 10 (Revised), 'Property, Plant and Equipment'*)

Meaning given in AS 10 (Revised) on 'property, plant and equipment' is similar to Ind AS 16.

Essentially, there is no difference in the definition of 'depreciable amount' under AS 10 (Revised), 'Property, Plant and Equipment', Ind AS 16 and the Companies Act, 2013.

(vi) **Residual value**: The estimated amount that an enterprise would currently obtain from the disposal of the asset after deducting the estimated costs of disposal, if the asset were already of the age and in the condition expected at the end of its useful life. *(Para 6 of AS 10 (Revised), 'Property, Plant and Equipment').*

Meaning given in AS 10 (Revised) on 'Property, Plant and Equipment' is similar to Ind AS 16.

(vii) **Amortisation:** Amortisation is the systematic allocation of the depreciable amount of an intangible asset over its useful life. (*Para 6.7 of AS 26 on 'Intangible Assets'*)

1.5.2 How should an enterprise ascertain the amount of depreciation to be charged?

Depreciable amount of a depreciable asset is its cost, or other amount substituted for historical cost, *less* the estimated residual value. Thus, assessment of depreciation depends on the following factors:

(*i*) cost or other amount substituted for the cost of the depreciable asset when the asset has been revalued;

(*ii*) expected useful life of the depreciable asset; and

(*iii*) estimated residual value of the depreciable asset.

1.5.2.1 Cost

Cost refers to the acquisition cost (including the incidental expenses necessary to bring the asset to its present condition or location, e.g., freight, installation charges, etc.). The cost may also change subsequently on account of factors like:

- Change in long-term liability on account of exchange fluctuations
- Changes in duties
- Price adjustments, etc.

1.5.2.2 Expected useful life of the asset

Useful life is either (*i*) the period over which a depreciable asset is expected to be used by the enterprise; or (*ii*) the number of production or similar units expected to be obtained from the use of the asset by the enterprise.

Thus, useful life is not the same as physical life. An asset may still exist physically but it may not be capable of being put to use any more. What is relevant is the useful life and not the physical life.

Determination of useful life is a matter of estimation. For this purpose, there are a number of *guiding factors* such as:

- expected usage of the asset. Usage is assessed by reference to the expected capacity or physical output of the asset.
- expected physical wear and tear, which depends on operational factors such as the number of shifts for which the asset is to be used and the repair and maintenance programme, and the care and maintenance of the asset while idle.
- technical or commercial obsolescence arising from changes or improvements in production, or from a change in the market demand for the product or service output of the asset. Expected future reductions in the selling price of an item that was produced using an asset could indicate the expectation of technical or commercial

obsolescence of the asset, which, in turn, might reflect a reduction of the future economic benefits embodied in the asset.

- legal or similar limits on the use of the asset, such as the expiry dates of related leases.

Useful life, in certain cases, gets over prematurely due to factors such as:

- technological changes;
- improvement in production methods;
- change in market demand for the product or service output of the asset; or
- legal or other restrictions.

1.5.2.3 Estimated residual value

If the residual value is considered as insignificant, it may be regarded as nil and if it is likely to be significant, it is taken into account for calculating depreciation. Estimation of useful life is normally difficult. One of the bases for determining the residual value could be the realisable value of similar assets which have reached the end of their useful lives and have operated under conditions similar to those in which the asset will be used.

Part A of Schedule II to the Companies Act, 2013 provides that the residual value of an asset should not be more than five per cent of the original cost of the asset. However, in case a company uses a residual value different from this limit, the financial statements should disclose such difference and provide justification in this behalf duly supported by technical advice.

(*MCA Notification G.S.R. 627(E) dated 29th August, 2014*)

1.5.2.4 Important points for consideration

Depreciation for shut-down period, etc.

Depreciation should be provided for the period such as shut-down period, lock-out period, period of strike, etc. (*A Study on Compliance of Financial Reporting Requirements - Financial Reporting Review Board, ICAI*)

Depreciation based on 'ready to use'

As soon as an item of an asset is installed and is fit for use, depreciation should be provided even though the said asset is not actually used for the whole or part of the relevant financial year. However, if the items are not installed and are, thus, not ready to use, depreciation is not provided. (*EAC Opinion, 2.16*)

Section 205(2) of the Companies Act, 1956, does not deal with the manner of provision for depreciation on assets remaining idle owing to labour trouble, etc, since according to accepted accounting principles, depreciation also arises out of efflux of time, it would be necessary for the purpose of section 205 to provide for depreciation even in respect of assets which are not in use during any financial year, if it purposes to declare to pay dividend. Section 205(1) of the Companies Act specifically requires that full depreciation for the year, as well as the arrears of depreciation of earlier years, must be provided before the company can declare dividend. (*EAC Opinion, 5.2*)

Depreciation should be charged for the period between the date when a project is ready to commence commercial production and the date on which it actually starts commercial production. (*EAC Opinion, 23.10*)

Pro rata depreciation

In cases where difference between pro rata depreciation and full year depreciation is not material in amount, the depreciation for the full year may be charged with appropriate disclosure of the said accounting policy. The concept of materiality has been recognised in the 'Guidance Note on Accounting for Depreciation in Companies', which recommends charging 100% depreciation on low-value items. If, during any financial year, any addition has been made to any asset, or where any asset has been sold, discarded, demolished or destroyed, the depreciation on such assets should be calculated on a pro rata basis from the date of such addition or, as the case may be, up to the date on which such asset has been sold, discarded, demolished or destroyed. A company may group additions and disposals in appropriate time period(s), e.g., 15 days, a month, a quarter, etc., for the purpose of charging pro rata depreciation in respect of additions and disposals of its assets keeping in view the materiality of the amounts involved. (*EAC Opinion, 12.7*)

1.5.3 What are the most commonly employed methods of charging depreciation?

The most commonly adopted methods are:

- Straight-line Method (SLM)
- Reducing Value Method / Written Down Value Method (WDV)

In SLM, the amount of annual depreciation is calculated as:

$$\frac{\text{Capitalised Cost} - \text{Estimated Residual Value}}{\text{Estimated Useful Life}}$$

In this method, the amount of annual depreciation remains uniform. On the other hand, in WDV method, the amount of annual depreciation is calculated as:

$$1 - \sqrt[n]{\frac{\text{Estimated Residual Value}}{\text{Capitalised Cost}}}$$

Where n = useful life (in years)

Thus, under WDV method, the amount of depreciation to be charged goes on declining every year.

EXAMPLE 1

From the following information, you are required to calculate the depreciation rate and illustrate the application under the following methods:

I. Straight-line method (SLM)

II. Written Down Value method (WDV)

(*INR in lakhs*)

Cost of the machine (acquired on 1 April 2014)	INR 30,000
Erection Charges	INR 3,000
Estimated useful life	10 years
Estimated Scrap Value	INR 3,000

SOLUTION

I. Straight Line Method

The asset will be capitalised at INR 33,000 lakh, being the purchase price and erection charges.

$$\text{Depreciation} = \frac{\text{Capitalised Cost} - \text{Estimated Residual Value}}{\text{Estimated Useful Life}}$$

= INR (33,000 lakh – 3,000 lakh)/10

= INR 3,000 lakh

Thus, the amount of depreciation would be INR 3,000 lakh p.a.

Effective rate of depreciation = Annual Depreciation × 100/Cost of Asset

= INR 3,000 lakh × 100/INR 33,000 lakh

= 9.09%

Accounting treatment for three years is given below:

Dr. **Fixed Asset A/c** **Cr.**

Date	Particulars	Amount (INR in lakhs)	Date	Particulars	Amount (INR in lakhs)
1-4-2014	Bank A/c	33,000	31-3-2015	Depreciation A/c	3,000
				Balance c/d	30,000
		33,000			33,000
1-4-2015	Balance b/d	30,000	31-3-2016	Depreciation A/c	3,000
				Balance c/d	27,000

Date	Particulars	Amount (INR in lakhs)	Date	Particulars	Amount (INR in lakhs)
		30,000			30,000
1-4-2016	Balance b/d	27,000	31-3-2017	Depreciation A/c	3,000
				Balance c/d	24,000
		27,000			27,000

Dr. Depreciation A/c Cr.

Date	Particulars	Amount (INR in lakhs)	Date	Particulars	Amount (INR in lakhs)
1-4-2014	Fixed Asset A/c	3,000	31-3-2015	Profit & Loss A/c	3,000
		3,000			3,000
1-4-2015	Fixed Asset A/c	3,000	31-3-2016	Profit & Loss A/c	3,000
		3,000			3,000
1-4-2016	Fixed Asset A/c	3,000	31-3-2017	Profit & Loss A/c	3,000
		3,000			3,000

II. Written down Value method:

Computation of depreciation rate:

Rate = 1 – (INR 3,000 lakh/INR 33,000 lakh)^0.1

= 21.32%

Computation of depreciation amount:

INR in lakhs

Depreciable amount		33,000
Depreciation for the First year at 21.32% of INR 33,000	7,036	
		25,964
Depreciation for the Second year at 21.32% of INR 25,964	5,536	
		20,428
Depreciation for the third year at 21.32% of INR 20,428	4,355	
		16,073

Dr **Fixed Asset A/c** Cr.

Date	Particulars	Amount (INR in lakhs)	Date	Particulars	Amount (INR in lakhs)
1-4-2014	Bank A/c	33,000	31-3-2015	Depreciation A/c	7,036
				Balance c/d	25,964
		33,000			33,000
1-4-2015	Balance b/d	25,964	31-3-2016	Depreciation A/c	5,536
				Balance c/d	20,428
		25,964			25,964
1-4-2016	Balance b/d	20,428	31-3-2017	Depreciation A/c	4,355
				Balance c/d	16,073
		20,428			20,428

Dr **Depreciation A/c** Cr.

Date	Particulars	Amount (INR in lakhs)	Date	Particulars	Amount (INR in lakhs)
1-4-2014	Fixed Asset A/c	7,036	31-3-2015	Profit & Loss A/c	7,036
		7,036			7,036
1-4-2015	Fixed Asset A/c	5,536	31-3-2016	Profit & Loss A/c	5,536
		5,536			5,536
1-4-2016	Fixed Asset A/c	4,355	31-3-2017	Profit & Loss A/c	4,355
		4,355			4,355

The management may choose a particular method or a combination of methods having regard to factors such as:

- Legal requirements such as Companies Act, 2013
- Type of asset
- Nature of the use of such asset
- Circumstances prevailing in the business, etc.

An enterprise may also adopt more than one method of depreciation for different assets or class of assets.

Unit of Production (UOP) Method of Depreciation

The depreciation on an asset can be provided, where appropriate, on the basis of the units expected to be obtained from the use of the asset. This method of providing depreciation is generally known as 'Unit of Production' method (UOP).

A company may use UOP method, where appropriate. UOP method is generally considered appropriate where the number of units that can be produced or serviced from the use of the asset is the major limiting factor for the use of the asset rather than the time. Following are some examples where UOP method can be identified appropriate:

(i) Useful life of Aircraft engine is restricted by number of flying hours

(ii) Useful life of Boiler is limited to number of hours

(iii) Useful life of Mould is limited by the number of imprints

A company will have to review the number of units that can be produced or serviced from the asset in the future periodically. The carrying amount of such an asset will be depreciated over the revised remaining number of units expected to be obtained or serviced on a prospective basis. Where, such an asset is idle for a long period of time, the company should assess whether the use of UOP method is still appropriate.

In accordance with AS 10 (revised) read with AS 5, change in method of depreciation from SLM to UOP or WDV to UOP would be considered as a change in an accounting estimate and need to be applied prospectively.

1.5.4 How should addition or extension to an existing asset be treated?

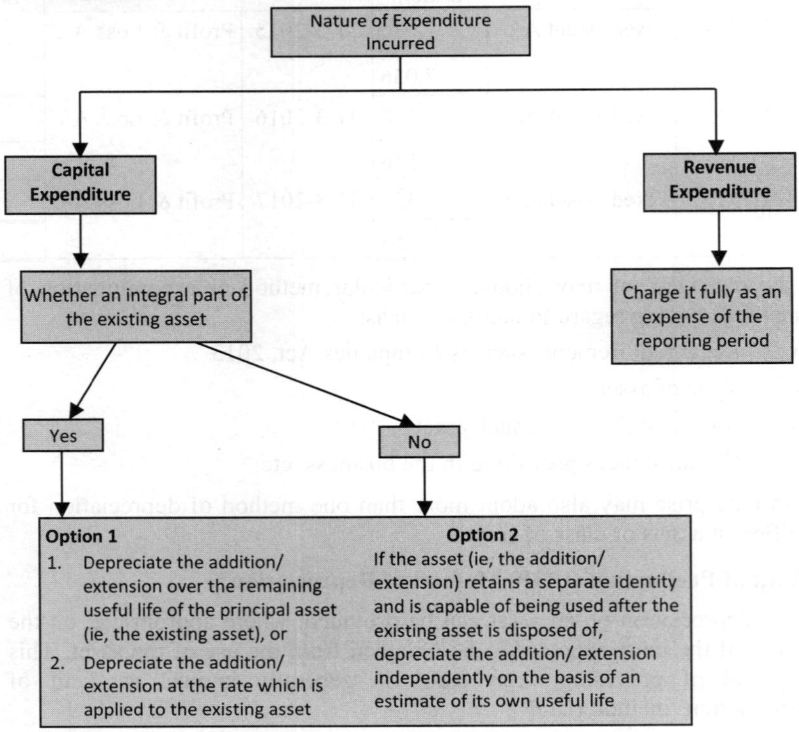

Note: The above two options should be in line with the requirement of 'componentisation' under the Companies Act, 2013.

EXAMPLE 2

X Ltd. acquired a plant and machinery on 01-04-2010 for INR 10 lakh. Incidental expenses of INR 50,000 were also incurred for this purpose. Residual value of the plant and machinery after its useful life of five years was estimated to INR 50,000. On 01-04-2012, X Ltd. made an important addition to the existing plant and machinery at a cost of INR 2,00,000. However, no residual value is likely to be realised for this addition. What is the amount of depreciation that X Ltd. should charge for the accounting year ending on 31-03-2013, assuming that the company follows straight line method of charging depreciation?

SOLUTION

The issue could be dealt with the following two different assumptions:

(i) The addition is a separate asset and can be used even after the existing asset is disposed of. Let us say the useful life is 8 years from the date of acquisition.

(ii) The addition is an integral part of the existing asset.

Let us now calculate depreciation for the year ending 31-3-2013 in both these cases:

Assumption I

Depreciable amount = INR 2,00,000 (as there is no residual value)

Estimated useful life = 8 years

Amount of annual depreciation (for year 2012-13 and later years) = $\frac{INR\ 2,00,000}{8}$

= INR 25,000

Assumption II

There are two options with X Ltd.

Option 1

Depreciate the addition over the remaining useful life of the existing asset, ie, 3 years

Annual depreciation = $\frac{\text{INR } 2,00,000}{3}$

= INR 66,667 (approx)

Option 2

Depreciate the addition at the rate applied to existing asset, ie, 20% in the present case, as the useful life is 5 years

Annual depreciation = INR 2,00,000 × 20%

= INR 40,000

Of course, in this case, X Ltd. will be able to write-off only INR 1,20,000 over the remaining useful life of the principal asset. The unamortised amount of INR 80,000 in such a case will be charged to the profit and loss account at the time of disposal of the asset (ie, the addition) along with the principal asset.

1.5.5 Can an enterprise provide depreciation at rates which are different from those laid down by the relevant Statute?

We shall examine the issue in two parts.

1.5.5.1 Position under the Companies Act, 1956

Can the management apply depreciation rates higher than those laid down by the relevant Statute?

The answer to this is yes, eg, the rates specified in the Companies Act, 1956 are the minimum rates of depreciation. Where the management's estimate of the useful life of an asset is shorter than that envisaged under the relevant Statute, depreciation can be calculated by applying a higher rate.

Can the depreciation rates be lower than that envisaged under the relevant Statute?

If the management's estimate of the useful life of the asset is longer than that envisaged under the Statute, depreciation rate lower than that envisaged by the Statute can be applied only in accordance with requirements of the Statute.

Since, the Companies Act, 1956 prescribed the minimum rates of depreciation, it was not possible to charge depreciation at rates lower than the ones prescribed in Schedule XIV of the Companies Act, 1956. In other words, there is no problem if an enterprise wants to charge depreciation at rates that are higher than the prescribed rates. However, depreciation rates cannot be lower than that prescribed under the Schedule XIV of the Companies Act, 1956.

1.5.5.2 Position under the Companies Act, 2013

Part A of Schedule II to the Companies Act, 2013 provides the indicative useful lives instead of rates as compared to Schedule XIV to the Companies Act, 1956. Useful lives and residual value have been prescribed for different class of companies which are mentioned below:

I. Tangible assets

(i) For regulated entities

The useful life or residual value of any specific asset, as notified for accounting purposes by a Regulatory Authority constituted under an Act of Parliament or by the Central Government should be applied in calculating the depreciation to be provided for such asset irrespective of the requirements of this Schedule.

(ii) Other Entities

Earlier the Companies Act, 2013 prescribed two different treatments for companies that were supposed to be prescribed for this purpose and other companies. It, *inter alia,* provided that:

(a) Prescribed class of companies whose financial statements comply with the Accounting Standards prescribed for such class of companies:

Useful life and the residual value of an asset should not be different from the useful life and the residual value as indicated in Part C (prescribes the useful lives of tangible assets) unless the justification for the same is disclosed.

(b) Other Companies:

Useful life of an asset and the residual value should not be more than what is specified in Schedule II.

However, the Ministry of Corporate Affairs *vide* notification G.S.R. 237(E), dated 31st March, 2014 amended this requirement and provided that:

"The useful life of an asset shall not be longer than the useful life specified in Part 'C' and the residual value of an asset shall not be more than five per cent of the original cost of the asset. Provided that where a company uses a useful life or residual value of the asset which is different from the above limits, justification for the difference shall be disclosed in its financial statement."

Further clarification that the useful lives and the residual values specified in Part C are indicative in nature was given by the Ministry of Corporate Affairs *vide* notification G.S.R. 627(E) dated 29th August, 2014.The amendment provides as under:

"The useful life of an asset shall not ordinarily be different from the useful life specified in Part 'C' and the residual value of an asset shall not be more than five per cent of the original cost of the asset.

Provided that where a company adopts a useful life different from what is specified in Part C or uses a residual value different from the limit specified above, the financial statements shall disclose such difference and provide justification in this behalf duly supported by technical advice."

Thus, now the position is as under:

All the companies (other than the entities in respect of which a Regulatory Authority has specified the useful life or residual value) will have the flexibility of deciding the useful life and residual value of the asset, however, in case the useful life and residual value differs from what is stated in Schedule II, they are required to give reasons justifying the same. By virtue of this, a level playing field has been provided to the Indian Companies *vis a vis* the international practices in this regard.

II. Intangible assets

For intangible assets, the provisions of the Accounting Standards applicable for the time being in force will apply, except in case of intangible assets (Toll Roads) created under 'Build, Operate and Transfer', 'Build, Own, Operate and Transfer' or any other form of Public Private Partnership route in case of road projects.

1.5.5.3 Comparison with Schedule XIV of the Companies Act, 1956

<table>
<tr><th colspan="3"></th><th>Companies Act, 2013</th><th>Companies Act, 1956</th></tr>
<tr><td rowspan="4">Companies other than regulated entities</td><td rowspan="2">Useful Life</td><td>Can it be higher</td><td rowspan="4">Yes, if the justification for the difference is disclosed in the financial statements</td><td>No</td></tr>
<tr><td>Can it be lower</td><td>Yes</td></tr>
<tr><td rowspan="2">Residual Value</td><td>Can it be higher than 5% of the original cost of the asset</td><td rowspan="2">Having regard to Sec 205 of the Companies Act, 1956, residual value could have been a maximum of 5% the original cost *</td></tr>
<tr><td>Can it be lower than 5% of the original cost of the asset</td></tr>
</table>

*Residual value was inbuilt in depreciation rates prescribed under Schedule XIV.

1.5.6 How should disposal, etc, of depreciable assets be treated in accounts?

When the depreciable assets are disposed of, discarded, demolished or destroyed, we need to ascertain and disclose the surplus or deficiency (as the case may be). The surplus or deficiency is to be calculated in the following manner:

Step 1: Ascertain the cost of the asset or any other amount substituted for the cost.

Step 2: Deduct:

(*i*) depreciation till the date of sale;

(*ii*) net selling price.

Step 3: If the balance left after deducting the items specified in Step 2 above is positive then there is a loss which should be charged to Profit and Loss Account, else if it is negative then it is a surplus to be credited to Profit and Loss Account.

EXAMPLE 3

X Ltd. acquired a plant and machinery on 01-01-2013 for INR 5,00,000. On 01-05-2016, due to change in technology, the same was sold for INR 95,000. In carrying out the sale an expense of INR 5,000 was also incurred. Assuming that till the date of sale, depreciation of INR 1,50,000 was provided, suggest how the surplus or deficiency, (if any), should be determined and treated in the accounts.

SOLUTION

The surplus or deficiency on sale of plant and machinery can be calculated as follows:

(*Amount in INR*)

Historical Cost of the asset	5,00,000		
Less: Depreciation till the date of sale	1,50,000		
Net selling price	95,000		
	– 5,000	90,000	2,40,000
Loss (Deficiency) on sale			2,60,000

This deficiency of INR 2,60,000 should be charged to the Profit & Loss Account in 2016-17 (ie, the year of sale of asset).

1.5.7 Under what circumstances can an enterprise change the method of depreciation and how should such a change be treated

1.5.7.1 Treatment under Ind AS

Treatment specified under Ind AS 16 on *'Property, Plant and Equipment'*

The depreciation method applied to an asset should be reviewed at least at each financial year-end and, if there has been a significant change in the expected pattern of consumption of the future economic benefits embodied in the asset, the method should be changed to reflect the changed pattern. Such a change should be accounted for as a change in an accounting estimate in accordance with Ind AS 8 on *'Accounting Policies, Changes in Accounting Estimates and Errors'*. The change will be applied PROSPECTIVELY.

Treatment of changes in accounting estimates specified under Ind AS 8

To the extent that a change in an accounting estimate gives rise to changes in assets and liabilities, or relates to an item of equity, it should be recognised by adjusting the carrying amount of the related asset, liability or equity item in the period of the change.

The effect of change in an accounting estimate, other than a change specified above shall be recognised prospectively by including it in profit or loss in:

(a) the period of the change, if the change affects that period only; or

(b) the period of the change and future periods, if the change affects both.

1.5.7.2 Treatment under Revised AS 10 on 'Property, Plant and Equipment'

The depreciation method applied to an asset should be reviewed at least at each financial year-end and, if there has been a significant change in the expected pattern of consumption of the future economic benefits embodied in the asset, the method should be changed to reflect the changed pattern. Such a change should be accounted for as a change in an accounting estimate in accordance with AS 5. The change should be applied PROSPECTIVELY. It may be noted that under the earlier AS 6 on 'Depreciation Accounting' (prior to the issuance of AS 10 (Revised) AS 6 used to deal with depreciation and a change in the method of depreciation was required to be applied RETROSPECTIVELY.

Treatment of change in an accounting estimate as per AS 5

The effect of a change in an accounting estimate should be included in the determination of net profit or loss in:

(a) the period of the change, if the change affects the period only; or

(b) the period of the change and future periods, if the change affects both.

The effect of a change in an accounting estimate should be classified using the same classification in the statement of profit and loss as was used previously for the estimate.

To ensure the comparability of financial statements of different periods, the effect of a change in an accounting estimate which was previously included in the profit or loss from ordinary activities is included in that component of net profit or loss. The effect of a change in an accounting estimate that was previously included as an extraordinary item is reported as an extraordinary item.

The nature and amount of a change in an accounting estimate which has a material effect in the current period, or which is expected to have a material effect in subsequent periods, should be disclosed. If it is impracticable to quantify the amount, this fact should be disclosed.

1.5.7.3 Treatment under IFRS

Treatment specified under IAS 16 on *'Property, Plant and Equipment'*

The depreciation method applied to an asset should be reviewed at least at each financial year-end and, if there has been a significant change in the expected pattern of consumption of the future economic benefits embodied in the asset, the method should be changed to reflect the changed pattern. Such a change should be accounted for as a change in an accounting estimate in accordance with IAS 8 on *'Accounting Policies, Accounting Estimates and Errors'*.

Treatment of changes in accounting estimates specified under IAS 8

An entity should recognise prospectively changes in accounting estimates by including the effects in profit or loss in the period that is affected (the period of the change and future periods), except if the change in estimate gives rise to changes in assets, liabilities or equity. In this case, it is recognised by adjusting the carrying amount of the related asset, liability or equity in the period of the change.

Thus, under AS, Ind AS and IFRS, a change in the method of depreciation is treated as change in an accounting estimate and the change is applied prospectively.

1.5.8 How should depreciation be ascertained when the cost has undergone a change?

As discussed above the cost of a depreciable asset may undergo subsequent changes arising as a result of increase or decrease in long term liability on account of exchange fluctuations, price adjustments, changes in duties or similar factors.

For this purpose, a three step approach given below should be followed:

Step 1: Ascertain the revised unamortised depreciable amount (i.e., amount not yet written off as depreciation, after considering cost change).

Step 2: Ascertain the residual useful life of the asset.

Step 3: Calculate revised depreciation by applying the relevant method using revised unamortised depreciable amount and remaining useful life. It may be noted here that the revised depreciation is to be applied prospectively.

EXAMPLE 7

X Ltd. acquired an item of furniture for INR 15 lakhs on 01-04-2009. Due to a change in the foreign exchange rate, the amount of unpaid liability increased by INR 40,000 in the year 2013-14. By the end of the year 2012-13, X Ltd. has already charged a depreciation of INR 7 lakh. Assuming that the asset has useful life of 10 year, determine the amount of depreciation to be changed for the year 2013-14 and later years.

SOLUTION:

Step 1 Revised unamortised depreciable amount INR 8,40,000 (INR 15,00,000 – INR 7,00,000 + INR 40,000)

Step 2 Residual useful life of the asset: 6 years (including year 2013-14)

Step 3 Revised annual depreciation

$$= \frac{\text{Revised unamirtised depreciable amout}}{\text{Remaining useful life}}$$

$$= \frac{\text{INR } 840000}{6} = \text{INR } 1{,}40{,}000$$

1.5.9 How to calculate depreciation when the asset has been revalued?

For this purpose, the following three step approach should be followed:

Step 1: Ascertain the revalued amount.

Step 2: Ascertain the residual useful life of the asset.

Step 3: Calculate revised depreciation by applying the relevant method using revalued amount and remaining useful life. It may be noted here that the revised depreciation is to be applied prospectively.

Note 1: Transfers from revaluation surplus (to the extent of additional depreciation) to the revenue reserves are not made through the statement of profit and loss.

Note 2: A company that followed the policy of recouping additional depreciation as a credit to the statement of profit and loss, with Schedule II becoming applicable starts recouping additional depreciation on account of revaluation as a credit to revenue reserves, such a company should disclose the change as a change in accounting policy in accordance with AS 5.

EXAMPLE 8

X Ltd. purchased a building for INR 75 lakh on 01-04-2008. The building has a useful life of 10 years. In the year 2013-14, the enterprise revalued the building at INR 25 lakh. By the end of year 2012-13, depreciation of INR 35 lakh has already been charged on the building. Ascertain the amount of depreciation to be charged for the year 2013-14, in the later years and also explain the treatment of revaluation amount.

SOLUTION

Step 1: Revalued amount: INR 25 lakh

Step 2: Remaining useful life of the building: 5 years (including year 2013-14)

Step 3: Revised annual depreciation

$$= \frac{\text{Revalued amount}}{\text{Remaining useful life}} = \frac{\text{INR 2500000}}{\text{5 years}}$$

= INR 5,00,000

The difference of INR 15,00,000 [ie, the difference between the unamortised depreciable amount (had there been no revaluation, i.e., INR 40 lakhs) and the revalued amount, i.e., INR 25 lakhs will be charged to the profit and loss account for the year ending 31-3-2014.]

EXAMPLE 9

Shivaji Ltd. purchased fixed assets worth INR 90,00,000 on 1 April 2012. The life of the assets is 10 years and they are to be depreciated on straight-line basis. The assets were revalued on 1 April 2014 when 50% of the assets was assessed at 10% less than the book value, and the remaining assets were revalued at 15% higher than book value. The assets were ultimately sold on 01-04-2016 for INR 54,80,000.

Show Fixed Assets A/c, Depreciation A/c and Revaluation Reserve A/c, supported by Working wherever necessary.

SOLUTION

Position before the Companies Act, 2013

Dr. Fixed Asset A/c Cr.

Date	Particulars	Amount INR	Date	Particulars	Amount INR
1-4-2012	Bank A/c	90,00,000	31-3-2013	Depreciation A/c	9,00,000
				Balance c/d	81,00,000
		90,00,000			90,00,000
1-4-2013	Balance b/d	81,00,000	31-3-2014	Depreciation A/c	9,00,000

Date	Particulars	Amount INR	Date	Particulars	Amount INR
				Balance c/d	72,00,000
		81,00,000			81,00,000
1-4-2014	Balance b/d	72,00,000	1-4-2014	Profit & Loss A/c (Downward Revaluation)	3,60,000
	Revaluation Reserve A/c (Upward Revaluation)	5,40,000			
			31-3-2015	Depreciation A/c	9,22,500
				Balance c/d	64,57,500
		77,40,000			77,40,000
1-4-2015	Balance b/d	64,57,500	31-3-2016	Depreciation A/c	9,22,500
				Balance c/d	55,35,000
		64,57,500			64,57,500
1-4-2016	Balance b/d	55,35,000	1-4-2016	Bank A/c	54,80,000
				Profit & Loss A/c (Loss on sale)	55,000
		55,35,000			55,35,000

Dr Depreciation A/c Cr

Date	Particulars	Amount INR	Date	Particulars	Amount INR
31-3-2013	Fixed Assets A/c	9,00,000	31-3-2013	Profit & Loss A/c	9,00,000
31-3-2014	Fixed Asset A/c	9,00,000	31-3-2014	Profit & Loss A/c	9,00,000
31-3-2015	Fixed Assets A/c	9,22,500	31-3-2015	Profit & Loss A/c	9,00,000
				Revaluation Reserve A/c	22,500
		9,22,500			9,22,500

Date	Particulars	Amount INR	Date	Particulars	Amount INR
31-3-2016	Fixed Assets A/c	9,22,500	31-3-2016	Profit & Loss A/c	9,00,000
				Revaluation Reserve A/c	22,500
		9,22,500			9,22,500

Dr **Revaluation Reserve A/c** **Cr**

Date	Particulars	Amount INR	Date	Particulars	Amount INR
1-4-2014	Fixed Assets A/c (Downward revaluation)	3,60,000	1-4-2014	Fixed Assets A/c (Upward revaluation)	5,40,000
31-3-2015	Depreciation A/c	22,500			
	Balance c/d	1,57,500			
		5,40,000			5,40,000
31-3-2016	Depreciation A/c	22,500	1-4-2015	Balance b/d	1,57,500
	Balance c/d	1,35,000			
		1,57,500			1,57,500
1-4-2016	General Reserve	1,35,000	1-4-2016	Balance b/d	1,35,000
		1,35,000			1,35,000

Workings

1. Computation of Revaluation Reserve

	INR
Book value of entire assets as on 01-04-2014	72,00,000
Revalued amount of 50% block of assets (say Block A)	
(INR 36,00,000 – 10% of INR 36,00,000)	32,40,000
Downward Revaluation (INR 36,00,000 - INR 32,40,000)	3,60,000
Revalued amount of balance block of assets (say Block B)	
(INR 36,00,000 + 15% of INR 36,00,000)	41,40,000
Upward Revaluation (INR 41,40,000 - INR 36,00,000)	5,40,000

Value of fixed assets after revaluation as on 01-04-2014 73,80,000

2. Annual depreciation for remaining useful life

Revalued amount of fixed assets = INR 73,80,000

Remaining useful life = 8 years

Revised annual depreciation = INR 73,80,000/8

= INR 9,22,500

3. Depreciation to be charged to Revaluation Reserve A/c

Revised annual depreciation = INR 9,22,500

Earlier annual depreciation = INR 9,00,000

Depreciation to be charged to Revaluation Reserve A/c (being the excess depreciation on revaluation) = INR 22,500

Position after the Companies Act, 2013

After the introduction of Companies Act, 2013, additional depreciation arising on revaluation cannot be recouped out of revaluation reserve. INR 22,500, being the additional depreciation arising on revaluation, will be charged to the statement of profit and loss only. In such case, 'depreciation' and 'revaluation reserve account' will be as under[1]:

Dr Depreciation A/c Cr

Date	Particulars	Amount INR	Date	Particulars	Amount INR
31-3-2013	Fixed Assets A/c	9,00,000	31-3-2013	Profit & Loss A/c	9,00,000
31-3-2014	Fixed Asset A/c	9,00,000	31-3-2014	Profit & Loss A/c	9,00,000
31-3-2015	Fixed Assets A/c	9,22,500	31-3-2015	Profit & Loss A/c	9,22,500
		9,22,500			9,22,500
31-3-2016	Fixed Assets A/c	9,22,500	31-3-2016	Profit & Loss A/c	9,22,500
		9,22,500			9,22,500

[1] In our view, an entity should be permitted to transfer an amount equivalent to the extra depreciation *from revaluation reserve to general reserve.*

Dr Revaluation Reserve A/c Cr

Date	Particulars	Amount INR	Date	Particulars	Amount INR
1-4-2014	Fixed Assets A/c (Downward revaluation)	3,60,000	1-4-2014	Fixed Assets A/c (Upward revaluation)	5,40,000
31-3-2015	Balance c/d	1,80,000			
		5,40,000			5,40,000
31-3-2016	Balance c/d	1,80,000	1-4-2015	Balance b/d	1,80,000
		1,80,000			1,80,000
1-4-2016	General Reserve	1,80,000	1-4-2016	Balance b/d	1,80,000
		1,80,000			1,80,000

The following chart may also be used as a reference point for requirements of AS 10 (Revised) on 'Property, Plant and Equipment' relating to revaluation:

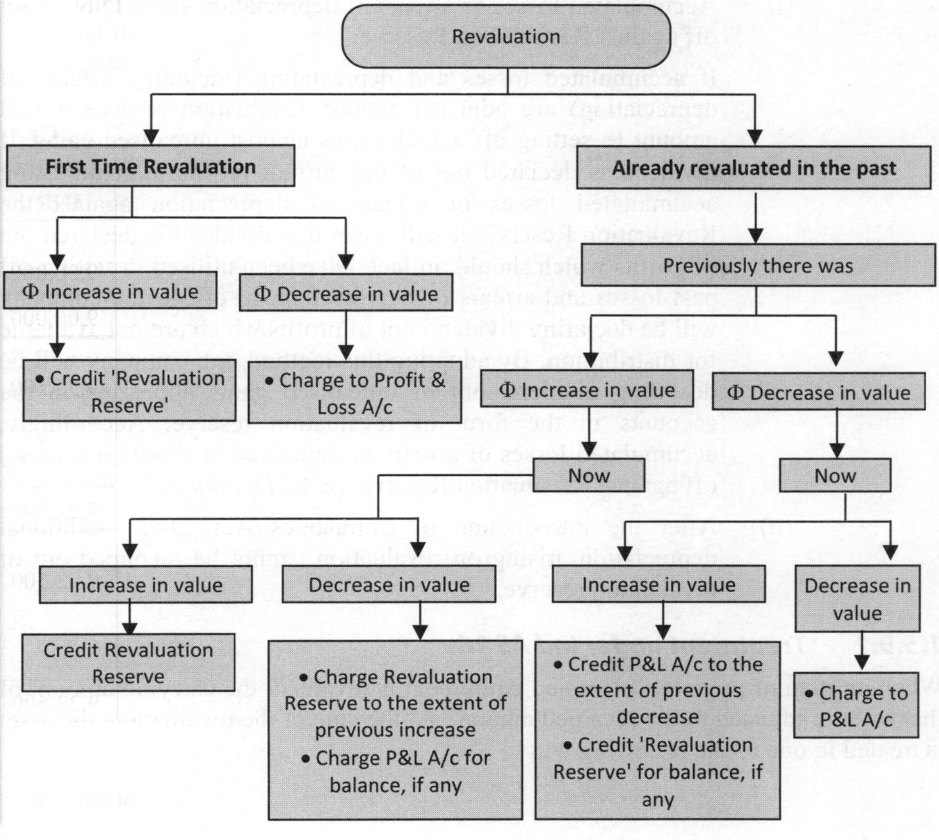

Certain points to be noted in respect of depreciation in case the assets are revalued:

(a) A company providing depreciation on revalued amount on two different bases (i) on original amount at the rates specified in Schedule XIV to the Companies Act, 1956 and (ii) on the amount added on revaluation, over the residual life as estimated by the valuers, is not a correct accounting treatment. In case of revaluation of fixed assets, depreciation on total revalued amount is required to be provided on one single basis, i.e., the remaining useful lives of assets concerned. If the useful life or depreciation rates of the assets are different from the principal rates specified in the Schedule, they should be disclosed. (*A Study on Compliance of Financial Reporting Requirements - Financial Reporting Review Board, ICAI*)

(b) Revaluation of assets does not, in itself, call for a change in the method of depreciation. (*EAC Opinion, 20.35*)

(c) Treatment of Reserve created on Revaluation of Fixed Assets:

(i) Accumulated losses or arrears of depreciation should not be set off against Revaluation Reserve.

If accumulated losses and depreciation (including arrears of depreciation) are adjusted against revaluation reserve it will amount to setting off actual losses against unrealised gains. If dividend is declared out of the current profits after adjusting accumulated losses or arrears of depreciation against the Revaluation Reserve, it will mean that dividend is declared out of profits which should, in fact, have been utilised in setting-off past losses and arrears of depreciation. In effect, the company will be declaring dividend out of profits which are not available for distribution. By adopting this method, the company will be declaring dividend out of unrealised gains appearing in the accounts in the form of revaluation reserve. Accordingly, accumulated losses or arrears of depreciation should not be set off against Revaluation Reserve. (*EAC Opinion, 14.21*)

(ii) After the introduction of Companies Act, 2013, additional depreciation arising on revaluation cannot be recouped out of revaluation reserve.

1.5.9.1 Treatment under Ind AS 16

When an item of property, plant and equipment is revalued, the carrying amount of that asset is adjusted to the revalued amount. At the date of the revaluation, the asset is treated in one of the following ways:

(a) the gross carrying amount is adjusted in a manner that is consistent with the revaluation of the carrying amount of the asset, e.g., the gross carrying amount may be restated by reference to observable market data or it may be restated proportionately to the change in the carrying amount. The accumulated depreciation at the date of the revaluation is adjusted to equal the difference between the gross carrying amount and the carrying amount of the asset after taking into account accumulated impairment losses; or

(b) the accumulated depreciation is eliminated against the gross carrying amount of the asset.

The amount of the adjustment of accumulated depreciation forms part of the increase or decrease in carrying amount

Upward Revaluation

If an asset's carrying amount is increased as a result of a revaluation, the increase should be recognised in other comprehensive income and accumulated in equity under the heading of revaluation surplus. However, the increase should be recognised in profit or loss to the extent that it reverses a revaluation decrease of the same asset previously recognised in profit or loss.

Downward Revaluation

If an asset's carrying amount is decreased as a result of a revaluation, the decrease should be recognised in profit or loss. However, the decrease should be recognised in other comprehensive income to the extent of any credit balance existing in the revaluation surplus in respect of that asset. The decrease recognised in other comprehensive income reduces the amount accumulated in equity under the heading of revaluation surplus.

Transfers from Revaluation Surplus on the disposal of the asset

The revaluation surplus included in equity in respect of an item of property, plant and equipment may be transferred directly to retained earnings when the asset is derecognised. This may involve transferring the whole of the surplus when the asset is retired or disposed off. However, some of the surplus may be transferred as the asset is used by an entity. In such a case, the amount of the surplus transferred would be the difference between depreciation based on the revalued carrying amount of the asset and depreciation based on the asset's original cost. Transfers from revaluation surplus to retained earnings are not made through profit or loss.

1.5.9.2 *Treatment under AS 10 (Revised) on 'Property, Plant and Equipment'*

Treatment given in AS 10 (Revised) on 'Property, Plant and Equipment' is similar to Ind AS 16.

1.5.10 How to calculate depreciation when the useful life of the depreciable asset has undergone a change?

For this purpose, the following three-step approach may be followed:

Step 1: Ascertain the revised remaining useful life of the asset.

Step 2: Ascertain the unamortised depreciable amount.

Step 3: Calculate the revised depreciation by applying the relevant method using unamortised depreciable amount and revised remaining useful life. In this case also, depreciation is to be calculated on the revalued amount prospectively.

EXAMPLE 10

The useful life of a machinery acquired by X Ltd. on 01-04-2010, at a price of INR 10 lakh, was 10 years. Till the end of year 2012-13, the total depreciation of INR 3 lakh has already been charged. In the year 2013-14 the remaining useful life of the machinery was reviewed. It was estimated at 2 years. Ascertain the amount of depreciation to be charged from the year 2013-14 onwards.

SOLUTION

Step 1: Revised remaining useful life = 2 years

Step 2: Unamortised depreciable amount = INR 7 lakh

Step 3: Revised annual depreciation

$$= \frac{\text{Unamortised depreciable amount}}{\text{Revised remaining useful life}}$$

= INR 7,00,000/2

= INR 3,50,000

Chapter 2

Key Highlights of Schedule II to the Companies Act, 2013

Under the Companies Act, 2013, depreciation provisions are mainly given in Schedule II. Schedule II has made sweeping changes vis-à-vis the earlier Schedule XIV to the Companies Act, 1956. In this Chapter, we have explained in detail the provisions of Schedule II and comparison with Schedule XIV. The Chapter also provides guidance on component accounting.

2.1 SCHEDULE II OF THE COMPANIES ACT, 2013: KEY HIGHLIGHTS

The salient features of the Schedule II are as under:

2.1.1 Useful life

Unlike the Companies Act, 1956, useful life of the assets has been prescribed in place of rates of depreciation in the Part 'C' Schedule II of the Companies Act, 2013 as a base for computing depreciation.

2.1.2 Effect of double shift and triple shift

The useful lives of assets working on shift basis have been specified in the Schedule II of the Companies Act, 2013, based on their single shift working. Except for assets in respect of which no extra shift depreciation is permitted (indicated by NESD in Part C), if an asset is used for any time during the year for double shift, the depreciation will increase by 50% for that period and, in case of the triple shift, the depreciation will be calculated on the basis of 100% for that period. (*Note no. 5 to Part-C of the schedule II of the Companies Act, 2013*)

Determination of useful life

A company has to determine the useful life at the beginning of the year for all fixed assets, existing as at the end of the immediately preceding period and for newly acquired assets, as and when acquired. All fixed assets existing at the beginning of the year should be classified into assets for which no extra shift depreciation is applicable which would include continuous process plant (CPP) and assets for which extra shift depreciation applies. Of the assets for which extra shift depreciation applies, assets which are going to be used on single shift, double shift or triple shift are segregated. This segregation is required as the extra shift depreciation is applicable only to those assets whose useful life is determined on single shift basis. After segregation, the remaining useful life of the asset is estimated. A company recognises depreciation expense based on the useful life estimated by the management. Where the useful life estimated by the management is different from that specified by Schedule II, the same is disclosed in notes.

2.1.2.1 How to ascertain if the assets have been used in double shift or triple shift?

The term 'shift' has not been defined in the Companies Act, 1956 or Companies Act, 2013. So, it is understood in the common commercial parlance. Section 2(r) of the Factories Act, 1948, defines the term 'shift' as follows:

> *"Where work of the same kind is carried out by two or more sets of workers working during different periods of the day, each of such sets is called 'group' or 'relay' and each of such periods is called a 'shift'".*

The basic feature of the system of extra shifts is employment of a different set of workers for the period additional to the normal working hours. Generally, the shift system is operative for a certain number of consecutive working days and not extra hours worked on isolated working days. The extra hours worked by the same set of workers is generally termed and treated as overtime and is not referred to as shift. Manifestation of extra shift can also be a situation where a significant number of extra hours are worked beyond the normal working hours in a day, say, four hours or more over and above a shift of eight hours. However, calculation of a shift has to be with reference to a working day and not with reference to the entire year. (*EAC Opinion, 13.22*)

As per the requirements of Schedule XIV, the unit of usage of assets is 'shift' and non utilisation of capacity. If the plant has worked triple shift, and although there is a substantial under-utilisation of capacity, the depreciation thereon should be charged on triple-shift basis. (*EAC Opinion, 17.15*)

Extra shift depreciation

Extra shift depreciation does not apply to CPP and the assets which have been marked as No Extra Shift Depreciation (NESD) under Schedule II. The concept of extra shift depreciation applies only to those assets for which the useful life has been estimated on single shift basis at the beginning of the year.

Where a company, which estimated the useful life of an asset on single shift basis at the beginning of the year, used the asset on double or triple shifts during the year, the depreciation expense should be increased by 50% or 100% as the case may be for that period. Further, for such asset/s, the company at the beginning of the next year should determine whether the asset used in extra shift during the past year was on sporadic basis and is expected to be used on sporadic basis in future also. In such a case, the useful life to be on single shift basis and if in future the asset is used on double or triple shift then as in the past, the depreciation expense for the double or triple shift should be increased by 50% or 100% as the case may be for the period of use. In case the company estimates that the use of the asset for extra shift would not be on sporadic basis i.e. the extra shift working for the asset would be on regular or continuous basis, it should reassess its useful life considering its use on extra shift basis. The reassessed useful life should then be used for the purpose of charging depreciation expense henceforth.

For assets which are not marked as NESD under Schedule II and for which the useful life has been estimated on double/triple shift basis at the beginning of the year, the concept of extra shift deprecation will not apply. For such assets, a company should consider whether there is any change in circumstances on which the useful life of asset was based or any new developments have taken place which may have impact on the estimated useful life of the asset. If there is no such indication, the company should continue to depreciate such assets on the basis of previous estimates. If there is any such indication, the company should reassess the remaining useful life of the assets on the basis of changed circumstances or new developments, e.g., use of the asset on single shift basis in future.

(*Para 24-26 of Guidance Note on Accounting for Depreciation in companies in the context of Schedule II to the Companies Act, 2013*)

2.1.2.2 Calculation of extra shift depreciation

The calculation of the extra depreciation for double shift working and for triple shift working should be made separately in the proportion which the number of days for which the concern worked double shift or triple shift, as the case may be, bears to the normal number of working days during the year. For this purpose, the normal number of working days during the year shall be deemed to be:

(a) In the case of a seasonal factory or concern, the number of days on which the factory or concern actually worked during the year or 180 days, whichever is greater;

(b) In any other case, the number of days on which the factory or concern actually worked during the year or 240 days, whichever is greater. (*Note 6 to Schedule XIV of the Companies Act, 1956*).

Schedule XIV requires that where the concern has worked extra shift, the multiple or extra shift depreciation will have to be provided on the plant and machinery, wherever applicable. In this regard, various units/departments/ mills/factories should be taken as separate concerns. (*EAC Opinion, 13.25*)

Extra depreciation for double shift working should be the difference between the depreciation for double shift working and the depreciation for single shift working, adjusted in the proportion which the number of days for which concern worked double shift bears to the normal working days during the year. The extra depreciation for double shift working, so calculated, has to be added to the depreciation for single shift working to arrive at the total depreciation for double shift working. (*EAC Opinion, 10.3.3*)

Extra depreciation for double or triple shifts has to be worked out on the basis of number of days for which the 'concern' worked double or triple shift. Thus, the actual utilisation of capacity of the plant and machinery items in the concern is not relevant for the purpose of computing extra shift deprecation. (*EAC Opinion 17.15*)

The rates of depreciation specified in respect of single shift have been determined based on two factors – effluxion of time and wear and tear. However, in case of double shift and triple shift, the factor of effluxion of time remains constant. Therefore, rates for extra shifts include only the incremental/extra depreciation due to extra wear and tear. Thus, single shift depreciation rate should be applied for the time period when the asset is held by the company irrespective of the fact whether such asset is in use or not. As regards 'extra depreciation' to be computed for items of plant and machinery operating for extra shifts, the incremental depreciation should be determined by applying the differential rate of depreciation, i.e., depreciation rate as specified for the relevant shift *less* the rate specified for the single shift in the proportion in which the company worked for the double/triple shift bears to the number the number of days on which the factory or 'concern' actually worked during the year. The formula for arriving at the 'depreciation' is as under:

Depreciation for single shift working + (Depreciation for double/triple shift working – Depreciation for single shift working) × (Number of days worked double or triple shift / Normal working days during the year)

(*EAC Opinion 31.13*)

2.1.2.3 Calculation of normal working days

Schedule XIV to the Companies Act, 1956, requires that normal number of working days during the year should be the number of days on which the factory or 'concern' actually worked during the year. Thus, it is not the working days of individual plant and machinery items which should be considered for the purpose of computing extra depreciation. For calculating extra shift depreciation on addition to plant items of an existing factory or a concern, the normal number of working days for the concern or factory as a whole should be considered (*EAC Opinion, 15.1.10 and EAC Opinion 31.13*).

For working out 'normal number of working days during the year', the higher of (a) 'number of days on which the concern actually worked during the year', and (b) 180 days in case of seasonal factory or concern and 240 days in other cases, is to be taken. For computing the number of days on which the concern actually worked, idle days on account of maintenance, etc, for which the factory/concern has worked should be included even though the individual machines/labourers in the factory/concern might not have actually worked during these days. When machines are shut down for maintenance in a factory/concern, the maintenance work is carried on although no production takes place. (*EAC Opinion, 13.26*)

2.1.3 Component accounting

Useful life specified in Part C of the Schedule II of the Companies Act, 2013, is for whole of the asset. Where cost of a part of the asset is significant to total cost of the asset and useful life of that part is different from the useful life of the remaining asset, useful life of that significant part should be determined separately.

Note: As per the notification dated 29th August, 2014, the requirement will be voluntary in respect of the financial year commencing on or after the 1st April, 2014 and mandatory for financial statements in respect of financial years commencing on or after the 1st April, 2015.

Till now, component accounting was not mandatory under Indian GAAP. However, Schedule II to the Companies Act, 2013 and AS 10 (Revised) on 'Property, Plant and Equipment' mandates component accounting. Para 45 and 46 of AS 10 (revised) provides as under:

> *"45. Each part of an item of property, plant and equipment with a cost that is significant in relation to the total cost of the item should be depreciated separately.*
>
> *46. An enterprise allocates the amount initially recognised in respect of an item of property, plant and equipment to its significant parts and depreciates each such part separately. For example, it may be appropriate to depreciate separately the airframe and engines of an aircraft, whether owned or subject to a finance lease."*

It is not necessary that all companies have been following component accounting under the Companies Act, 1956. There are companies which would be following component accounting for the first time after the introduction of Companies Act, 2013. For such companies, separate cost of each significant component of an asset will not be available in the books of accounts of companies. In order to determine the separate cost of each significant component, any of the following criteria can be used:

(a) Break-up cost provided by the vendor;

(b) Cost break-up given by internal/external technical expert;

(c) Fair values of various components; or

(d) Current replacement cost of component of the related asset and applying the same basis on the historical cost of asset

(*Please note that the above criteria is only illustrative and some other appropriate criteria can also be applied*)

2.1.3.1 Identification of components

Identification of significant/material components of an asset is a matter of judgment and is to be determined keeping in view the facts and circumstances of each case, e.g., a component having original cost less than or equal to 5% of original cost of asset may not be material. However, a component having original cost less than or equal to 30% of original cost of asset may be material.

The company may consider 10% of the original cost of the asset as a threshold to determine whether the component is significant/material. A company should also consider impact on retained earnings, current and future years' profit or loss to decide materiality. In case, there is a material impact from either of the perspective, the component should be considered as material and recognised separately.

Identification of significant components of an asset and determination of their useful life is not merely an accounting exercise, rather, it involves technical expertise as well.

Determination as to whether a part of an asset is significant requires a careful assessment of the facts and circumstances. This assessment would include at a minimum:

- Determine the threshold value to determine which asset requires componentisation.
- Threshold value in percentage of cost of component to the total cost of the asset
- Proportion of useful life of that part as compared to the useful life of the asset
- Potential impact on the total depreciation expenditure

Step by Step approach for identification of the components is given as under:

Step 1

In order to identify the components, a company should segregate the asset into various identifiable parts to the extent possible.

Example:

- Part 1
- Part 2
- Part 3
- Part 4
- Other insignificant parts

Step 2

Compare the identified parts on the basis of their

- useful lives; and
- pattern of consumption

Step 3

Group the identified parts if they have the same or similar useful lives or pattern of consumption. Other insignificant parts may be combined together in the remainder of the asset or with the principal asset.

Example:

- Component 1: Part 1 and 3
- Component 2: Part 2
- Component 3: Part 4 and 5
- Remainder

For instance:

A Ship may be bifurcated into the following components –

(i) Hull

(ii) Keel

(iii) Engine

(iv) Navigation system

(v) Major overhaul/ inspections

(vi) Other fit out assets

2.1.3.2 Determining the useful Life of components

Schedule II to the Companies Act, 2013 requires component accounting only when both the following conditions are satisfied:

- cost of a part of the asset is significant to total cost of the asset; and
- useful life of that part is different from the useful life of the remaining asset

As far as useful life is concerned, the following situations are possible:

Case 1 Useful life of the component is less than the useful life of the principal asset specified in Schedule II

Lower useful life should be used for depreciating the relevant component

Case 2 Useful life of the component is more than the useful life of the principal asset specified in Schedule II

Company may use either the higher useful life or the lower useful life for depreciating the component. However, higher useful life can only be used in case the company intends to use the component even after the expiry of useful life of the principal asset.

EXAMPLE 1

Useful life of principal asset as specified in Schedule II to the Companies Act, 2013 is 12 years. Management also estimates the life of the principal asset to be 12 years.

Case 1: Useful life of the component is 10 years

Useful life of the component is less than the useful life of the principal asset specified in Schedule II to the Companies Act, 2013.

Component should be depreciated using the useful life of 10 years only.

Case 2: Useful life of the component is 15 years

Useful life of the component is more than the useful life of the principal asset specified in Schedule II to the Companies Act, 2013.

Component should be depreciated using the higher useful life of 15 years in case the company intends to use the component even after the expiry of useful life of the principal asset, i.e., 12 years. However, company may also depreciate the component using 12 years life as prescribed in the Schedule II to the Companies Act, 2013.

EXAMPLE 2

X Ltd., a steel company, is in the process of enhancing its production capacity. The company has got another furnace commissioned. Based on its historical experience, the company determines the life of furnace to be 30 years. The cost of the furnace is INR 90 crore. The break-down of the cost is as below:

	Useful life	Cost (INR in crores)
Structure	30	45
Internal lining of refractory	5	11
Heating components	7	14
Motors and other operating parts for controlling temperature	10	20
Total		90

Give the impact of component accounting on depreciation after introduction of the Companies Act, 2013 and compare with the earlier situation under the Companies Act, 1956. Residual value may be assumed to be nil.

SOLUTION

Treatment under the Companies Act, 1956

The component accounting was not mandatory under the Companies Act, 1956. The replacement cost was charged to the statement of profit and loss in the year in which it was incurred.

Annual depreciation of the furnace = INR 90 crore/30

= INR 3 crore

Replacement cost of various components will be charged to the statement of profit and loss.

Companies Act, 2013

Statement showing component-wise annual depreciation

Furnace	Depreciable amount (INR in crores) (A)	Useful life (B)	Depreciation (INR in crores)(SLM) (A)/(B)
Structure	45	30	1.5
Internal lining of refractory	11	5	2.2
Heating components	14	7	2
Motors and other operating parts for controlling temperature	20	10	2
Total			7.7

When at the end of the respective useful lives of the components, the components will be replaced, the replacement cost should be capitalised because by that time, they are fully depreciated and the carrying value at the end of their respective useful lives is nil.

Thus, although the overall amount that will be charged to the statement of profit and loss will be same during the entire life of the furnace, the annual charge to the statement of profit and loss will differ significantly.

EXAMPLE 3

X Ltd. has purchased a ship for INR 38 crore. The components of ship along with the cost allocated to each component, replacement cost at the end of the useful life and the useful life are as follows:

Ship	Allocated cost (INR)	Residual Value (INR)	Useful life (Years)
Life raft	1,00,00,000	10,00,000	10
Others	5,00,00,000	50,00,000	10
Decks	10,00,00,000	50,00,000	15
Boiler	10,00,00,000	10,00,000	15
Bulkhead	9,00,00,000	99,00,000	30
Propulsion system	3,00,00,000	30,00,000	30
Total	**38,00,00,000**	**2,49,00,000**	

The overall useful life of the ship was 30 years.
Give the impact of component accounting on depreciation after introduction of the Companies Act, 2013 and compare with the earlier situation under the Companies Act, 1956.

SOLUTION

Companies Act, 1956

The component accounting was not mandatory under the Companies Act, 1956. The replacement cost will be charged to the statement of profit and loss in the year in which incurred.

Annual depreciation of the ship = (INR 38,00,00,000 – INR 2,49,00,000)/30
= INR 1,18,36,667

Replacement cost of various components will be charged to the statement of profit and loss.

Companies Act, 2013

Statement showing component-wise annual depreciation

Ship	Depreciable amount (INR) (A)	Useful life (B)	Depreciation (INR)(SLM) (A)/(B)
Life raft	1,00,00,000 – 10,00,000 = 90,00,000	10	9,00,000
Others	5,00,00,000 – 50,00,000 = 4,50,00,000	10	45,00,000
Decks	10,00,00,000 – 50,00,000 = 9,50,00,000	15	63,33,333
Boiler	10,00,00,000 – 10,00,000 = 9,90,00,000	15	66,00,000
Bulkhead	9,00,00,000 – 99,00,000 = 8,01,00,000	30	26,70,000
Propulsion system	3,00,00,000 – 30,00,000 = 2,70,00,000	30	9,00,000
Total			**2,19,03,333**

When at the end of the respective useful lives of the components, the components will be replaced, the replacement cost should be capitalised and the existing carrying value, if any, should be decapitalised.

Thus, although the overall amount that will be charged to the statement of profit and loss will be same during the entire life of the ship, the annual charge to the statement of profit and loss will differ significantly.

2.1.3.3 Guidance under AS 10 (Revised), 'Property, Plant and Equipment' and Ind AS 16 for component Accounting

(a) Each part of an item of property, plant and equipment with a cost that is significant in relation to the total cost of the item should be depreciated separately.

(b) An entity allocates the amount initially recognised in respect of an item of property, plant and equipment to its significant parts and depreciates separately each such part, eg, it may be appropriate to depreciate separately the airframe and engines of an aircraft, whether owned or subject to a finance lease.

(c) A significant part of an item of property, plant and equipment may have a useful life and a depreciation method that are the same as the useful life and the depreciation method of another significant part of that same item. Such parts may be grouped in determining the depreciation charge.

(d) To the extent that an entity depreciates separately some parts of an item of property, plant and equipment, it also depreciates separately the remainder of the item. The remainder consist of the parts of the item that are individually not significant. If an entity has varying expectations for these parts, approximation techniques may be necessary to depreciate the remainder in a manner that faithfully represents the consumption pattern and/or useful life of its parts.

(e) An entity may choose to depreciate the parts of an item separately which do not have a cost that is significant in relation to the total cost of the item.

2.1.3.4 Impact of component accounting on replacement of components

Parts of some items of property, plant and equipment may require replacement at regular intervals, eg, a furnace may require relining after a specified number of hours of use, or aircraft interiors such as seats and galleys may require replacement several times during the life of the airframe. Items of property, plant and equipment may also be acquired to make a less frequently recurring replacement, such as replacing the interior walls of a building, or to make a non-recurring replacement. Under the recognition principle, an entity recognises in the carrying amount of an item of property, plant and equipment the cost of replacing part of such an item when that cost is incurred if the recognition criteria are met. The carrying amount of those parts that are replaced is derecognised.

If an entity recognises in the carrying amount of an item of property, plant and equipment the cost of a replacement for part of the item, then it derecognises the carrying amount of the replaced part regardless of whether the replaced part had been depreciated separately. If it is not practicable for an entity to determine the carrying amount of the replaced part, it may use the cost of the replacement as an indication of what the cost of the replaced part was at the time it was acquired or constructed.

EXAMPLE 4

A manufacturing company has recently acquired a new factory building for a cost of INR 23,00,000 with a residual value of INR 300,000. This factory building has a flat roof, which needs replacing every ten years at a cost of INR 5,00,000.

The company is considering two alternative approaches:

To regard the item as one asset and, therefore, to depreciate the whole factory building over its useful economic life of 20 years, charging INR 1,00,000 per annum.

To regard the roof as a significant part of the item and depreciate the cost of the roof of INR 500,000 over 10 years, giving a depreciation charge of INR 50,000 per annum and to depreciate the remainder of the factory building of INR 18,00,000 down to its residual value of INR 3,00,000 over 20 years, giving a depreciation charge of INR 75,000.

Which approach is more suitable?

SOLUTION

Whichever approach is adopted, in year 10 when the roof is replaced the carrying amount attributable to the replaced roof will be written off.

The cost and accumulated depreciation of the old roof will be INR 5,00,000 and INR 2,50,000 respectively under the first approach described above. There will be a loss on disposal of INR 2,50,000 to be recognised in the income statement (the INR 5,00,000 replacement cost is used as a proxy for the original cost of the old roof as the actual cost is not determinable. No residual value is assumed for the old roof in calculating the accumulated depreciation).

The carrying amount of the old roof in year 10 will be nil under the second approach. The cost and accumulated depreciation of INR 5,00,000 are written off, with no profit or loss on disposal arising.

The second approach is suitable because this approach more accurately reflects the consumption of economic benefits of the factory building.

2.1.4 Option to take a useful life and residual value different from the prescribed useful life and residual value in Schedule II

The useful life of an asset should not ordinarily be different from the useful life specified in Part 'C' and the residual value of an asset should not be more than five per cent of the original cost of the asset.

However, where a company adopts a useful life different from what is specified in Part C or uses a residual value different from the limit specified above, the financial statements should disclose such difference and provide justification in this behalf duly supported by technical advice, whether external or internal.

Determination of residual value

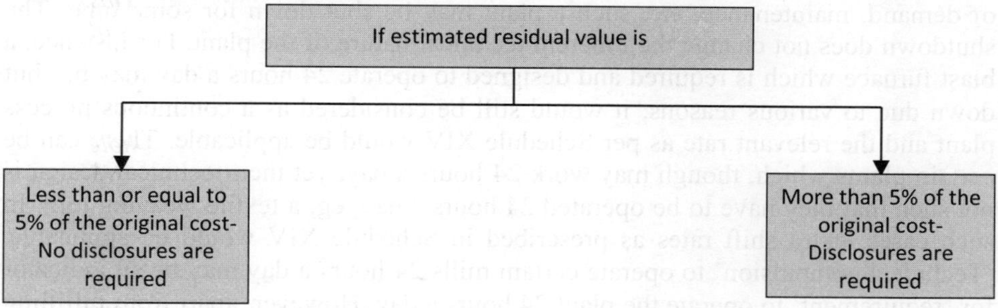

2.1.5 Regulated entities/assets

The useful life or residual value of any specific asset, as notified for accounting purposes by a Regulatory Authority constituted under an Act of Parliament or by the Central Government should be applied in calculating the depreciation to be provided for such asset irrespective of the requirements of Schedule II of the Companies Act, 2013.

Where a Regulatory Authority prescribes useful life, rate of depreciation or residual value for any specific asset for accounting purposes, the company should use that useful life, rate of depreciation or residual value even though it is different from that as estimated by the management. For example, Govt. Of India, Ministry of Power vide resolution dated 6th January, 2006 has notified Tariff Policy in terms of section 3 of the Electricity Act, 2003. The said policy inter-alia provides that rates of depreciation as notified by Central Electricity Regulatory Commission (CERC) would be applicable for the purpose of tariffs as well as accounting. Therefore, in accordance with Part B of Schedule II, companies which are regulated by the above-mentioned tariff policy should apply the rate of depreciation as specified in the above-mentioned tariff policy. *(Para 40 of Guidance Note on Accounting for Depreciation in companies in the context of Schedule II to the Companies Act, 2013)*

2.1.6 Continuous process plant

The concept of continuous process plant is same under both the Acts which is described as follows:

> *"Continuous process plant is a plant which is required and designed to operate 24 hours a day".*

The words 'required and designed to operate 24 hours a day' are very significant and should be interpreted with reference to the inherent technical nature of the plant, ie, the technical design of a continuous process plant is such that there is a requirement to run it continuously for 24 hours a day. If not so run, there are significant shutdown and/or start-up costs. If such a plant is shut down, there may be significant spoilage of material-in-process / some damage to the plant itself / significant energy loss. It is, however, possible that due to various reasons, eg, lack of demand, maintenance, etc, such a plant may be shut down for some time. The shutdown does not change the inherent technical nature of the plant. For instance, a blast furnace which is required and designed to operate 24 hours a day may be shut down due to various reasons; it would still be considered as a continuous process plant and the relevant rate as per Schedule XIV would be applicable. There can be certain plants which, though may work 24 hours a day, yet their technical design is not such that they have to be operated 24 hours a day, eg, a textile weaving mill. In such cases, extra shift rates as prescribed in Schedule XIV would be applicable. 'Technical compulsion' to operate certain mills 24 hours a day may be an indicator for 'requirement' to operate the plant 24 hours a day. However, apart from fulfilling the aforesaid condition, the plant should also be 'designed' to operate 24 hours a day. The expression 'inherent technical nature' does not only refer to the technological compulsion, but also to the design aspect of the plant. Whether a particular mill/plant is a continuous process plant is a technical question and should be determined keeping in view the individual facts and circumstance of each case on the basis of the inherent technical nature of plant (*EAC Opinion, 15.1.8*)

Repetitive process plant or assembly-line type plants should not be considered as the continuous process plants since these plants do not involve significant shut down and/or start-up costs and are not technically required and designed to operate 24 hours a day, e.g., an automobile manufacturing plant.

2.1.7 Depreciation on additions/deletions during the year

Schedule II of the Companies Act, 2013 provides that where, during any financial year, any addition has been made to any asset, or where any asset has been sold, discarded, demolished or destroyed, the depreciation on such assets should be calculated on a pro rata basis from the date of such addition or, as the case may be, up to the date on which such asset has been sold, discarded, demolished or destroyed.

This provision is similar to the requirements of the Companies Act, 1956 in this regard.

2.1.8 Depreciation on assets with value less than rupees five thousand

Treatment under Schedule XIV of the Companies Act, 1956

Notwithstanding anything mentioned in this Schedule depreciation on assets, whose actual cost does not exceed five thousand rupees, shall be provided depreciation at the rate of hundred per cent.

However, where the aggregate actual cost of individual items of plant and machinery costing INR 5,000 or less constitutes more than 10 per cent of the total actual cost of plant and machinery, rates of depreciation applicable to such items shall be the rates as specified in Item II of the Schedule.

Treatment under Schedule II of the Companies Act, 2013

There is no specified provision in the Companies Act, 2013. Thus, it may be inferred that the requirement of fully depreciating the assets up to INR 5,000 does not exist in the Companies Act, 2013. However, it should be noted that the provision under Schedule XIV to the Companies Act, 1956 to allow 100% depreciation in case of assets costing INR 5,000 or less was based on practices followed by the companies based on the materiality of the financial impact of such charge. Materiality of the financial impact of such charge should be considered with reference to the cost of the asset and size of the company. Accordingly, even after the introduction of Companies Act, 2013, a company may have the policy of 100% depreciation of assets upto certain threshold limits considering the aspect of materiality in the year of acquisition of the asset.

Chapter 3

Comparison of SLM Depreciation rates under Schedule II to the Companies Act, 1956 and Schedule XIV to the Companies Act, 2013

In this chapter, the comparison between SLM depreciation rates on various assets under the Companies Act, 2013 and Companies Act, 1956 has been given. The single shift depreciation rates has been computed on the basis of useful life and for double shift, the depreciation will increase by 50% for the period during which the asset is used for double shift. In case of the triple shift, the depreciation shall be calculated on the basis of 100% for the period during which the asset is used for triple shift.

The comparison have been given assuming both, i.e., nil residual value and residual value as 5% of original cost.

(*It may be noted that the depreciation rates have been rounded off to two decimal places*)

3.1 ITEM-BY-ITEM COMPARISON AND ASCERTAINMENT OF IMPACT IN SINGLE SHIFT (ASSUMING NIL RESIDUAL VALUE)

Nature of Assets	**Useful Life (Co. Act, 2013)**	**SLM BASIS**		**Impact Increase/ (decrease) (1)-(2)**
		Single Shift rate (Co. Act, 2013) (1)	**Single Shift rate (Co. Act, 1956) (2)**	
	(*Years*)	(%)	(%)	(%)
I. Buildings [NESD]				
(a) Buildings (other than factory buildings) RCC Frame Structure	60	1.67	1.63	0.04

Nature of Assets	**Useful Life (Co. Act, 2013)**	**SLM BASIS**		**Impact Increase/ (decrease) (1)-(2)**
		Single Shift rate (Co. Act, 2013) (1)	**Single Shift rate (Co. Act, 1956) (2)**	
	(Years)	(%)	(%)	(%)
(b) Buildings (other than factory buildings) other than RCC Frame Structure	30	3.33	1.63	1.70
(c) Factory buildings	30	3.33	3.34	(0.01)
(d) Fences, wells, tube wells	5	20	1.63 (Note 1)	18.37
(e) Others (including temporary structure, etc)	3	33.33	100 (Note 2)	(66.67)
II. Bridges, culverts, bunders, etc [NESD]	30	3.33	1.63 (Note 1)	1.70
III. Roads [NESD]				
(a) Carpeted roads				
(i) Carpeted Roads - RCC	10	10	1.63 (Note 1)	8.37
(ii) Carpeted Roads - other than RCC	5	20	1.63 (Note 1)	18.37
(b) Non-carpeted roads	3	33.33	1.63 (Note 1)	31.70
IV. Plant and Machinery				
(i) General rate applicable to plant and machinery not covered under special plant and machinery				
(a) Plant and Machinery other than continuous process plant not covered under specific industries	15	6.67	4.75	1.92
(b) continuous process plant for which no special rate has been prescribed under (ii) below [NESD]	25	4	5.28	(1.28)
(ii) Special Plant and Machinery				

Nature of Assets	Useful Life (Co. Act, 2013)	SLM BASIS		Impact Increase/ (decrease) (1)-(2)
		Single Shift rate (Co. Act, 2013) (1)	Single Shift rate (Co. Act, 1956) (2)	
	(*Years*)	(%)	(%)	(%)
(a) Plant and Machinery related to production and exhibition of Motion Picture Films				
Cinematograph films—Machinery used in the production and exhibition of cinematograph films, recording and equipment, developing machines, printing machines, editing reproducing machines, synchronisers and studio lights except bulbs	13	7.69	7.07	0.62
Projecting equipment for exhibition of films	13	7.69	7.07	0.62
(b) Plant and Machinery used in glass manufacturing				
1. Plant and Machinery except direct fire glass melting furnaces Recuperative and regenerative glass melting furnaces	13	7.69	7.07	0.62
2. Plant and Machinery except direct fire glass melting furnaces Moulds [NESD]	8	12.50	11.31	1.19
3. Float Glass Melting Furnaces [NESD]	10	10	10	-

Nature of Assets	**Useful Life (Co. Act, 2013)**	**SLM BASIS**		**Impact Increase/ (decrease) (1)-(2)**
		Single Shift rate (Co. Act, 2013) (1)	**Single Shift rate (Co. Act, 1956) (2)**	
	(Years)	(%)	(%)	(%)
(c) Plant and Machinery used in mines and quarries: Portable underground machinery and earth moving machinery used in open cast mining [NESD]	8	12.50	11.31	1.19
(d) Plant and Machinery used in Telecommunications [NESD]				
1. Towers	18	5.56	4.75 (Note 5)	0.81
2. Telecom transceivers, switching centres, transmission and other network equipment	13	7.69	4.75 (Note 5)	2.94
3. Telecom: Ducts, Cables and optical fibre	18	5.56	4.75 (Note 5)	0.81
4. Satellites	18	5.56	4.75 (Note 5)	0.81
(e) Plant and Machinery used in exploration, production and refining oil and gas [NESD]				
1. Refineries	25	4	4.75 (Note 5)	(0.75)
2. Oil and gas assets (including wells), processing plant and facilities	25	4	4.75 (Note 5)	(0.75)
3. Petrochemical Plant	25	4	4.75 (Note 5)	(0.75)
4. Storage tanks and related equipment	25	4	4.75 (Note 5)	(0.75)
5. Pipelines	30	3.33	4.75 (Note 5)	(1.42)
6. Drilling Rig	30	3.33	11.31	(7.98)

Nature of Assets	Useful Life (Co. Act, 2013)	SLM BASIS		Impact Increase/ (decrease) (1)-(2)
		Single Shift rate (Co. Act, 2013) (1)	Single Shift rate (Co. Act, 1956) (2)	
	(*Years*)	(%)	(%)	(%)
7. Field operations (above ground) Portable boilers, drilling tools, well-head tanks, etc	8	12.50	11.31	1.19
8. Loggers	8	12.50	4.75 (Note 5)	7.75
(f) Plant and Machinery used in generation, transmission and distribution of power [NESD]				
1. Thermal/ Gas/ Combined Cycle Power Generation Plant	40	2.50	4.75 (Note 5)	(2.25)
2. Hydro Power Generation Plant	40	2.50	4.75 (Note 5)	(2.25)
3. Nuclear Power Generation Plant	40	2.50	4.75 (Note 5)	(2.25)
4. Transmission lines, cables and other network assets	40	2.50	4.75 (Note 5)	(2.25)
5. Wind Power Generation Plant	22	4.55	4.75 (Note 5)	(0.20)
6. Electric Distribution Plant	35	2.86	4.75 (Note 5)	(1.89)
7. Gas Storage and Distribution Plant	30	3.33	4.75 (Note 5)	(1.42)
8. Water Distribution Plant including pipelines	30	3.33	4.75 (Note 5)	(1.42)
(g) Plant and Machinery used in manufacture of steel				

Nature of Assets	Useful Life (Co. Act, 2013)	SLM BASIS		Impact Increase/ (decrease) (1)-(2)
		Single Shift rate (Co. Act, 2013) (1)	Single Shift rate (Co. Act, 1956) (2)	
	(*Years*)	(%)	(%)	(%)
Plant and Machinery used in manufacture of steel				
1. Sinter Plant	20	5	4.75 (Note 5)	0.25
2. Blast Furnace	20	5	4.75 (Note 5)	0.25
3. Coke ovens	20	5	4.75 (Note 5)	0.25
4. Rolling mill in steel plant	20	5	4.75 (Note 5)	0.25
5. Basic oxygen Furnace Converter	25	4	4.75 (Note 5)	(0.75)
(h) Plant and Machinery used in manufacture of non-ferrous metals				
1. Metal pot line [NESD]	40	2.50	4.75 (Note 5)	(2.25)
2. Bauxite crushing and grinding section [NESD]	40	2.50	4.75 (Note 5)	(2.25)
3. Digester Section [NESD]	40	2.50	4.75 (Note 5)	(2.25)
4. Turbine [NESD]	40	2.50	4.75 (Note 5)	(2.25)
5. Equipment for Calcination [NESD]	40	2.50	4.75 (Note 5)	(2.25)
6. Copper Smelter [NESD]	40	2.50	4.75 (Note 5)	(2.25)
7. Roll Grinder	40	2.50	4.75 (Note 5)	(2.25)
8. Soaking Pit	30	3.33	4.75 (Note 5)	(1.42)
9. Annealing Furnace	30	3.33	4.75 (Note 5)	(1.42)
10. Rolling Mills	30	3.33	4.75 (Note 5)	(1.42)
11. Equipment for Scalping, Slitting , etc [NESD]	30	3.33	4.75 (Note5)	(1.42)
12. Surface Miner, Ripper Dozer, etc, used in mines	25	4.00	4.75 (Note 5)	(0.75)
13. Copper refining plant [NESD]	25	4.00	4.75 (Note 5)	(0.75)
(i) Plant and Machinery used in medical and surgical operations [NESD]				

Nature of Assets	Useful Life (Co. Act, 2013)	SLM BASIS		Impact Increase/ (decrease) (1)-(2)
		Single Shift rate (Co. Act, 2013) (1)	Single Shift rate (Co. Act, 1956) (2)	
	(*Years*)	(%)	(%)	(%)
1. Electrical Machinery, X-ray and electrotherapeutic apparatus and accessories thereto, medical, diagnostic equipment, namely, Cat-scan, Ultrasound Machines, ECG Monitors, etc	13	7.69	7.07	0.62
2. Other Equipment	15	6.67	4.75 (Note 5)	1.92
(j) Plant and Machinery used in manufacture of pharmaceuticals and chemicals [NESD]				
1. Reactors	20	5	4.75 (Note 5)	0.25
2. Distillation Columns	20	5	4.75 (Note 5)	0.25
3. Drying equipment/Centrifuges and Decanters	20	5	4.75 (Note 5)	0.25
4. Vessel/storage tanks	20	5	4.75 (Note 5)	0.25
(k) Plant and Machinery used in civil construction				
1. Concreting, Crushing, Piling Equipment and Road Making Equipment	12	8.33	4.75 (Note 5)	3.58
2. Heavy Lift Equipment				
Cranes with capacity of more than 100 tons	20	5	4.75 (Note 5)	0.25
Cranes with capacity of less than 100 tons	15	6.67	4.75 (Note 5)	1.92
3. Transmission line, Tunnelling Equipment [NESD]	10	10.00	4.75 (Note 5)	5.25

Nature of Assets	Useful Life (Co. Act, 2013)	SLM BASIS		Impact Increase/ (decrease) (1)-(2)
		Single Shift rate (Co. Act, 2013) (1)	Single Shift rate (Co. Act, 1956) (2)	
	(*Years*)	(%)	(%)	(%)
4. Earth-moving equipment	9	11.11	11.31	(0.2)
5. Others including Material Handling /Pipeline/Welding Equipment [NESD]	12	8.33	4.75 (Note 5)	3 .58
(l) Plant and Machinery used in salt works [NESD]	15	6.67	4.75 (Note 4)	1.92
V. Furniture and fittings [NESD]				
(i) General furniture and fittings	10	10	6.33	3.67
(ii) Furniture and fittings used in hotels, restaurants and boarding houses, schools, colleges and other educational institutions, libraries; welfare centres; meeting halls, cinema houses; theatres and circuses; and furniture and fittings let out on hire for use on the occasion of marriages and similar functions.	8	12.50	9.5	3.00
VI. Motor Vehicles [NESD]				
1. Motor cycles, scooters and other mopeds	10	10	9.5	0.50
2. Motor buses, motor lorries, motor cars and motor taxies used in a business of running them on hire	6	16.67	16.21	0.46

Nature of Assets	Useful Life (Co. Act, 2013)	SLM BASIS		Impact Increase/ (decrease) (1)-(2)
		Single Shift rate (Co. Act, 2013) (1)	Single Shift rate (Co. Act, 1956) (2)	
	(*Years*)	(%)	(%)	(%)
3. Motor buses, motor lorries and motor cars other than those used in a business of running them on hire	8	12.50	11.31	1.19
4. Motor tractors, harvesting combines and heavy vehicles	8	12.50	11.31	1.19
5. Electrically operated vehicles including battery powered or fuel cell powered vehicles	8	12.50	7.07	5.43
VII. Ships [NESD]				
1. Ocean-going ships				
(i) Bulk Carriers and liner vessels	25	4	5 (Note 3)	(1.00)
(ii) Crude tankers, product carriers and easy chemical carriers with or without conventional tank coatings	20	5	5 (Note 3)	-
(iii) Chemicals and Acid Carriers:				
(a) With Stainless steel tanks	25	4	5 (Note 3)	(1.00)
(b) With other tanks	20	5	5 (Note 3)	-
(iv) Liquefied gas carriers	30	3.33	5 (Note 3)	(1.67)
(v) Conventional large passenger vessels which are used for cruise purpose also	30	3.33	5 (Note 3)	(1.67)
(vi) Coastal service ships of all categories	30	3.33	5 (Note 3)	(1.67)
(vii) Offshore supply and support vessels	20	5	5 (Note 3)	-
(viii) Catamarans and other high speed passenger for ships or boats	20	5	5 (Note 3)	-

Nature of Assets	**Useful Life (Co. Act, 2013)**	**SLM BASIS**		**Impact Increase/ (decrease) (1)-(2)**
		Single Shift rate (Co. Act, 2013) (1)	**Single Shift rate (Co. Act, 1956) (2)**	
	(*Years*)	(%)	(%)	(%)
(ix) Drill ships	25	4	5(Note 3)	(1.00)
(x) Hovercrafts	15	6.67	5(Note 3)	1.67
(xi) Fishing vessels with wooden hull	10	10	10	-
(xii) Dredgers, tugs, barges, survey launches and other similar ships used mainly for dredging purposes	14	7.14	7	0.14
2. Vessels ordinarily operating on inland waters				
(i) Speed boats	13	7.69	7.07	0.62
(ii) Other vessels	28	3.57	3.34	0.23
VIII. Aircrafts or Helicopters [NESD]	20	5	5.6	(0.60)
IX. Railways sidings, locomotives, rolling stocks, tramways and railways used by concerns, excluding railway concerns [NESD]	15	6.67	4.75(Note5)	1.92
X. Ropeway structures [NESD]	15	6.67	11.31	(4.64)
XI. Office equipment [NESD]	5	20	4.75(Note 5)	15.25
XII. Computers and data processing units [NESD]				
(i) Servers and networks	6	16.67	16.21	0.46
(ii) End user devices, such as, desktops, laptops, etc.	3	33.33	16.21	17.12
XIII. Laboratory equipment [NESD]				
(i) General laboratory equipment	10	10	4.75(Note 5)	5.25

Nature of Assets	Useful Life (Co. Act, 2013)	SLM BASIS		Impact Increase/ (decrease) (1)-(2)
		Single Shift rate (Co. Act, 2013) (1)	Single Shift rate (Co. Act, 1956) (2)	
	(*Years*)	(%)	(%)	(%)
(ii) Laboratory equipment used in educational institutions	5	20	4.75(Note 5)	15.25
XIV. Electrical Installations and Equipment [NESD]	10	10	4.75(Note 5)	5.25
XV. Hydraulic works, pipelines and sluices [NESD]	15	6.67	4.75(Note 5)	1.92

Notes:

1. 'Buildings' includes roads, bridges, culverts, wells and tubewells; 'factory buildings' does not include offices, godowns, officers and employees' quarters, roads, bridges, culverts, wells and tubewells according to the Schedule XIV of the Companies Act, 1956. Hence the corresponding Schedule XIV rates considered for comparison for the following categories prescribed in Schedule II to the Companies Act, 2013 are those of *'buildings* (*other than factory buildings*) *NESD'* specified in Schedule XIV*:*
   (a) 'Fences, wells and tubewells' under the head 'Buildings (NESD)'
   (b) Bridges, culverts, bunders, etc (NESD)
   (c) Roads (NESD)
2. Corresponding Schedule XIV rate considered for comparison for the sub-category 'others (including temporary structure etc)' under the category 'buildings (NESD)' prescribed in Schedule II to the Companies Act, 2013 is that of 'Purely temporary erections such as wooden structures' prescribed in Schedule XIV of the Companies Act, 1956.
3. Corresponding Schedule XIV rate considered for comparison for the following sub-categories are those of sub-category 'other ships (NESD)' under the category 'Ships' prescribed in the schedule XIV:
   (a) Bulk Carriers and liner vessels
   (b) Crude tankers, product carriers and easy chemical carriers with or without conventional tank coatings
   (c) Chemicals and Acid Carriers
   (d) Liquefied gas carriers

(e) Conventional large passenger vessels which are used for cruise purpose also

(f) Coastal service ships of all categories

(g) Offshore supply and support vessels

(h) Catamarans and other high speed passenger for ships or boats

(i) Drill ships

(j) Hovercrafts

4. Corresponding Schedule XIV rate considered for comparison for the item 'plant and machinery used in salt works' are those of general plant and machinery (other than continuous process plant and ship) for which no specific rates have been prescribed.

5. There are various items which were clubbed earlier under general plant and machinery category and now separate useful life has been prescribed for them after the introduction of Schedule II. For such items, Schedule XIV rate for comparison is taken to be the rate prescribed in Schedule XIV for the general category, ie, 'other than continuous process plant for which no special rate has been prescribed'.

3.2 ITEM-BY-ITEM COMPARISON AND ASCERTAINMENT OF IMPACT IN DOUBLE SHIFT (ASSUMING NIL RESIDUAL VALUE)

(*Note: The useful lives of assets working on shift basis have been specified in the Schedule II of the Companies Act, 2013, based on their single shift working. Except for assets in respect of which no extra shift depreciation is permitted (indicated by NESD), if an asset is used for any time during the year for double shift, the depreciation will increase by 50% for that period. Accordingly, the double shift SLM rate in column 1 below is computed by adding an increase of 50% in the single shift SLM rate.*)

Nature of Assets	Useful Life for Single shift (Co. Act, 2013)	SLM BASIS		Impact Increase/ (decrease) (1)-(2)
		Double Shift rate (Co. Act, 2013) (1)	Double Shift rate (Co. Act, 1956) (2)	
	(*Years*)	(%)	(%)	(%)
Plant and Machinery				
General rate applicable to plant and machinery not covered under special plant and machinery				

Nature of Assets	**Useful Life for Single shift (Co. Act, 2013)**	**SLM BASIS**		**Impact Increase/ (decrease) (1)-(2)**
		Double Shift rate (Co. Act, 2013) (1)	**Double Shift rate (Co. Act, 1956) (2)**	
	(*Years*)	(%)	(%)	(%)
(a) Plant and Machinery other than continuous process plant not covered under specific industries	15	10.00	7.42	2.58
Special Plant and Machinery				
(a) Plant and Machinery related to production and exhibition of Motion Picture Films				
1. Cinematograph films—Machinery used in the production and exhibition of cinematograph films, recording and equipment, developing machines, printing machines, editing reproducing machines, synchronisers and studio lights except bulbs	13	11.54	7.07 (*NESD*)	4.47
2. Projecting equipment for exhibition of films	13	11.54	7.07 (*NESD*)	4.47
(b) Plant and Machinery used in glass manufacturing				
1. Plant and Machinery except direct fire glass melting furnaces Recuperative and regenerative glass melting furnaces	13	11.54	11.31	0.23
(c) Plant and Machinery used in manufacture of steel				
1. Sinter Plant	20	7.50	7.42	0.08
2. Blast Furnace	20	7.50	7.42	0.08
3. Coke ovens	20	7.50	7.42	0.08
4. Rolling mill in steel plant	20	7.50	7.42	0.08
5. Basic oxygen Furnace Converter	25	6.00	7.42	(1.42)

Nature of Assets	Useful Life for Single shift (Co. Act, 2013)	SLM BASIS		Impact Increase/ (decrease) (1)-(2)
		Double Shift rate (Co. Act, 2013) (1)	Double Shift rate (Co. Act, 1956) (2)	
	(Years)	(%)	(%)	(%)
(d) Plant and Machinery used in civil construction				
1. Concreting, Crushing, Piling Equipment and Road Making Equipment	12	12.50	7.42	5.08
2. Heavy Lift Equipment				
Cranes with capacity of more than 100 tons	20	7.50	7.42	0.08
Cranes with capacity of less than 100 tons	15	10.00	7.42	2.58
3. Transmission line, Tunnelling Equipment [NESD]	10	10 *(NESD)*	7.42	2.58
4. Earth-moving equipment	9	16.67	11.31 *(NESD)*	5.36
5. Others including Material Handling /Pipeline/Welding Equipment [NESD]	12	8.33 *(NESD)*	7.42	0.91
(e) Plant and Machinery used in Telecommunications [NESD]				
1. Towers	18	5.56 *(NESD)*	7.42	(1.86)
2. Telecom transceivers, switching centres, transmission and other network equipment	13	7.69 *(NESD)*	7.42	0.27
3. Telecom: Ducts, Cables and optical fibre	18	5.56 *(NESD)*	7.42	(1.86)
4. Satellites	18	5.56 *(NESD)*	7.42	(1.86)
(f) Plant and Machinery used in exploration, production and refining oil and gas [NESD]				

Nature of Assets	Useful Life for Single shift (Co. Act, 2013)	SLM BASIS		Impact Increase/ (decrease) (1)-(2)
		Double Shift rate (Co. Act, 2013) (1)	Double Shift rate (Co. Act, 1956) (2)	
	(*Years*)	(%)	(%)	(%)
1. Refineries	25	4 (*NESD*)	7.42	(3.42)
2. Oil and gas assets (including wells), processing plant and facilities	25	4 (*NESD*)	7.42	(3.42)
3. Petrochemical Plant	25	4 (*NESD*)	7.42	(3.42)
4. Storage tanks and related equipments	25	4 (*NESD*)	7.42	(3.42)
5. Pipelines	30	3.33 (*NESD*)	7.42	(4.09)
6. Loggers	8	12.5 (*NESD*)	7.42	5.08
(g) Plant and Machinery used in generation, transmission and distribution of power [NESD]				
1. Thermal/ Gas/ Combined Cycle Power Generation Plant	40	2.5 (*NESD*)	7.42	(4.92)
2. Hydro Power Generation Plant	40	2.5 (*NESD*)	7.42	(4.92)
3. Nuclear Power Generation Plant	40	2.5 (*NESD*)	7.42	(4.92)
4. Transmission lines, cables and other network assets	40	2.5 (*NESD*)	7.42	(4.92)
5. Wind Power Generation Plant	22	4.55 (*NESD*)	7.42	(2.87)
6. Electric Distribution Plant	35	2.86 (*NESD*)	7.42	(4.56)
7. Gas Storage and Distribution Plant	30	3.33 (*NESD*)	7.42	(4.09)
8. Water Distribution Plant including pipelines	30	3.33 (*NESD*)	7.42	(4.09)

Nature of Assets	Useful Life for Single shift (Co. Act, 2013)	SLM BASIS		Impact Increase/ (decrease) (1)-(2)
		Double Shift rate (Co. Act, 2013) (1)	Double Shift rate (Co. Act, 1956) (2)	
	(*Years*)	(%)	(%)	(%)
(h) Plant and Machinery used in manufacture of non-ferrous metals				
1. Metal pot line [NESD]	40	2.5 (*NESD*)	7.42	(4.92)
2. Bauxite crushing and grinding section [NESD]	40	2.5 (*NESD*)	7.42	(4.92)
3. Digester Section [NESD]	40	2.5 (*NESD*)	7.42	(4.92)
4. Turbine [NESD]	40	2.5 (*NESD*)	7.42	(4.92)
5. Equipment for Calcination [NESD]	40	2.5 (*NESD*)	7.42	(4.92)
6. Copper Smelter [NESD]	40	2.5 (*NESD*)	7.42	(4.92)
		3.75		
7. Roll Grinder	40	5	7.42	(3.67)
8. Soaking Pit	30	5	7.42	(2.42)
9. Annealing Furnace	30	5	7.42	(2.42)
10. Rolling Mills	30	3.33	7.42	(2.42)
11. Equipment for Scalping, Slitting , etc [NESD]	30	(*NESD*)	7.42	(4.09)
		6		
12. Surface Miner, Ripper Dozer, etc, used in mines	25		7.42	(1.42)
		4 (*NESD*)		
13. Copper refining plant [NESD]	25		7.42	(3.42)
(i) Plant and Machinery used in medical and surgical operations [NESD]				
1. Other Equipment	15	6.67 (*NESD*)	7.42	(0.75)
(j) Plant and Machinery used in manufacture of pharmaceuticals and chemicals [NESD]				
1. Reactors	20	5 (*NESD*)	7.42	(2.42)
2. Distillation Columns	20	5 (*NESD*)	7.42	(2.42)
3. Drying equipment/Centrifuges and	20	5 (*NESD*)	7.42	(2.42)

Nature of Assets	Useful Life for Single shift (Co. Act, 2013)	SLM BASIS		Impact Increase/ (decrease) (1)-(2)
		Double Shift rate (Co. Act, 2013) (1)	Double Shift rate (Co. Act, 1956) (2)	
	(*Years*)	(%)	(%)	(%)
Decanters 4. Vessel/storage tanks	20	5 (*NESD*)	7.42	(2.42)
(k) Plant and Machinery used in salt works [NESD]	15	6.67 (*NESD*)	7.42	(0.75)
Laboratory equipment [NESD]				
(i) General laboratory equipment	10	10 (*NESD*)	7.42	2.58
(ii) Laboratory equipment used in educational institutions	5	20 (*NESD*)	7.42	12.58

3.3 ITEM-BY-ITEM COMPARISON AND ASCERTAINMENT OF IMPACT IN TRIPLE SHIFT (ASSUMING NIL RESIDUAL VALUE)

(***Note:*** *The useful lives of assets working on shift basis have been specified in the Schedule II of the Companies Act, 2013, based on their single shift working. Except for assets in respect of which no extra shift depreciation is permitted (indicated by NESD), if an asset is used for any time during the year for triple shift, the depreciation should be calculated on the basis of 100% for that period. Accordingly, the triple shift SLM rate in column 1 below is taken as 200% of the single shift SLM rate*)

Nature of Assets	Useful Life for Single shift (Co. Act, 2013)	SLM BASIS		Impact Increase/ (decrease) (1)-(2)
		Triple Shift rate (Co. Act, 2013) (1)	Triple Shift rate (Co. Act, 1956) (2)	
	(*Years*)	(%)	(%)	(%)
Plant and Machinery				
General rate applicable to plant and machinery not covered under special plant and machinery				
(a) Plant and Machinery other than continuous process plant	15	13.33	10.34	2.99

Nature of Assets	Useful Life for Single shift (Co. Act, 2013)	SLM BASIS		Impact Increase/ (decrease) (1)-(2)
		Triple Shift rate (Co. Act, 2013) (1)	Triple Shift rate (Co. Act, 1956) (2)	
	(*Years*)	(%)	(%)	(%)
not covered under specific industries				
Special Plant and Machinery				
(a) Plant and Machinery related to production and exhibition of Motion Picture Films				
1. Cinematograph films: Machinery used in the production and exhibition of cinematograph films, recording and equipment, developing machines, printing machines, editing reproducing machines, synchronizers and studio lights except bulbs	13	15.38	7.07 (*NESD*)	8.31
2. Projecting equipment for exhibition of films	13	15.38	7.07 (*NESD*)	8.31
(b) Plant and Machinery used in glass manufacturing				
1. Plant and Machinery except direct fire glass melting furnaces Recuperative and regenerative glass melting furnaces	13	15.38	16.21	(0.83)
(c) Plant and Machinery used in manufacture of steel				
1. Sinter Plant	20	10.00	10.34	(0.34)
2. Blast Furnace	20	10.00	10.34	(0.34)
3. Coke ovens	20	10.00	10.34	(0.34)
4. Rolling mill in steel plant	20	10.00	10.34	(0.34)
5. Basic oxygen Furnace Converter	25	8.00	10.34	(2.34)

Nature of Assets	Useful Life for Single shift (Co. Act, 2013)	SLM BASIS		Impact Increase/ (decrease) (1)-(2)
		Triple Shift rate (Co. Act, 2013) (1)	Triple Shift rate (Co. Act, 1956) (2)	
	(Years)	(%)	(%)	(%)
(d) Plant and Machinery used in civil construction				
1. Concreting, Crushing, Piling Equipment and Road Making Equipment	12	16.67	10.34	6.33
2. Heavy Lift Equipment				
Cranes with capacity of more than 100 tons	20	10.00	10.34	(0.34)
Cranes with capacity of less than 100 tons	15	13.33	10.34	2.99
3. Transmission line, Tunnelling Equipment [NESD]	10	10 *(NESD)*	10.34	(0.34)
4. Earth-moving equipment	9	22.22	11.31 *(NESD)*	10.91
5. Others including Material Handling /Pipeline/ Welding Equipment [NESD]	12	8.33 *(NESD)*	10.34	(2.01)
(e) Plant and Machinery used in Telecommunications [NESD]				
1. Towers	18	5.56 *(NESD)*	10.34	(4.78)
2. Telecom transceivers, switching centres, transmission and other network equipment	13	7.69 *(NESD)*	10.34	(2.65)
3. Telecom: Ducts, Cables and optical fibre	18	5.56 *(NESD)*	10.34	(4.78)
4. Satellites	18	5.56 *(NESD)*	10.34	(4.78)
(f) Plant and Machinery used in exploration, production and refining oil and gas [NESD]				

Nature of Assets	Useful Life for Single shift (Co. Act, 2013)	SLM BASIS		Impact Increase/ (decrease) (1)-(2)
		Triple Shift rate (Co. Act, 2013) (1)	Triple Shift rate (Co. Act, 1956) (2)	
	(*Years*)	(%)	(%)	(%)
1. Refineries	25	4 (*NESD*)	10.34	(6.34)
2. Oil and gas assets (including wells), processing plant and facilities	25	4 (*NESD*)	10.34	(6.34)
3. Petrochemical Plant	25	4 (*NESD*)	10.34	(6.34)
4. Storage tanks and related equipments	25	4 (*NESD*)	10.34	(6.34)
5. Pipelines	30	3.33 (*NESD*)	10.34	(7.01)
6. Loggers	8	12.5 (*NESD*)	10.34	2.16
(g) Plant and Machinery used in generation, transmission and distribution of power [NESD]				
1. Thermal/ Gas/ Combined Cycle Power Generation Plant	40	2.5 (*NESD*)	10.34	(7.84)
2. Hydro Power Generation Plant	40	2.5 (*NESD*)	10.34	(7.84)
3. Nuclear Power Generation Plant	40	2.5 (*NESD*)	10.34	(7.84)
4. Transmission lines, cables and other network assets	40	2.5 (*NESD*)	10.34	(7.84)
5. Wind Power Generation Plant	22	4.55 (*NESD*)	10.34	(5.79)
6. Electric Distribution Plant	35	2.86 (*NESD*)	10.34	(7.48)
7. Gas Storage and Distribution Plant	30	3.33 (*NESD*)	10.34	(7.01)
8. Water Distribution Plant including pipelines	30	3.33 (*NESD*)	10.34	(7.01)

Nature of Assets	Useful Life for Single shift (Co. Act, 2013)	SLM BASIS		Impact Increase/ (decrease) (1)-(2)
		Triple Shift rate (Co. Act, 2013) (1)	Triple Shift rate (Co. Act, 1956) (2)	
	(*Years*)	(%)	(%)	(%)
(h) Plant and Machinery used in manufacture of non-ferrous metals				
1. Metal pot line [NESD]	40	2.5 (*NESD*)	10.34	(7.84)
2. Bauxite crushing and grinding section [NESD]	40	2.5 (*NESD*)	10.34	(7.84)
3. Digester Section [NESD]	40	2.5 (*NESD*)	10.34	(7.84)
4. Turbine [NESD]	40	2.5 (*NESD*)	10.34	(7.84)
5. Equipment for Calcination [NESD]	40	2.5 (*NESD*)	10.34	(7.84)
6. Copper Smelter [NESD]	40	2.5 (*NESD*)	10.34	(7.84)
7. Roll Grinder	40	5	10.34	(5.34)
8. Soaking Pit	30	6.67	10.34	(3.67)
9. Annealing Furnace	30	6.67	10.34	(3.67)
10. Rolling Mills	30	6.67	10.34	(3.67)
11. Equipment for Scalping, Slitting , etc [NESD]	30	3.33 (*NESD*)	10.34	(7.01)
12. Surface Miner, Ripper Dozer, etc., used in mines	25	8	10.34	(2.34)
13. Copper refining plant [NESD]	25	4 (*NESD*)	10.34	(6.34)
(i) Plant and Machinery used in medical and surgical operations [NESD]				
1. Other Equipment	15	6.67 (*NESD*)	10.34	(3.67)
(j) Plant and Machinery used in manufacture of pharmaceuticals and chemicals [NESD]				
1. Reactors	20	5 (*NESD*)	10.34	(5.34)
2. Distillation Columns	20	5 (*NESD*)	10.34	(5.34)

Nature of Assets	Useful Life for Single shift (Co. Act, 2013)	SLM BASIS		Impact Increase/ (decrease) (1)-(2)
		Triple Shift rate (Co. Act, 2013) (1)	Triple Shift rate (Co. Act, 1956) (2)	
	(*Years*)	(%)	(%)	(%)
3. Drying equipment/Centrifuges and Decanters	20	5 (*NESD*)	10.34	(5.34)
4. Vessel/storage tanks	20	5 (*NESD*)	10.34	(5.34)
(k) Plant and Machinery used in salt works [NESD]	15	6.67 (*NESD*)	10.34	(3.67)
Laboratory equipment [NESD]				
(i) General laboratory equipment	10	10 (*NESD*)	10.34	(0.34)
(ii) Laboratory equipment used in educational institutions	5	20 (*NESD*)	10.34	9.66

3.4 ITEM BY ITEM COMPARISON AND ASCERTAINMENT OF IMPACT IN SINGLE SHIFT (ASSUMING 5% RESIDUAL VALUE)

Nature of Assets	Useful Life (Co. Act, 2013)	SLM BASIS		Impact Increase/ (decrease) (1)-(2)
		Single Shift rate (Co. Act, 2013) (1)	Single Shift rate (Co. Act, 1956) (2)	
	(*Years*)	(%)	(%)	(%)
I. Buildings [NESD]				
(a) Buildings (other than factory buildings) RCC Frame Structure	60	1.58	1.63	(0.05)
(b) Buildings (other than factory buildings) other than RCC Frame Structure	30	3.17	1.63	1.54
(c) Factory buildings	30	3.17	3.34	(0.17)
(d) Fences, wells, tube wells	5	19.00	1.63	17.37

		SLM BASIS		
Nature of Assets	Useful Life (Co. Act, 2013)	Single Shift rate (Co. Act, 2013) (1)	Single Shift rate (Co. Act, 1956) (2)	Impact Increase/ (decrease) (1)-(2)
	(*Years*)	(%)	(%)	(%)
			(Note 1)	
(e) Others (including temporary structure, etc.)	3	31.67	100 (Note 2)	(68.33)
II. Bridges, culverts, bunders, etc. [NESD]	30	3.17	1.63 (Note 1)	1.54
III. Roads [NESD]				
(a) Carpeted roads				
(i) Carpeted Roads-RCC	10	9.50	1.63 (Note 1)	7.87
(ii) Carpeted Roads-other than RCC	5	19.00	1.63 (Note 1)	17.37
(b) Non-carpeted roads	3	31.67	1.63 (Note 1)	30.04
IV. Plant and Machinery				
(i) General rate applicable to plant and machinery not covered under special plant and machinery				
(a) Plant and Machinery other than continuous process plant not covered under specific industries	15	6.33	4.75	1.58
(b) continuous process plant for which no special rate has been prescribed under (ii) below [NESD]	25	3.80	5.28	(1.48)
(ii) Special Plant and Machinery				
(a) Plant and Machinery related to production and exhibition of Motion				

Nature of Assets	Useful Life (Co. Act, 2013)	SLM BASIS Single Shift rate (Co. Act, 2013) (1)	Single Shift rate (Co. Act, 1956) (2)	Impact Increase/ (decrease) (1)-(2)
	(*Years*)	(%)	(%)	(%)
Picture Films				
Cinematograph films—Machinery used in the production and exhibition of cinematograph films, recording and equipments, developing machines, printing machines, editing reproducing machines, synchronizers and studio lights except bulbs	13	7.31	7.07	0.24
Projecting equipment for exhibition of films	13	7.31	7.07	0.24
(b) Plant and Machinery used in glass manufacturing				-
1. Plant and Machinery except direct fire glass melting furnaces Recuperative and regenerative glass melting furnaces	13	7.31	7.07	0.24
2. Plant and Machinery except direct fire glass melting furnaces Moulds [NESD]	8	11.88	11.31	0.57
3. Float Glass Melting Furnaces [NESD]	10	9.50	10	(0.50)
(c) Plant and Machinery used in mines and quarries—Portable underground machinery and earth moving machinery used in open cast mining [NESD]	8	11.88	11.31	0.57
(d) Plant and Machinery used in Telecommunications [NESD]				

Nature of Assets	Useful Life (Co. Act, 2013)	SLM BASIS: Single Shift rate (Co. Act, 2013) (1)	Single Shift rate (Co. Act, 1956) (2)	Impact: Increase/ (decrease) (1)-(2)
	(*Years*)	(%)	(%)	(%)
1. Towers	18	5.28	4.75 (Note 4)	0.53
2. Telecom transceivers, switching centres, transmission and other network equipment	13	7.31	4.75 (Note 4)	2.56
3. Telecom—Ducts, Cables and optical fibre	18	5.28	4.75 (Note 4)	0.53
4. Satellites	18	5.28	4.75 (Note 4)	0.53
(e) Plant and Machinery used in exploration, production and refining oil and gas [NESD]				
1. Refineries	25	3.80	4.75 (Note 4)	(0.95)
2. Oil and gas assets (including wells), processing plant and facilities	25	3.80	4.75 (Note 4)	(0.95)
3. Petrochemical Plant	25	3.80	4.75 (Note 4)	(0.95)
4. Storage tanks and related equipment	25	3.80	4.75 (Note 4)	(0.95)
5. Pipelines	30	3.17	4.75 (Note 4)	(1.58)
6. Drilling Rig	30	3.17	11.31	(8.14)
7. Field operations (above ground) Portable boilers, drilling tools, well-head tanks, etc.	8	11.88	11.31	0.57
8. Loggers	8	11.88	4.75 (Note 4)	7.13

Nature of Assets	Useful Life (Co. Act, 2013)	SLM BASIS Single Shift rate (Co. Act, 2013) (1)	Single Shift rate (Co. Act, 1956) (2)	Impact Increase/ (decrease) (1)-(2)
	(*Years*)	(%)	(%)	(%)
(f) Plant and Machinery used in generation, transmission and distribution of power [NESD]				
1. Thermal/ Gas/ Combined Cycle Power Generation Plant	40	2.38	4.75 (Note 4)	(2.38)
2. Hydro Power Generation Plant	40	2.38	4.75 (Note 4)	(2.38)
3. Nuclear Power Generation Plant	40	2.38	4.75 (Note 4)	(2.38)
4. Transmission lines, cables and other network assets	40	2.38	4.75 (Note 4)	(2.38)
5. Wind Power Generation Plant	22	4.32	4.75 (Note 4)	(0.43)
6. Electric Distribution Plant	35	2.71	4.75 (Note 4)	(2.04)
7. Gas Storage and Distribution Plant	30	3.17	4.75 (Note 4)	(1.58)
8. Water Distribution Plant including pipelines	30	3.17	4.75 (Note 4)	(1.58)
(g) Plant and Machinery used in manufacture of steel				
1. Sinter Plant	20	4.75	4.75 (Note 4)	-
2. Blast Furnace	20	4.75	4.75 (Note 4)	-
3. Coke ovens	20	4.75	4.75 (Note 4)	-
4. Rolling mill in steel plant	20	4.75	4.75 (Note 4)	-
5. Basic oxygen Furnace	25	3.80	4.75	(0.95)

Nature of Assets	Useful Life (Co. Act, 2013)	SLM BASIS Single Shift rate (Co. Act, 2013) (1)	Single Shift rate (Co. Act, 1956) (2)	Impact Increase/ (decrease) (1)-(2)
	(*Years*)	(%)	(%)	(%)
Converter			(Note 4)	
(h) Plant and Machinery used in manufacture of non-ferrous metals				
1. Metal pot line [NESD]	40	2.38	4.75 (Note 4)	(2.38)
2. Bauxite crushing and grinding section [NESD]	40	2.38	4.75 (Note 4)	(2.38)
3. Digester Section [NESD]	40	2.38	4.75 (Note 4)	(2.38)
4. Turbine [NESD]	40	2.38	4.75 (Note 4)	(2.38)
5. Equipments for Calcination [NESD]	40	2.38	4.75 (Note 4)	(2.38)
6. Copper Smelter [NESD]	40	2.38	4.75 (Note 4)	(2.38)
7. Roll Grinder	40	2.38	4.75 (Note 4)	(2.38)
8. Soaking Pit	30	3.17	4.75 (Note 4)	(1.58)
9. Annealing Furnace	30	3.17	4.75 (Note 4)	(1.58)
10. Rolling Mills	30	3.17	4.75 (Note 4)	(1.58)
11. Equipments for Scalping, Slitting , etc. [NESD]	30	3.17	4.75 (Note 4)	(1.58)
12. Surface Miner, Ripper Dozer, etc., used in mines	25	3.80	4.75 (Note 4)	(0.95)
13. Copper refining plant [NESD]	25	3.80	4.75 (Note 4)	(0.95)

Nature of Assets	Useful Life (Co. Act, 2013)	SLM BASIS Single Shift rate (Co. Act, 2013) (1)	SLM BASIS Single Shift rate (Co. Act, 1956) (2)	Impact Increase/ (decrease) (1)-(2)
	(*Years*)	(%)	(%)	(%)
(i) Plant and Machinery used in medical and surgical operations [NESD]				
1. Electrical Machinery, X-ray and electrotherapeutic apparatus and accessories thereto, medical, diagnostic equipments, namely, Cat-scan, Ultrasound Machines, ECG Monitors, etc.	13	7.31	7.07	0.24
2. Other Equipments.	15	6.33	4.75 (Note 4)	1.58
(j) Plant and Machinery used in manufacture of pharmaceuticals and chemicals [NESD]				
1. Reactors	20	4.75	4.75 (Note 4)	-
2. Distillation Columns	20	4.75	4.75 (Note 4)	-
3. Drying equipments/Centrifuges and Decanters	20	4.75	4.75 (Note 4)	-
4. Vessel/storage tanks	20	4.75	4.75 (Note 4)	-
(k) Plant and Machinery used in civil construction				
1. Concreting, Crushing, Piling Equipments and Road Making Equipments	12	7.92	4.75 (Note 4)	3.17
2. Heavy Lift Equipments				

Nature of Assets	Useful Life (Co. Act, 2013)	SLM BASIS Single Shift rate (Co. Act, 2013) (1)	Single Shift rate (Co. Act, 1956) (2)	Impact Increase/ (decrease) (1)-(2)
	(*Years*)	(%)	(%)	(%)
Cranes with capacity of more than 100 tons	20	4.75	4.75 (Note 4)	-
Cranes with capacity of less than 100 tons	15	6.33	4.75 (Note 4)	1.58
3. Transmission line, Tunneling Equipments [NESD]	10	9.50	4.75 (Note 4)	4.75
4. Earth-moving equipments	9	10.56	11.31	(0.75)
5. Others including Material Handling /Pipeline/Welding Equipments [NESD]	12	7.92	4.75 (Note 4)	3.17
(l) Plant and Machinery used in salt works [NESD]	15	6.33	4.75 (Note 5)	1.58
V. Furniture and fittings [NESD]				
(i) General furniture and fittings	10	9.50	6.33	3.17
(ii) Furniture and fittings used in hotels, restaurants and boarding houses, schools, colleges and other educational institutions, libraries; welfare centres; meeting halls, cinema houses; theatres and circuses; and furniture and fittings let out on hire for use on the occasion of marriages and similar functions.	8	11.88	9.5	2.38
VI. Motor Vehicles [NESD]				
1. Motor cycles, scooters and other mopeds	10	9.50	9.5	-

Nature of Assets	Useful Life (Co. Act, 2013)	SLM BASIS Single Shift rate (Co. Act, 2013) (1)	Single Shift rate (Co. Act, 1956) (2)	Impact Increase/ (decrease) (1)-(2)
	(*Years*)	(%)	(%)	(%)
2. Motor buses, motor lorries, motor cars and motor taxies used in a business of running them on hire	6	15.83	16.21	(0.38)
3. Motor buses, motor lorries and motor cars other than those used in a business of running them on hire	8	11.88	11.31	0.57
4. Motor tractors, harvesting combines and heavy vehicles	8	11.88	11.31	0.57
5. Electrically operated vehicles including battery powered or fuel cell powered vehicles	8	11.88	7.07	4.81
VII. Ships [NESD]				
1. Ocean-going ships				
(i) Bulk Carriers and liner vessels	25	3.80	5 (Note 3)	(1.20)
(ii) Crude tankers, product carriers and easy chemical carriers with or without conventional tank coatings	20	4.75	5 (Note 3)	(0.25)
(iii) Chemicals and Acid Carriers:				
(a) With Stainless steel tanks	25	3.80	5 (Note 3)	(1.20)
(b) With other tanks	20	4.75	5 (Note 3)	(0.25)
(iv) Liquified gas carriers	30	3.17	5 (Note 3)	(1.83)
(v) Conventional large passenger vessels which are used for cruise purpose also	30	3.17	5 (Note 3)	(1.83)

Nature of Assets	Useful Life (Co. Act, 2013)	SLM BASIS: Single Shift rate (Co. Act, 2013) (1)	SLM BASIS: Single Shift rate (Co. Act, 1956) (2)	Impact: Increase/ (decrease) (1)-(2)
	(*Years*)	(%)	(%)	(%)
(vi) Coastal service ships of all categories	30	3.17	5 (Note 3)	(1.83)
(vii) Offshore supply and support vessels	20	4.75	5 (Note 3)	(0.25)
(viii) Catamarans and other high speed passenger for ships or boats	20	4.75	5 (Note 3)	(0.25)
(ix) Drill ships	25	3.80	5 (Note 3)	(1.20)
(x) Hovercrafts	15	6.33	5 (Note 3)	1.33
(xi) Fishing vessels with wooden hull	10	9.50	10	(0.50)
(xii) Dredgers, tugs, barges, survey launches and other similar ships used mainly for dredging purposes	14	6.79	7	(0.21)
2. Vessels ordinarily operating on inland waters				
(i) Speed boats	13	7.31	7.07	0.24
(ii) Other vessels	28	3.39	3.34	0.05
VIII. Aircrafts or Helicopters [NESD]	20	4.75	5.6	(0.85)
IX. Railways sidings, locomotives, rolling stocks, tramways and railways used by concerns, excluding railway concerns [NESD]	15	6.33	4.75 (Note 4)	1.58
X. Ropeway structures [NESD]	15	6.33	11.31	(4.98)

		SLM BASIS		
Nature of Assets	**Useful Life (Co. Act, 2013)**	**Single Shift rate (Co. Act, 2013) (1)**	**Single Shift rate (Co. Act, 1956) (2)**	**Impact Increase/ (decrease) (1)-(2)**
	(*Years*)	(%)	(%)	(%)
XI. Office equipment [NESD]	5	19.00	4.75 (Note 4)	14.25
XII. Computers and data processing units [NESD]				
(i) Servers and networks	6	15.83	16.21	(0.38)
(ii) End user devices, such as, desktops, laptops, etc.	3	31.67	16.21	15.46
XIII. Laboratory equipment [NESD]				-
(i) General laboratory equipment	10	9.50	4.75 (Note 4)	4.75
(ii) Laboratory equipments used in educational institutions	5	19.00	4.75 (Note 4)	14.25
XIV. Electrical Installations and Equipment [NESD]	10	9.50	4.75 (Note 4)	4.75
XV. Hydraulic works, pipelines and sluices [NESD]	15	6.33	4.75 (Note 4)	1.58

Notes:

1. 'Buildings' includes roads, bridges, culverts, wells and tubewells; 'factory buildings' does not include offices, godowns, officers and employees' quarters, roads, bridges, culverts, wells and tubewells according to the Schedule XIV of the Companies Act, 1956. Hence the corresponding Schedule XIV rates considered for comparison for the following categories prescribed in Schedule II to the Companies Act, 2013 are those of *'buildings (other than factory buildings) NESD'* specified in Schedule XIV:
   (a) 'Fences, wells and tubewells' under the head 'Buildings (NESD)'
   (b) Bridges, culverts, bunders, etc (NESD)
   (c) Roads (NESD)
2. Corresponding Schedule XIV rate considered for comparison for the sub-category 'others (including temporary structure etc)' under the category

'buildings (NESD)' prescribed in Schedule II to the Companies Act, 2013 is that of 'Purely temporary erections such as wooden structures' prescribed in Schedule XIV of the Companies Act, 1956.

3. Corresponding Schedule XIV rate considered for comparison for the following sub-categories are those of sub-category 'other ships (NESD)' under the category 'Ships' prescribed in the schedule XIV:
   (a) Bulk Carriers and liner vessels
   (b) Crude tankers, product carriers and easy chemical carriers with or without conventional tank coatings
   (c) Chemicals and Acid Carriers
   (d) Liquefied gas carriers
   (e) Conventional large passenger vessels which are used for cruise purpose also
   (f) Coastal service ships of all categories
   (g) Offshore supply and support vessels
   (h) Catamarans and other high speed passenger for ships or boats
   (i) Drill ships
   (j) Hovercrafts
4. Corresponding Schedule XIV rate considered for comparison for the item 'plant and machinery used in salt works' are those of general plant and machinery (other than continuous process plant and ship) for which no specific rates have been prescribed.
5. There are various items which were clubbed earlier under general plant and machinery category and now separate useful life has been prescribed for them after the introduction of Schedule II. For such items, Schedule XIV rate for comparison is taken to be the rate prescribed in Schedule XIV for the general category, ie, 'other than continuous process plant for which no special rate has been prescribed'.

3.5 ITEM BY ITEM COMPARISON AND ASCERTAINMENT OF IMPACT IN DOUBLE SHIFT (ASSUMING 5% RESIDUAL VALUE)

(***Note:*** *The useful lives of assets working on shift basis have been specified in the Schedule based on their single shift working. Except for assets in respect of which no extra shift depreciation is permitted (indicated by NESD), if an asset is used for any time during the year for double shift, the depreciation will increase by 50% for that period. Accordingly, the double shift SLM rate in column 1 below is computed by adding an increase of 50% in the single shift SLM rate.*)

Nature of Assets	Useful Life for Single shift (Co. Act, 2013)	SLM BASIS		Impact
		Double Shift rate (Co. Act, 2013) (1)	Double Shift rate (Co. Act, 1956) (2)	Increase/ (decrease) (1)-(2)
	(*Years*)	(%)	(%)	(%)
Plant and Machinery				
General rate applicable to plant and machinery not covered under special plant and machinery				
(a) Plant and Machinery other than continuous process plant not covered under specific industries	15	9.5	7.42	2.08
Special Plant and Machinery				
(a) Plant and Machinery related to production and exhibition of Motion Picture Films				
1. Cinematograph films—Machinery used in the production and exhibition of cinematograph films, recording and equipments, developing machines, printing machines, editing reproducing machines, synchronizers and studio lights except bulbs	13	10.96	7.07 *(NESD)*	3.89
2. Projecting equipment for exhibition of films	13	10.96	7.07 *(NESD)*	3.89
(b) Plant and Machinery used in glass manufacturing				
1. Plant and Machinery except direct fire glass melting furnaces Recuperative and regenerative glass melting furnaces	13	10.96	11.31	(0.35)
(c) Plant and Machinery used in manufacture of steel				
1. Sinter Plant	20	7.13	7.42	(0.30)

Nature of Assets	Useful Life for Single shift (Co. Act, 2013)	SLM BASIS		
		Double Shift rate (Co. Act, 2013) (1)	Double Shift rate (Co. Act, 1956) (2)	Impact Increase/ (decrease) (1)-(2)
	(*Years*)	(%)	(%)	(%)
2. Blast Furnace	20	7.13	7.42	(0.30)
3. Coke ovens	20	7.13	7.42	(0.30)
4. Rolling mill in steel plant	20	7.13	7.42	(0.30)
5. Basic oxygen Furnace Converter	25	5.7	7.42	(1.72)
(d) Plant and Machinery used in civil construction				
1. Concreting, Crushing, Piling Equipments and Road Making Equipments	12	11.88	7.42	4.46
2. Heavy Lift Equipments				
Cranes with capacity of more than 100 tons	20	7.13	7.42	(0.29)
Cranes with capacity of less than 100 tons	15	9.5	7.42	2.08
3. Transmission line, Tunneling Equipments [NESD]	10	9.50 *(NESD)*	7.42	2.08
4. Earth-moving equipments	9	15.83	11.31 *(NESD)*	4.52
5. Others including Material Handling /Pipeline/Welding Equipments [NESD]	12	7.92 *(NESD)*	7.42	0.5
(e) Plant and Machinery used in Telecommunications [NESD]				
1. Towers	18	5.28 *(NESD)*	7.42	(2.14)
2. Telecom transceivers, switching centres, transmission and other network equipment	13	7.31 *(NESD)*	7.42	(0.11)
3. Telecom—Ducts, Cables and optical fibre	18	5.28 *(NESD)*	7.42	(2.14)
4. Satellites	18	5.28	7.42	(2.14)

		SLM BASIS		
Nature of Assets	**Useful Life for Single shift (Co. Act, 2013)**	**Double Shift rate (Co. Act, 2013) (1)**	**Double Shift rate (Co. Act, 1956) (2)**	**Impact Increase/ (decrease) (1)-(2)**
	(*Years*)	(%)	(%)	(%)
		(*NESD*)		
(f) Plant and Machinery used in exploration, production and refining oil and gas [NESD]				
1. Refineries	25	3.80 (*NESD*)	7.42	(3.62)
2. Oil and gas assets (including wells), processing plant and facilities	25	3.8 (*NESD*)	7.42	(3.62)
3. Petrochemical Plant	25	3.8 (*NESD*)	7.42	(3.62)
4. Storage tanks and related equipment	25	3.80 (*NESD*)	7.42	(3.62)
5. Pipelines	30	3.17 (*NESD*)	7.42	(4.25)
6. Loggers	8	11.88 (*NESD*)	7.42	4.46
(g) Plant and Machinery used in generation, transmission and distribution of power [NESD]				
1. Thermal/ Gas/ Combined Cycle Power Generation Plant	40	2.38 (*NESD*)	7.42	(5.05)
2. Hydro Power Generation Plant	40	2.38 (*NESD*)	7.42	(5.05)
3. Nuclear Power Generation Plant	40	2.38 (*NESD*)	7.42	(5.05)
4. Transmission lines, cables and other network assets	40	2.38 (*NESD*)	7.42	(5.05)
5. Wind Power Generation Plant	22	4.32 (*NESD*)	7.42	(3.10)
6. Electric Distribution Plant	35	2.71 (*NESD*)	7.42	(4.71)

Nature of Assets	Useful Life for Single shift (Co. Act, 2013)	SLM BASIS		
		Double Shift rate (Co. Act, 2013) (1)	Double Shift rate (Co. Act, 1956) (2)	Impact Increase/ (decrease) (1)-(2)
	(*Years*)	(%)	(%)	(%)
7. Gas Storage and Distribution Plant	30	3.17 *(NESD)*	7.42	(4.25)
8. Water Distribution Plant including pipelines	30	3.17 *(NESD)*	7.42	(4.25)
(h) Plant and Machinery used in manufacture of non-ferrous metals				
1. Metal pot line [NESD]	40	2.38 *(NESD)*	7.42	(5.05)
2. Bauxite crushing and grinding section [NESD]	40	2.38 *(NESD)*	7.42	(5.05)
3. Digester Section [NESD]	40	2.38 *(NESD)*	7.42	(5.05)
4. Turbine [NESD]	40	2.38 *(NESD)*	7.42	(5.05)
5. Equipments for Calcination [NESD]	40	2.38 *(NESD)*	7.42	(5.05)
6. Copper Smelter [NESD]	40	2.38 *(NESD)*	7.42	(5.05)
7. Roll Grinder	40	3.56	7.42	(3.86)
8. Soaking Pit	30	4.75	7.42	(2.67)
9. Annealing Furnace	30	4.75	7.42	(2.67)
10. Rolling Mills	30	4.75	7.42	(2.67)
11. Equipments for Scalping, Slitting , etc. [NESD]	30	3.17 *(NESD)*	7.42	(4.25)
12. Surface Miner, Ripper Dozer, etc., used in mines	25	5.7	7.42	(1.72)
13. Copper refining plant [NESD]	25	3.8 *(NESD)*	7.42	(3.62)

Nature of Assets	Useful Life for Single shift (Co. Act, 2013)	SLM BASIS Double Shift rate (Co. Act, 2013) (1)	Double Shift rate (Co. Act, 1956) (2)	Impact Increase/ (decrease) (1)-(2)
	(Years)	(%)	(%)	(%)
(i) Plant and Machinery used in medical and surgical operations [NESD]				
1. Other Equipments.	15	6.33 *(NESD)*	7.42	(1.09)
(j) Plant and Machinery used in manufacture of pharmaceuticals and chemicals [NESD]				
1. Reactors	20	4.75 *(NESD)*	7.42	(2.67)
2. Distillation Columns	20	4.75 *(NESD)*	7.42	(2.67)
3. Drying equipments/Centrifuges and Decanters	20	4.75 *(NESD)*	7.42	(2.67)
4. Vessel/storage tanks	20	4.75 *(NESD)*	7.42	(2.67)
(k) Plant and Machinery used in salt works [NESD]	15	6.33 *(NESD)*	7.42	(1.09)
Laboratory equipment [NESD]				
(i) General laboratory equipment	10	9.5 *(NESD)*	7.42	2.08
(ii) Laboratory equipments used in educational institutions	5	19 *(NESD)*	7.42	11.58

3.6 ITEM BY ITEM COMPARISON AND ASCERTAINMENT OF IMPACT IN TRIPLE SHIFT (ASSUMING 5% RESIDUAL VALUE)

(***Note:*** *The useful lives of assets working on shift basis have been specified in the Schedule based on their single shift working. Except for assets in respect of which no extra shift depreciation is permitted (indicated by NESD), if an asset is used for any time during the year for triple shift, the depreciation should be calculated on* *the basis of 100% for that period. Accordingly, the triple shift SLM rate in column 1 below is taken as 200% of the single shift SLM rate)*

Nature of Assets	SLM BASIS			Impact
	Useful Life for Single shift (Co. Act, 2013)	Triple Shift rate (Co. Act, 2013) (1)	Triple Shift rate (Co. Act, 1956) (2)	Increase/ (decrease) (1)-(2)
	(Years)	(%)	(%)	(%)
Plant and Machinery				
General rate applicable to plant and machinery not covered under special plant and machinery				
(a) Plant and Machinery other than continuous process plant not covered under specific industries	15	12.67	10.34	2.33
Special Plant and Machinery				
(a) Plant and Machinery related to production and exhibition of Motion Picture Films				
1. Cinematograph films—Machinery used in the production and exhibition of cinematograph films, recording and equipments, developing machines, printing machines, editing reproducing machines, synchronizers and studio lights except bulbs	13	14.62	7.07 *(NESD)*	7.55
2. Projecting equipment for exhibition of films	13	14.62	7.07 *(NESD)*	7.55
(b) Plant and Machinery used in glass manufacturing				
1. Plant and Machinery except direct fire glass melting furnaces Recuperative and regenerative glass melting furnaces	13	14.62	16.21	(1.59)
(c) Plant and Machinery used in manufacture of steel				
1. Sinter Plant	20	9.50	10.34	(0.84)
2. Blast Furnace	20	9.50	10.34	(0.84)

		SLM BASIS		
Nature of Assets	**Useful Life for Single shift (Co. Act, 2013)**	**Triple Shift rate (Co. Act, 2013) (1)**	**Triple Shift rate (Co. Act, 1956) (2)**	**Impact Increase/ (decrease) (1)-(2)**
	(*Years*)	(%)	(%)	(%)
3. Coke ovens	20	9.50	10.34	(0.84)
4. Rolling mill in steel plant	20	9.50	10.34	(0.84)
5. Basic oxygen Furnace Converter	25	7.60	10.34	(2.74)
(d) Plant and Machinery used in civil construction				
1. Concreting, Crushing, Piling Equipments and Road Making Equipments	12	15.83	10.34	5.49
2. Heavy Lift Equipments				
Cranes with capacity of more than 100 tons	20	9.50	10.34	(0.84)
Cranes with capacity of less than 100 tons	15	12.67	10.34	2.33
3. Transmission line, Tunneling Equipments [NESD]	10	9.50 *(NESD)*	10.34	(0.84)
4. Earth-moving equipments	9	21.11	11.31 *(NESD)*	9.80
5. Others including Material Handling /Pipeline/Welding Equipments [NESD]	12	7.92 *(NESD)*	10.34	(2.42)
(e) Plant and Machinery used in Telecommunications [NESD]				
1. Towers	18	5.28 *(NESD)*	10.34	(5.06)
2. Telecom transceivers, switching centres, transmission and other network equipment	13	7.31 *(NESD)*	10.34	(3.03)
3. Telecom—Ducts, Cables and optical fibre	18	5.28 *(NESD)*	10.34	(5.06)
4. Satellites	18	5.28 *(NESD)*	10.34	(5.06)
(f) Plant and Machinery used in exploration, production and refining oil and gas [NESD]				

		SLM BASIS		
Nature of Assets	**Useful Life for Single shift (Co. Act, 2013)**	**Triple Shift rate (Co. Act, 2013) (1)**	**Triple Shift rate (Co. Act, 1956) (2)**	**Impact Increase/ (decrease) (1)-(2)**
	(*Years*)	(%)	(%)	(%)
1. Refineries	25	3.80 *(NESD)*	10.34	(6.54)
2. Oil and gas assets (including wells), processing plant and facilities	25	3.80 *(NESD)*	10.34	(6.54)
3. Petrochemical Plant	25	3.80 *(NESD)*	10.34	(6.54)
4. Storage tanks and related equipment	25	3.80 *(NESD)*	10.34	(6.54)
5. Pipelines	30	3.17 *(NESD)*	10.34	(7.17)
6. Loggers	8	11.88 *(NESD)*	10.34	1.54
(g) Plant and Machinery used in generation, transmission and distribution of power [NESD]				
1. Thermal/ Gas/ Combined Cycle Power Generation Plant	40	2.38 *(NESD)*	10.34	(7.97)
2. Hydro Power Generation Plant	40	2.38 *(NESD)*	10.34	(7.97)
3. Nuclear Power Generation Plant	40	2.38 *(NESD)*	10.34	(7.97)
4. Transmission lines, cables and other network assets	40	2.38 *(NESD)*	10.34	(7.97)
5. Wind Power Generation Plant	22	4.32 *(NESD)*	10.34	(6.02)
6. Electric Distribution Plant	35	2.71 *(NESD)*	10.34	(7.63)
7. Gas Storage and Distribution Plant	30	3.17 *(NESD)*	10.34	(7.17)
8. Water Distribution Plant including pipelines	30	3.17 *(NESD)*	10.34	(7.17)
(h) Plant and Machinery used in manufacture of non-ferrous metals				
1. Metal pot line [NESD]	40	2.38	10.34	(7.97)

Nature of Assets	Useful Life for Single shift (Co. Act, 2013)	SLM BASIS Triple Shift rate (Co. Act, 2013) (1)	Triple Shift rate (Co. Act, 1956) (2)	Impact Increase/ (decrease) (1)-(2)
	(*Years*)	(%)	(%)	(%)
		(NESD)		
2. Bauxite crushing and grinding section [NESD]	40	2.38 *(NESD)*	10.34	(7.97)
3. Digester Section [NESD]	40	2.38 *(NESD)*	10.34	(7.97)
4. Turbine [NESD]	40	2.38 *(NESD)*	10.34	(7.97)
5. Equipments for Calcination [NESD]	40	2.38 *(NESD)*	10.34	(7.97)
6. Copper Smelter [NESD]	40	2.38 *(NESD)*	10.34	(7.97)
7. Roll Grinder	40	4.75	10.34	(5.59)
8. Soaking Pit	30	6.33	10.34	(4.01)
9. Annealing Furnace	30	6.33	10.34	(4.01)
10. Rolling Mills	30	6.33	10.34	(4.01)
11. Equipments for Scalping, Slitting , etc. [NESD]	30	3.17 *(NESD)*	10.34	(7.17)
12. Surface Miner, Ripper Dozer, etc., used in mines	25	7.60	10.34	(2.74)
13. Copper refining plant [NESD]	25	3.80 *(NESD)*	10.34	(6.54)
(i) Plant and Machinery used in medical and surgical operations [NESD]				
1. Other Equipments.	15	6.33 *(NESD)*	10.34	(4.01)
(j) Plant and Machinery used in manufacture of pharmaceuticals and chemicals [NESD]				
1. Reactors	20	4.75 *(NESD)*	10.34	(5.59)
2. Distillation Columns	20	4.75 *(NESD)*	10.34	(5.59)
3. Drying equipments/Centrifuges and Decanters	20	4.75 *(NESD)*	10.34	(5.59)

Nature of Assets	SLM BASIS			
	Useful Life for Single shift (Co. Act, 2013)	Triple Shift rate (Co. Act, 2013) (1)	Triple Shift rate (Co. Act, 1956) (2)	Impact Increase/ (decrease) (1)-(2)
	(Years)	(%)	(%)	(%)
4. Vessel/storage tanks	20	4.75 *(NESD)*	10.34	(5.59)
(k) Plant and Machinery used in salt works [NESD]	15	6.33 *(NESD)*	10.34	(4.01)
Laboratory equipment [NESD]				
(i) General laboratory equipment	10	9.50 *(NESD)*	10.34	(0.84)
(ii) Laboratory equipments used in educational institutions	5	19.00 *(NESD)*	10.34	8.66

3.7 ITEMS AGAINST WHICH NESD IS PRESCRIBED IN BOTH THE COMPANIES ACT, 2013 AS WELL AS COMPANIES ACT, 1956

It may be noted that the following categories of assets prescribed under Schedule II of the Companies Act, 2013 against which NESD is mentioned in the Schedule are also the items to which no extra shift depreciation is applicable under Schedule XIV to the Companies Act, 1956.

I. Buildings

II. Bridges, culverts, bunders, etc

III. Roads

Note: Bridges, culverts, bunders, fences, wells, tubewells etc, and roads are covered in 'Buildings' as per the Note 1 to the Schedule XIV of the Companies Act, 1956; ie 'Buildings' include roads, bridges, culverts, wells and tubewells.

I. General rate applicable to plant and machinery not covered under special plant and machinery

  (a) Continuous process plant for which no special rate has been prescribed under special plant and machinery category

II. Following categories of special plant and machinery

  (a) *Plant and Machinery used in glass manufacturing*

    (i) Plant and Machinery except direct fire glass melting furnaces-Moulds

    (ii) Float Glass Melting Furnaces

(b) *Plant and Machinery used in exploration, production and refining oil and gas:*

(i) Drilling Rig

(ii) Field operations (above ground) Portable boilers, drilling tools, well-head tanks, etc.

(c) *Plant and Machinery used in mines and quarries-*

Portable underground machinery and earth moving machinery used in open cast mining

(d) *Plant and Machinery used in medical and surgical operations:*

Electrical Machinery, X-ray and electrotherapeutic apparatus and accessories thereto, medical, diagnostic equipments, namely, Cat-scan, Ultrasound Machines, ECG Monitors, etc.

III Furniture and fittings

IV. Motor Vehicles

V. Ships

VI. Aircrafts or Helicopters

VII. Railways sidings, locomotives, rolling stocks, tramways and railways used by concerns, excluding railway concerns

VIII. Ropeway structures

IX. Office equipment

X. Computers and data processing units

XI. Electrical Installations and Equipment

XII. Hydraulic works, pipelines and sluices

Chapter 4
Comparison of WDV Depreciation rates under Schedule II to the Companies Act, 1956 and Schedule XIV to the Companies Act, 2013

In this chapter, the comparison between WDV depreciation rates on various assets under the Companies Act, 2013 and Companies Act, 1956 has been given. The single shift depreciation rates has been computed on the basis of useful life and for double shift, the depreciation will increase by 50% for the period during which the asset is used for double shift and in case of the triple shift the depreciation shall be calculated on the basis of 100% for the period during which the asset is used for triple shift.

The comparison have been given assuming residual value as 5% of original cost, 1% of original cost and 0.01% of original cost.

(*It may be noted that the depreciation rates have been rounded off to two decimal places*)

4.1 ITEM-BY-ITEM COMPARISON AND ASCERTAINMENT OF IMPACT IN SINGLE SHIFT (ASSUMING 5% RESIDUAL VALUE)

		WDV BASIS		
Nature of Assets	**Useful Life (Co. Act, 2013)**	**Single Shift rate (Co. Act, 2013) (1)**	**Single Shift rate (Co. Act, 1956) (2)**	**Impact Increase/ (decrease) (1)-(2)**
	(*Years*)	(%)	(%)	(%)
I. Buildings [NESD]				
(a) Buildings (other than factory buildings) RCC Frame Structure	60	4.87	5	(0.13)

Nature of Assets	**Useful Life (Co. Act, 2013)**	**WDV BASIS**		**Impact**
		Single Shift rate (Co. Act, 2013) (1)	**Single Shift rate (Co. Act, 1956) (2)**	**Increase/ (decrease) (1)-(2)**
	(*Years*)	(%)	(%)	(%)
(b) Buildings (other than factory buildings) other than RCC Frame Structure	30	9.50	5	4.50
(c) Factory buildings	30	9.50	10	(0.50)
(d) Fences, wells, tube wells	5	45.07	5 (Note 1)	40.07
(e) Others (including temporary structure, etc.)	3	63.16	100 (Note 2)	(36.84)
II. Bridges, culverts, bunders, etc. [NESD]	30	9.50	5 (Note 1)	4.50
III. Roads [NESD]				
(a) Carpeted roads				
(i) Carpeted Roads-RCC	10	25.89	5 (Note 1)	20.89
(ii) Carpeted Roads-other than RCC	5	45.07	5 (Note 1)	40.07
(b) Non-carpeted roads	3	63.16	5 (Note 1)	58.16
IV. Plant and Machinery				
(i) General rate applicable to plant and machinery not covered under special plant and machinery				
(a) Plant and Machinery other than continuous process plant not covered under specific industries	15	18.10	13.91	4.19
b) continuous process plant for which no special rate has been prescribed under (ii) below [NESD]	25	11.29	15.33	(4.04)
(ii) Special Plant and Machinery				
(a) Plant and Machinery related to production and exhibition of Motion Picture Films				

Nature of Assets	Useful Life (Co. Act, 2013)	WDV BASIS Single Shift rate (Co. Act, 2013) (1)	Single Shift rate (Co. Act, 1956) (2)	Impact Increase/ (decrease) (1)-(2)
	(*Years*)	(%)	(%)	(%)
Cinematograph films—Machinery used in the production and exhibition of cinematograph films, recording and equipments, developing machines, printing machines, editing reproducing machines, synchronizers and studio lights except bulbs	13	20.58	20	0.58
Projecting equipment for exhibition of films	13	20.58	20	0.58
(b) Plant and Machinery used in glass manufacturing				-
1. Plant and Machinery except direct fire glass melting furnaces Recuperative and regenerative glass melting furnaces	13	20.58	20	0.58
2. Plant and Machinery except direct fire glass melting furnaces Moulds [NESD]	8	31.23	30	1.23
3. Float Glass Melting Furnaces [NESD]	10	25.89	27	(1.11)
(c) Plant and Machinery used in mines and quarries—Portable underground machinery and earth moving machinery used in open cast mining [NESD]	8	31.23	30	1.23
(d) Plant and Machinery used in Telecommunications [NESD]				
1. Towers	18	15.33	13.91 (Note 5)	1.42
2. Telecom transceivers, switching centres, transmission and other network equipment	13	20.58	13.91 (Note 5)	6.67

Nature of Assets	Useful Life (Co. Act, 2013)	WDV BASIS Single Shift rate (Co. Act, 2013) (1)	Single Shift rate (Co. Act, 1956) (2)	Impact Increase/ (decrease) (1)-(2)
	(*Years*)	(%)	(%)	(%)
3. Telecom—Ducts, Cables and optical fibre	18	15.33	13.91 (Note 5)	1.42
4. Satellites	18	15.33	13.91 (Note 5)	1.42
(e) Plant and Machinery used in exploration, production and refining oil and gas [NESD]				
1. Refineries	25	11.29	13.91 (Note 5)	(2.62)
2. Oil and gas assets (including wells), processing plant and facilities	25	11.29	13.91 (Note 5)	(2.62)
3. Petrochemical Plant	25	11.29	13.91 (Note 5)	(2.62)
4. Storage tanks and related equipment	25	11.29	13.91 (Note 5)	(2.62)
5. Pipelines	30	9.50	13.91 (Note 5)	(4.41)
6. Drilling Rig	30	9.50	30	(20.50)
7. Field operations (above ground) Portable boilers, drilling tools, well-head tanks, etc.	8	31.23	30	1.23
8. Loggers	8	31.23	13.91 (Note 5)	17.32
(f) Plant and Machinery used in generation, transmission and distribution of power [NESD]				
1. Thermal/ Gas/ Combined Cycle Power Generation Plant	40	7.22	13.91 (Note 5)	(6.69)
2. Hydro Power Generation Plant	40	7.22	13.91 (Note 5)	(6.69)
3. Nuclear Power Generation Plant	40	7.22	13.91 (Note 5)	(6.69)

		WDV BASIS		
Nature of Assets	Useful Life (Co. Act, 2013)	Single Shift rate (Co. Act, 2013) (1)	Single Shift rate (Co. Act, 1956) (2)	Impact Increase/ (decrease) (1)-(2)
	(*Years*)	(%)	(%)	(%)
4. Transmission lines, cables and other network assets	40	7.22	13.91 (Note 5)	(6.69)
5. Wind Power Generation Plant	22	12.73	13.91 (Note 5)	(1.18)
6. Electric Distribution Plant	35	8.20	13.91 (Note 5)	(5.71)
7. Gas Storage and Distribution Plant	30	9.50	13.91 (Note 5)	(4.41)
8. Water Distribution Plant including pipelines	30	9.50	13.91 (Note 5)	(4.41)
(g) Plant and Machinery used in manufacture of steel				
1. Sinter Plant	20	13.91	13.91 (Note 5)	0.00
2. Blast Furnace	20	13.91	13.91 (Note 5)	0.00
3. Coke ovens	20	13.91	13.91 (Note 5)	0.00
4. Rolling mill in steel plant	20	13.91	13.91 (Note 5)	0.00
5. Basic oxygen Furnace Converter	25	11.29	13.91 (Note 5)	(2.62)
(h) Plant and Machinery used in manufacture of non-ferrous metals				
1. Metal pot line [NESD]	40	7.22	13.91 (Note 5)	(6.69)
2. Bauxite crushing and grinding section [NESD]	40	7.22	13.91 (Note 5)	(6.69)
3. Digester Section [NESD]	40	7.22	13.91 (Note 5)	(6.69)
4. Turbine [NESD]	40	7.22	13.91 (Note 5)	(6.69)

Nature of Assets	Useful Life (Co. Act, 2013)	WDV BASIS Single Shift rate (Co. Act, 2013) (1)	Single Shift rate (Co. Act, 1956) (2)	Impact Increase/ (decrease) (1)-(2)
	(*Years*)	(%)	(%)	(%)
5. Equipments for Calcination [NESD]	40	7.22	13.91 (Note 5)	(6.69)
6. Copper Smelter [NESD]	40	7.22	13.91 (Note 5)	(6.69)
7. Roll Grinder	40	7.22	13.91 (Note 5)	(6.69)
8. Soaking Pit	30	9.50	13.91 (Note 5)	(4.41)
9. Annealing Furnace	30	9.50	13.91 (Note 5)	(4.41)
10. Rolling Mills	30	9.50	13.91 (Note 5)	(4.41)
11. Equipments for Scalping, Slitting, etc. [NESD]	30	9.50	13.91 (Note 5)	(4.41)
12. Surface Miner, Ripper Dozer, etc., used in mines	25	11.29	13.91 (Note 5)	(2.62)
13. Copper refining plant [NESD]	25	11.29	13.91 (Note 5)	(2.62)
(i) Plant and Machinery used in medical and surgical operations [NESD]				
1. Electrical Machinery, X-ray and electrotherapeutic apparatus and accessories thereto, medical, diagnostic equipments, namely, Cat-scan, Ultrasound Machines, ECG Monitors, etc.	13	20.58	20	0.58
2. Other Equipments.	15	18.10	13.91 (Note 5)	4.19
(j) Plant and Machinery used in manufacture of pharmaceuticals and chemicals [NESD]				
1. Reactors	20	13.91	13.91 (Note 5)	0.00

Nature of Assets	Useful Life (Co. Act, 2013)	WDV BASIS Single Shift rate (Co. Act, 2013) (1)	Single Shift rate (Co. Act, 1956) (2)	Impact Increase/ (decrease) (1)-(2)
	(*Years*)	(%)	(%)	(%)
2. Distillation Columns	20	13.91	13.91 (Note 5)	0.00
3. Drying equipments/ Centrifuges and Decanters	20	13.91	13.91 (Note 5)	0.00
4. Vessel/storage tanks	20	13.91	13.91 (Note 5)	0.00
(k) Plant and Machinery used in civil construction				
1. Concreting, Crushing, Piling Equipments and Road Making Equipments	12	22.09	13.91 (Note 5)	8.18
2. Heavy Lift Equipments				
Cranes with capacity of more than 100 tons	20	13.91	13.91 (Note 5)	0.00
Cranes with capacity of less than 100 tons	15	18.10	13.91 (Note 5)	4.19
3. Transmission line, Tunneling Equipments [NESD]	10	25.89	13.91 (Note 5)	11.98
4. Earth-moving equipments	9	28.31	30	(1.69)
5. Others including Material Handling /Pipeline/Welding Equipments [NESD]	12	22.09	13.91 (Note 5)	8.18
(l) Plant and Machinery used in salt works [NESD]	15	18.10	13.91 (Note 4)	4.19
V. Furniture and fittings [NESD]				
(i) General furniture and fittings	10	25.89	18.1	7.79
(ii) Furniture and fittings used in hotels, restaurants and boarding houses, schools, colleges and other educational institutions, libraries; welfare centres; meeting halls, cinema houses; theatres and circuses; and furniture and fittings let out on	8	31.23	25.88	5.35

		WDV BASIS		
Nature of Assets	**Useful Life (Co. Act, 2013)**	**Single Shift rate (Co. Act, 2013) (1)**	**Single Shift rate (Co. Act, 1956) (2)**	**Impact Increase/ (decrease) (1)-(2)**
	(*Years*)	(%)	(%)	(%)
hire for use on the occasion of marriages and similar functions.				
VI. Motor Vehicles [NESD]				
1. Motor cycles, scooters and other mopeds	10	25.89	25.89	(0.00)
2. Motor buses, motor lorries, motor cars and motor taxies used in a business of running them on hire	6	39.30	40	(0.70)
3. Motor buses, motor lorries and motor cars other than those used in a business of running them on hire	8	31.23	30	1.23
4. Motor tractors, harvesting combines and heavy vehicles	8	31.23	30	1.23
5. Electrically operated vehicles including battery powered or fuel cell powered vehicles	8	31.23	20	11.23
VII. Ships [NESD]				
1. Ocean-going ships				
(i) Bulk Carriers and liner vessels	25	11.29	14.6 (Note 3)	(3.31)
(ii) Crude tankers, product carriers and easy chemical carriers with or without conventional tank coatings	20	13.91	14.6 (Note 3)	(0.69)
(iii) Chemicals and Acid Carriers:				
(a) With Stainless steel tanks	25	11.29	14.6 (Note 3)	(3.31)
(b) With other tanks	20	13.91	14.6 (Note 3)	(0.69)
(iv) Liquified gas carriers	30	9.50	14.6 (Note 3)	(5.10)
(v) Conventional large passenger	30	9.50	14.6	(5.10)

Nature of Assets	Useful Life (Co. Act, 2013)	WDV BASIS Single Shift rate (Co. Act, 2013) (1)	Single Shift rate (Co. Act, 1956) (2)	Impact Increase/ (decrease) (1)-(2)
	(*Years*)	(%)	(%)	(%)
vessels which are used for cruise purpose also			(Note 3)	
(vi) Coastal service ships of all categories	30	9.50	14.6 (Note 3)	(5.10)
(vii) Offshore supply and support vessels	20	13.91	14.6 (Note 3)	(0.69)
(viii) Catamarans and other high speed passenger for ships or boats	20	13.91	14.6 (Note 3)	(0.69)
(ix) Drill ships	25	11.29	14.6 (Note 3)	(3.31)
(x) Hovercrafts	15	18.10	14.6 (Note 3)	3.50
(xi) Fishing vessels with wooden hull	10	25.89	27.05	(1.16)
(xii) Dredgers, tugs, barges, survey launches and other similar ships used mainly for dredging purposes	14	19.26	19.8	(0.54)
2. Vessels ordinarily operating on inland waters				
(i) Speed boats	13	20.58	20	0.58
(ii) Other vessels	28	10.15	10	0.15
VIII. Aircrafts or Helicopters [NESD]	20	13.91	16.2	(2.29)
IX. Railways sidings, locomotives, rolling stocks, tramways and railways used by concerns, excluding railway concerns [NESD]	15	18.10	13.91 (Note 5)	4.19
X. Ropeway structures [NESD]	15	18.10	30	(11.90)
XI. Office equipment [NESD]	5	45.07	13.91 (Note 5)	31.16

Nature of Assets	Useful Life (Co. Act, 2013)	WDV BASIS Single Shift rate (Co. Act, 2013) (1)	Single Shift rate (Co. Act, 1956) (2)	Impact Increase/ (decrease) (1)-(2)
	(Years)	(%)	(%)	(%)
XII. Computers and data processing units [NESD]				
(i) Servers and networks	6	39.30	40	(0.70)
(ii) End user devices, such as, desktops, laptops, etc.	3	63.16	40	23.16
XIII. Laboratory equipment [NESD]				
(i) General laboratory equipment	10	25.89	13.91 (Note 5)	11.98
(ii) Laboratory equipments used in educational institutions	5	45.07	13.91 (Note 5)	31.16
XIV. Electrical Installations and Equipment [NESD]	10	25.89	13.91 (Note 5)	11.98
XV. Hydraulic works, pipelines and sluices [NESD]	15	18.10	13.91 (Note 5)	4.19

Notes:

1. 'Buildings' includes roads, bridges, culverts, wells and tubewells; 'factory buildings' does not include offices, godowns, officers and employees' quarters, roads, bridges, culverts, wells and tubewells according to the Schedule XIV of the Companies Act, 1956. Hence the corresponding Schedule XIV rates considered for comparison for the following categories prescribed in Schedule II to the Companies Act, 2013 are those of *'buildings* (*other than factory buildings*) *NESD'* specified in Schedule XIV*:*
   (a) 'Fences, wells and tubewells' under the head 'Buildings (NESD)'
   (b) Bridges, culverts, bunders, etc (NESD)
   (c) Roads (NESD)
2. Corresponding Schedule XIV rate considered for comparison for the sub-category 'others (including temporary structure etc)' under the category 'buildings (NESD)' prescribed in Schedule II to the Companies Act, 2013 is that of 'Purely temporary erections such as wooden structures' prescribed in Schedule XIV of the Companies Act, 1956.

3. Corresponding Schedule XIV rate considered for comparison for the following sub-categories are those of sub-category 'other ships (NESD)' under the category 'Ships' prescribed in the schedule XIV:
   (a) Bulk Carriers and liner vessels
   (b) Crude tankers, product carriers and easy chemical carriers with or without conventional tank coatings
   (c) Chemicals and Acid Carriers
   (d) Liquefied gas carriers
   (e) Conventional large passenger vessels which are used for cruise purpose also
   (f) Coastal service ships of all categories
   (g) Offshore supply and support vessels
   (h) Catamarans and other high speed passenger for ships or boats
   (i) Drill ships
   (j) Hovercrafts
4. Corresponding Schedule XIV rate considered for comparison for the item 'plant and machinery used in salt works' are those of general plant and machinery (other than continuous process plant and ship) for which no specific rates have been prescribed.
5. There are various items which were clubbed earlier under general plant and machinery category and now separate useful life has been prescribed for them after the introduction of Schedule II. For such items, Schedule XIV rate for comparison is taken to be the rate prescribed in Schedule XIV for the general category, ie, 'other than continuous process plant for which no special rate has been prescribed'.

4.2 ITEM-BY-ITEM COMPARISON AND ASCERTAINMENT OF IMPACT IN DOUBLE SHIFT (ASSUMING 5% RESIDUAL VALUE)

(***Note:*** *The useful lives of assets working on shift basis have been specified in the Schedule II of the Companies Act, 2013, based on their single shift working. Except for assets in respect of which no extra shift depreciation is permitted (indicated by NESD), if an asset is used for any time during the year for double shift, the depreciation will increase by 50% for that period. Accordingly, the double shift WDV rate is computed by adding an increase of 50% in the single shift WDV rate.*)

		WDV BASIS		
Nature of Assets	**Useful Life for Single shift (Co. Act, 2013)**	**Double Shift rate (Co. Act, 2013) (1)**	**Double Shift rate (Co. Act, 1956) (2)**	**Impact Increase/ (decrease) (1)-(2)**
	(*Years*)	(%)	(%)	(%)
Plant and Machinery				
General rate applicable to plant and machinery not covered under special plant and machinery				
(a) Plant and Machinery other than continuous process plant not covered under specific industries	15	27.16	20.87	6.29
Special Plant and Machinery				
(a) Plant and Machinery related to production and exhibition of Motion Picture Films				
1. Cinematograph films—Machinery used in the production and exhibition of cinematograph films, recording and equipments, developing machines, printing machines, editing reproducing machines, synchronizers and studio lights except bulbs	13	30.87	20.00 *(NESD)*	10.87
2. Projecting equipment for exhibition of films	13	30.87	20.00 *(NESD)*	10.87
(b) Plant and Machinery used in glass manufacturing				
1. Plant and Machinery except direct fire glass melting furnaces Recuperative and regenerative glass melting furnaces	13	30.87	30	0.87

		WDV BASIS		
Nature of Assets	**Useful Life for Single shift (Co. Act, 2013)**	**Double Shift rate (Co. Act, 2013) (1)**	**Double Shift rate (Co. Act, 1956) (2)**	**Impact Increase/ (decrease) (1)-(2)**
	(*Years*)	(%)	(%)	(%)
(c) Plant and Machinery used in manufacture of steel				
1. Sinter Plant	20	20.87	20.87	(0.00)
2. Blast Furnace	20	20.87	20.87	(0.00)
3. Coke ovens	20	20.87	20.87	(0.00)
4. Rolling mill in steel plant	20	20.87	20.87	(0.00)
5. Basic oxygen Furnace Converter	25	16.94	20.87	(3.93)
(d) Plant and Machinery used in civil construction				
1. Concreting, Crushing, Piling Equipments and Road Making Equipments	12	33.14	20.87	12.27
2. Heavy Lift Equipments				
Cranes with capacity of more than 100 tons	20	20.87	20.87	(0.00)
Cranes with capacity of less than 100 tons	15	27.16	20.87	6.29
3. Transmission line, Tunneling Equipments [NESD]	10	25.89 *(NESD)*	20.87	5.02
4. Earth-moving equipments	9	42.47	30.00 *(NESD)*	12.47
5. Others including Material Handling/ Pipeline/Welding Equipments [NESD]	12	22.09 *(NESD)*	20.87	1.22
(e) Plant and Machinery used in Telecommunications [NESD]				
1. Towers	18	15.33 *(NESD)*	20.87	(5.54)
2. Telecom transceivers, switching centres,	13	20.58 *(NESD)*	20.87	(0.29)

Nature of Assets	Useful Life for Single shift (Co. Act, 2013)	WDV BASIS Double Shift rate (Co. Act, 2013) (1)	Double Shift rate (Co. Act, 1956) (2)	Impact Increase/ (decrease) (1)-(2)
	(Years)	(%)	(%)	(%)
transmission and other network equipment				
3. Telecom—Ducts, Cables and optical fibre	18	15.33 *(NESD)*	20.87	(5.54)
4. Satellites	18	15.33 *(NESD)*	20.87	(5.54)
(f) Plant and Machinery used in exploration, production and refining oil and gas [NESD]				
1. Refineries	25	11.29 *(NESD)*	20.87	(9.58)
2. Oil and gas assets (including wells), processing plant and facilities	25	11.29 *(NESD)*	20.87	(9.58)
3. Petrochemical Plant	25	11.29 *(NESD)*	20.87	(9.58)
4. Storage tanks and related equipment	25	11.29 *(NESD)*	20.87	(9.58)
5. Pipelines	30	9.50 *(NESD)*	20.87	(11.37)
6. Loggers	8	31.23 *(NESD)*	20.87	10.36
(g) Plant and Machinery used in generation, transmission and distribution of power [NESD]				
1. Thermal/ Gas/ Combined Cycle Power Generation Plant	40	7.22 *(NESD)*	20.87	(13.65)
2. Hydro Power Generation Plant	40	7.22 *(NESD)*	20.87	(13.65)
3. Nuclear Power Generation Plant	40	7.22 *(NESD)*	20.87	(13.65)

		WDV BASIS		
Nature of Assets	**Useful Life for Single shift (Co. Act, 2013)**	**Double Shift rate (Co. Act, 2013) (1)**	**Double Shift rate (Co. Act, 1956) (2)**	**Impact Increase/ (decrease) (1)-(2)**
	(*Years*)	(%)	(%)	(%)
4. Transmission lines, cables and other network assets	40	7.22 *(NESD)*	20.87	(13.65)
5. Wind Power Generation Plant	22	12.73 *(NESD)*	20.87	(8.14)
6. Electric Distribution Plant	35	8.20 *(NESD)*	20.87	(12.67)
7. Gas Storage and Distribution Plant	30	9.50 *(NESD)*	20.87	(11.37)
8. Water Distribution Plant including pipelines	30	9.50 *(NESD)*	20.87	(11.37)
(h) Plant and Machinery used in manufacture of non-ferrous metals				
1. Metal pot line [NESD]	40	7.22 *(NESD)*	20.87	(13.65)
2. Bauxite crushing and grinding section [NESD]	40	7.22 *(NESD)*	20.87	(13.65)
3. Digester Section [NESD]	40	7.22 *(NESD)*	20.87	(13.65)
4. Turbine [NESD]	40	7.22 *(NESD)*	20.87	(13.65)
5. Equipments for Calcination [NESD]	40	7.22 *(NESD)*	20.87	(13.65)
6. Copper Smelter [NESD]	40	7.22 *(NESD)*	20.87	(13.65)
7. Roll Grinder	40	10.82	20.87	(10.05)
8. Soaking Pit	30	14.26	20.87	(6.61)
9. Annealing Furnace	30	14.26	20.87	(6.61)
10. Rolling Mills	30	14.26	20.87	(6.61)
11. Equipments for Scalping, Slitting , etc. [NESD]	30	9.50 *(NESD)*	20.87	(11.37)

		WDV BASIS		
Nature of Assets	**Useful Life for Single shift (Co. Act, 2013)**	**Double Shift rate (Co. Act, 2013) (1)**	**Double Shift rate (Co. Act, 1956) (2)**	**Impact Increase/ (decrease) (1)-(2)**
	(*Years*)	(%)	(%)	(%)
12. Surface Miner, Ripper Dozer, etc., used in mines	25	16.94	20.87	(3.93)
13. Copper refining plant [NESD]	25	11.29 *(NESD)*	20.87	(9.58)
(i) Plant and Machinery used in medical and surgical operations [NESD]				
1. Other Equipments.	15	18.10 *(NESD)*	20.87	(2.77)
(j) Plant and Machinery used in manufacture of pharmaceuticals and chemicals [NESD]				
1. Reactors	20	13.91 *(NESD)*	20.87	(6.96)
2. Distillation Columns	20	13.91 *(NESD)*	20.87	(6.96)
3. Drying equipments/ Centrifuges and Decanters	20	13.91 *(NESD)*	20.87	(6.96)
4. Vessel/storage tanks	20	13.91 *(NESD)*	20.87	(6.96)
(k) Plant and Machinery used in salt works [NESD]	15	18.10 *(NESD)*	20.87	(2.77)
Laboratory equipment [NESD]				
(i) General laboratory equipment	10	25.89 *(NESD)*	20.87	5.02
(ii) Laboratory equipments used in educational institutions	5	45.07 *(NESD)*	20.87	24.20

4.3 ITEM-BY-ITEM COMPARISON AND ASCERTAINMENT OF IMPACT IN TRIPLE SHIFT (ASSUMING 5% RESIDUAL VALUE)

(***Note:*** *The useful lives of assets working on shift basis have been specified in the Schedule II of the Companies Act, 2013, based on their single shift working. Except for assets in respect of which no extra shift depreciation is permitted (indicated by NESD), if an asset is used for any time during the year for triple shift, the depreciation should be calculated on the basis of 100% for that period. Accordingly, the triple shift WDV rate below is taken as 200% of the single shift WDV rate*).

		WDV BASIS		
Nature of Assets	**Useful Life for Single shift (Co. Act, 2013)**	**Triple Shift rate (Co. Act, 2013) (1)**	**Triple Shift rate (Co. Act, 1956) (2)**	**Impact Increase/ (decrease) (1)-(2)**
	(Years)	(%)	(%)	(%)
Plant and Machinery				
General rate applicable to plant and machinery not covered under special plant and machinery				
(a) Plant and Machinery other than continuous process plant not covered under specific industries	15	36.21	27.82	8.39
Special Plant and Machinery				
(a) Plant and Machinery related to production and exhibition of Motion Picture Films				
1. Cinematograph films—Machinery used in the production and exhibition of cinematograph films, recording and equipments, developing machines, printing machines, editing reproducing machines, synchronizers and studio lights except bulbs	13	41.16	20.00 *(NESD)*	21.16
2. Projecting equipment for exhibition of films	13	41.16	20.00 *(NESD)*	21.16

Nature of Assets	Useful Life for Single shift (Co. Act, 2013)	WDV BASIS Triple Shift rate (Co. Act, 2013) (1)	Triple Shift rate (Co. Act, 1956) (2)	Impact Increase/ (decrease) (1)-(2)
	(Years)	(%)	(%)	(%)
(b) Plant and Machinery used in glass manufacturing				
1. Plant and Machinery except direct fire glass melting furnaces Recuperative and regenerative glass melting furnaces	13	41.16	40	1.16
(c) Plant and Machinery used in manufacture of steel				
1. Sinter Plant	20	27.82	27.82	0.00
2. Blast Furnace	20	27.82	27.82	0.00
3. Coke ovens	20	27.82	27.82	0.00
4. Rolling mill in steel plant	20	27.82	27.82	0.00
5. Basic oxygen Furnace Converter	25	22.59	27.82	(5.23)
(d) Plant and Machinery used in civil construction				
1. Concreting, Crushing, Piling Equipments and Road Making Equipments	12	44.18	27.82	16.36
2. Heavy Lift Equipments				
Cranes with capacity of more than 100 tons	20	27.82	27.82	0.00
Cranes with capacity of less than 100 tons	15	36.21	27.82	8.39
3. Transmission line, Tunneling Equipments [NESD]	10	25.89 *(NESD)*	27.82	(1.93)
4. Earth-moving equipments	9	56.63	30.00 *(NESD)*	26.63
5. Others including Material Handling	12	22.09 *(NESD)*	27.82	(5.73)

Nature of Assets	Useful Life for Single shift (Co. Act, 2013)	WDV BASIS Triple Shift rate (Co. Act, 2013) (1)	Triple Shift rate (Co. Act, 1956) (2)	Impact Increase/ (decrease) (1)-(2)
	(*Years*)	(%)	(%)	(%)
/Pipeline/Welding Equipments [NESD]				
(e) Plant and Machinery used in Telecommunications [NESD]				
1. Towers	18	15.33 (*NESD*)	27.82	(12.49)
2. Telecom transceivers, switching centres, transmission and other network equipment	13	20.58 (*NESD*)	27.82	(7.24)
3. Telecom—Ducts, Cables and optical fibre	18	15.33 (*NESD*)	27.82	(12.49)
4. Satellites	18	15.33 (*NESD*)	27.82	(12.49)
(f) Plant and Machinery used in exploration, production and refining oil and gas [NESD]				
1. Refineries	25	11.29 (*NESD*)	27.82	(16.53)
2. Oil and gas assets (including wells), processing plant and facilities	25	11.29 (*NESD*)	27.82	(16.53)
3. Petrochemical Plant	25	11.29 (*NESD*)	27.82	(16.53)
4. Storage tanks and related equipment	25	11.29 (*NESD*)	27.82	(16.53)
5. Pipelines	30	9.50 (*NESD*)	27.82	(18.32)
6. Loggers	8	31.23 (*NESD*)	27.82	3.41
(g) Plant and Machinery used in generation, transmission and distribution of power [NESD]				

Nature of Assets	Useful Life for Single shift (Co. Act, 2013)	WDV BASIS		Impact Increase/ (decrease) (1)-(2)
		Triple Shift rate (Co. Act, 2013) (1)	Triple Shift rate (Co. Act, 1956) (2)	
	(*Years*)	(%)	(%)	(%)
1. Thermal/ Gas/ Combined Cycle Power Generation Plant	40	7.22 *(NESD)*	27.82	(20.60)
2. Hydro Power Generation Plant	40	7.22 *(NESD)*	27.82	(20.60)
3. Nuclear Power Generation Plant	40	7.22 *(NESD)*	27.82	(20.60)
4. Transmission lines, cables and other network assets	40	7.22 *(NESD)*	27.82	(20.60)
5. Wind Power Generation Plant	22	12.73 *(NESD)*	27.82	(15.09)
6. Electric Distribution Plant	35	8.20 *(NESD)*	27.82	(19.62)
7. Gas Storage and Distribution Plant	30	9.50 *(NESD)*	27.82	(18.32)
8. Water Distribution Plant. including pipelines	30	9.50 *(NESD)*	27.82	(18.32)
(h) Plant and Machinery used in manufacture of non-ferrous metals				
1. Metal pot line [NESD]	40	7.22 *(NESD)*	27.82	(20.60)
2. Bauxite crushing and grinding section [NESD]	40	7.22 *(NESD)*	27.82	(20.60)
3. Digester Section [NESD]	40	7.22 *(NESD)*	27.82	(20.60)
4. Turbine [NESD]	40	7.22 *(NESD)*	27.82	(20.60)
5. Equipments for Calcination [NESD]	40	7.22 *(NESD)*	27.82	(20.60)
6. Copper Smelter [NESD]	40	7.22 *(NESD)*	27.82	(20.60)
7. Roll Grinder	40	14.43	27.82	(13.39)

Nature of Assets	Useful Life for Single shift (Co. Act, 2013)	WDV BASIS Triple Shift rate (Co. Act, 2013) (1)	Triple Shift rate (Co. Act, 1956) (2)	Impact Increase/ (decrease) (1)-(2)
	(*Years*)	(%)	(%)	(%)
8. Soaking Pit	30	19.01	27.82	(8.81)
9. Annealing Furnace	30	19.01	27.82	(8.81)
10. Rolling Mills	30	19.01	27.82	(8.81)
11. Equipments for Scalping, Slitting , etc. [NESD]	30	9.50 *(NESD)*	27.82	(18.32)
12. Surface Miner, Ripper Dozer, etc., used in mines	25	22.59	27.82	(5.23)
13. Copper refining plant [NESD]	25	11.29 *(NESD)*	27.82	(16.53)
(i) Plant and Machinery used in medical and surgical operations [NESD]				
1. Other Equipments.	15	18.10 *(NESD)*	27.82	(9.72)
(j) Plant and Machinery used in manufacture of pharmaceuticals and chemicals [NESD]				
1. Reactors	20	13.91 *(NESD)*	27.82	(13.91)
2. Distillation Columns	20	13.91 *(NESD)*	27.82	(13.91)
3. Drying equipments/ Centrifuges and Decanters	20	13.91 *(NESD)*	27.82	(13.91)
4. Vessel/storage tanks	20	13.91 *(NESD)*	27.82	(13.91)
(k) Plant and Machinery used in salt works [NESD]	15	18.10 *(NESD)*	27.82	(9.72)
Laboratory equipment [NESD]				
(i) General laboratory equipment	10	25.89 *(NESD)*	27.82	(1.93)
(ii) Laboratory equipments used in educational institutions	5	45.07 *(NESD)*	27.82	17.25

4.4 ITEM-BY-ITEM COMPARISON AND ASCERTAINMENT OF IMPACT IN SINGLE SHIFT (ASSUMING 1% RESIDUAL VALUE)

		WDV BASIS		
Nature of Assets	**Useful Life (Co. Act, 2013)**	**Single Shift rate (Co. Act, 2013) (1)**	**Single Shift rate (Co. Act, 1956) (2)**	**Impact Increase/ (decrease) (1)-(2)**
	(*Years*)	(%)	(%)	(%)
I. Buildings [NESD]				
(a) Buildings (other than factory buildings) RCC Frame Structure	60	7.39	5	2.39
(b) Buildings (other than factory buildings) other than RCC Frame Structure	30	14.23	5	9.23
(c) Factory buildings	30	14.23	10	4.23
(d) Fences, wells, tube wells	5	60.19	5 (Note 1)	55.19
(e) Others (including temporary structure, etc.)	3	78.46	100 (Note 2)	(21.54)
II. Bridges, culverts, bunders, etc. [NESD]	30	14.23	5 (Note 1)	9.23
III. Roads [NESD]				
(a) Carpeted roads				
(i) Carpeted Roads-RCC	10	36.90	5 (Note 1)	31.90
(ii) Carpeted Roads-other than RCC	5	60.19	5 (Note 1)	55.19
(b) Non-carpeted roads	3	78.46	5 (Note 1)	73.46
IV. Plant and Machinery				
(i) General rate applicable to plant and machinery not covered under special plant and machinery				
(a) Plant and Machinery other than continuous process plant not covered	15	26.44	13.91	12.53

Nature of Assets	Useful Life (Co. Act, 2013)	WDV BASIS		Impact Increase/ (decrease) (1)-(2)
		Single Shift rate (Co. Act, 2013) (1)	Single Shift rate (Co. Act, 1956) (2)	
under specific industries				
(b) continuous process plant for which no special rate has been prescribed under (ii) below [NESD]	25	16.82	15.33	1.49
(ii) Special Plant and Machinery				
(a) Plant and Machinery related to production and exhibition of Motion Picture Films				
Cinematograph films—Machinery used in the production and exhibition of cinematograph films, recording and equipments, developing machines, printing machines, editing reproducing machines, synchronizers and studio lights except bulbs	13	29.83	20	9.83
Projecting equipment for exhibition of films	13	29.83	20	9.83
(b) Plant and Machinery used in glass manufacturing				
1. Plant and Machinery except direct fire glass melting furnaces Recuperative and regenerative glass melting furnaces	13	29.83	20	9.83
2. Plant and Machinery except direct fire glass melting furnaces Moulds [NESD]	8	43.77	30	13.77
3. Float Glass Melting Furnaces [NESD]	10	36.90	27	9.90

Nature of Assets	Useful Life (Co. Act, 2013)	WDV BASIS Single Shift rate (Co. Act, 2013) (1)	WDV BASIS Single Shift rate (Co. Act, 1956) (2)	Impact Increase/ (decrease) (1)-(2)
(c) Plant and Machinery used in mines and quarries—Portable underground machinery and earth moving machinery used in open cast mining [NESD]	8	43.77	30	13.77
(d) Plant and Machinery used in Telecommunications [NESD]				
1. Towers	18	22.57	13.91 (Note 5)	8.66
2. Telecom transceivers, switching centres, transmission and other network equipment	13	29.83	13.91 (Note 5)	15.92
3. Telecom—Ducts, Cables and optical fibre	18	22.57	13.91 (Note 5)	8.66
4. Satellites	18	22.57	13.91 (Note 5)	8.66
(e) Plant and Machinery used in exploration, production and refining oil and gas [NESD]				
1. Refineries	25	16.82	13.91 (Note 5)	2.91
2. Oil and gas assets (including wells), processing plant and facilities	25	16.82	13.91 (Note 5)	2.91
3. Petrochemical Plant	25	16.82	13.91 (Note 5)	2.91
4. Storage tanks and related equipment	25	16.82	13.91 (Note 5)	2.91
5. Pipelines	30	14.23	13.91 (Note 5)	0.32
6. Drilling Rig	30	14.23	30	(15.77)

Nature of Assets	Useful Life (Co. Act, 2013)	WDV BASIS		Impact Increase/ (decrease) (1)-(2)
		Single Shift rate (Co. Act, 2013) (1)	Single Shift rate (Co. Act, 1956) (2)	
7. Field operations (above ground) Portable boilers, drilling tools, well-head tanks, etc.	8	43.77	30	13.77
8. Loggers	8	43.77	13.91 (Note 5)	29.86
(f) Plant and Machinery used in generation, transmission and distribution of power [NESD]				
1. Thermal/ Gas/ Combined Cycle Power Generation Plant	40	10.87	13.91 (Note 5)	(3.04)
2. Hydro Power Generation Plant	40	10.87	13.91 (Note 5)	(3.04)
3. Nuclear Power Generation Plant	40	10.87	13.91 (Note 5)	(3.04)
4. Transmission lines, cables and other network assets	40	10.87	13.91 (Note 5)	(3.04)
5. Wind Power Generation Plant	22	18.89	13.91 (Note 5)	4.98
6. Electric Distribution Plant	35	12.33	13.91 (Note 5)	(1.58)
7. Gas Storage and Distribution Plant	30	14.23	13.91 (Note 5)	0.32
8. Water Distribution Plant including pipelines	30	14.23	13.91 (Note 5)	0.32
(g) Plant and Machinery used in manufacture of steel				
1. Sinter Plant	20	20.57	13.91 (Note 5)	6.66
2. Blast Furnace	20	20.57	13.91 (Note 5)	6.66
3. Coke ovens	20	20.57	13.91 (Note 5)	6.66
4. Rolling mill in steel plant	20	20.57	13.91 (Note 5)	6.66

Nature of Assets	Useful Life (Co. Act, 2013)	WDV BASIS		Impact Increase/ (decrease) (1)-(2)
		Single Shift rate (Co. Act, 2013) (1)	Single Shift rate (Co. Act, 1956) (2)	
5. Basic oxygen Furnace Converter	25	16.82	13.91 (Note 5)	2.91
(h) Plant and Machinery used in manufacture of non-ferrous metals				
1. Metal pot line [NESD]	40	10.87	13.91 (Note 5)	(3.04)
2. Bauxite crushing and grinding section [NESD]	40	10.87	13.91 (Note 5)	(3.04)
3. Digester Section [NESD]	40	10.87	13.91 (Note 5)	(3.04)
4. Turbine [NESD]	40	10.87	13.91 (Note 5)	(3.04)
5. Equipments for Calcination [NESD]	40	10.87	13.91 (Note 5)	(3.04)
6. Copper Smelter [NESD]	40	10.87	13.91 (Note 5)	(3.04)
7. Roll Grinder	40	10.87	13.91 (Note 5)	(3.04)
8. Soaking Pit	30	14.23	13.91 (Note 5)	0.32
9. Annealing Furnace	30	14.23	13.91 (Note 5)	0.32
10. Rolling Mills	30	14.23	13.91 (Note 5)	0.32
11. Equipments for Scalping, Slitting , etc. [NESD]	30	14.23	13.91 (Note 5)	0.32
12. Surface Miner, Ripper Dozer, etc., used in mines	25	16.82	13.91 (Note 5)	2.91
13. Copper refining plant [NESD]	25	16.82	13.91 (Note 5)	2.91
(i) Plant and Machinery used in medical and surgical operations [NESD]				

Nature of Assets	Useful Life (Co. Act, 2013)	WDV BASIS		Impact Increase/ (decrease) (1)-(2)
		Single Shift rate (Co. Act, 2013) (1)	Single Shift rate (Co. Act, 1956) (2)	
1. Electrical Machinery, X-ray and electrotherapeutic apparatus and accessories thereto, medical, diagnostic equipments, namely, Cat-scan, Ultrasound Machines, ECG Monitors, etc.	13	29.83	20	9.83
2. Other Equipments.	15	26.44	13.91 (Note 5)	12.53
(j) Plant and Machinery used in manufacture of pharmaceuticals and chemicals [NESD]				
1. Reactors	20	20.57	13.91 (Note 5)	6.66
2. Distillation Columns	20	20.57	13.91 (Note 5)	6.66
3. Drying equipments/ Centrifuges and Decanters	20	20.57	13.91 (Note 5)	6.66
4. Vessel/storage tanks	20	20.57	13.91 (Note 5)	6.66
(k) Plant and Machinery used in civil construction				
1. Concreting, Crushing, Piling Equipments and Road Making Equipments	12	31.87	13.91 (Note 5)	17.96
2. Heavy Lift Equipments				
Cranes with capacity of more than 100 tons	20	20.57	13.91 (Note 5)	6.66
Cranes with capacity of less than 100 tons	15	26.44	13.91 (Note 5)	12.53
3. Transmission line, Tunneling Equipments [NESD]	10	36.90	13.91 (Note 5)	22.99
4. Earth-moving equipments	9	40.05	30	10.05

Nature of Assets	Useful Life (Co. Act, 2013)	WDV BASIS Single Shift rate (Co. Act, 2013) (1)	Single Shift rate (Co. Act, 1956) (2)	Impact Increase/ (decrease) (1)-(2)
5. Others including Material Handling /Pipeline/Welding Equipments [NESD]	12	31.87	13.91 (Note 5)	17.96
(l) Plant and Machinery used in salt works [NESD]	15	26.44	13.91 (Note 4)	12.53
V. Furniture and fittings [NESD]				
(i) General furniture and fittings	10	36.90	18.1	18.80
(ii) Furniture and fittings used in hotels, restaurants and boarding houses, schools, colleges and other educational institutions, libraries; welfare centres; meeting halls, cinema houses; theatres and circuses; and furniture and fittings let out on hire for use on the occasion of marriages and similar functions.	8	43.77	25.88	17.89
VI. Motor Vehicles [NESD]				
1. Motor cycles, scooters and other mopeds	10	36.90	25.89	11.01
2. Motor buses, motor lorries, motor cars and motor taxies used in a business of running them on hire	6	53.58	40	13.58
3. Motor buses, motor lorries and motor cars other than those used in a business of running them on hire	8	43.77	30	13.77
4. Motor tractors, harvesting combines and heavy vehicles	8	43.77	30	13.77
5. Electrically operated vehicles including battery powered or fuel cell powered vehicles	8	43.77	20	23.77

Nature of Assets	Useful Life (Co. Act, 2013)	WDV BASIS		Impact Increase/ (decrease) (1)-(2)
		Single Shift rate (Co. Act, 2013) (1)	Single Shift rate (Co. Act, 1956) (2)	
VII. Ships [NESD]				
1. Ocean-going ships				
(i) Bulk Carriers and liner vessels	25	16.82	14.6 (Note 3)	2.22
(ii) Crude tankers, product carriers and easy chemical carriers with or without conventional tank coatings	20	20.57	14.6 (Note 3)	5.97
(iii) Chemicals and Acid Carriers:				
(a) With Stainless steel tanks	25	16.82	14.6 (Note 3)	2.22
(b) With other tanks	20	20.57	14.6 (Note 3)	5.97
(iv) Liquified gas carriers	30	14.23	14.6 (Note 3)	(0.37)
(v) Conventional large passenger vessels which are used for cruise purpose also	30	14.23	14.6 (Note 3)	(0.37)
(vi) Coastal service ships of all categories	30	14.23	14.6 (Note 3)	(0.37)
(vii) Offshore supply and support vessels	20	20.57	14.6 (Note 3)	5.97
(viii) Catamarans and other high speed passenger for ships or boats	20	20.57	14.6 (Note 3)	5.97
(ix) Drill ships	25	16.82	14.6 (Note 3)	2.22
(x) Hovercrafts	15	26.44	14.6 (Note 3)	11.84
(xi) Fishing vessels with wooden hull	10	36.90	27.05	9.85
(xii) Dredgers, tugs, barges, survey launches and other similar ships used mainly for dredging purposes	14	28.03	19.8	8.23

		WDV BASIS		
Nature of Assets	**Useful Life (Co. Act, 2013)**	**Single Shift rate (Co. Act, 2013) (1)**	**Single Shift rate (Co. Act, 1956) (2)**	**Impact Increase/ (decrease) (1)-(2)**
2. Vessels ordinarily operating on inland waters				
(i) Speed boats	13	29.83	20	9.83
(ii) Other vessels	28	15.17	10	5.17
VIII. Aircrafts or Helicopters [NESD]	20	20.57	16.2	4.37
IX. Railways sidings, locomotives, rolling stocks, tramways and railways used by concerns, excluding railway concerns [NESD]	15	26.44	13.91 (Note 5)	12.53
X. Ropeway structures [NESD]	15	26.44	30	(3.56)
XI. Office equipment [NESD]	5	60.19	13.91 (Note 5)	46.28
XII. Computers and data processing units [NESD]				
(i) Servers and networks	6	53.58	40	13.58
(ii) End user devices, such as, desktops, laptops, etc.	3	78.46	40	38.46
XIII. Laboratory equipment [NESD]				
(i) General laboratory equipment	10	36.90	13.91 (Note 5)	22.99
(ii) Laboratory equipments used in educational institutions	5	60.19	13.91 (Note 5)	46.28
XIV. Electrical Installations and Equipment [NESD]	10	36.90	13.91 (Note 5)	22.99
XV. Hydraulic works, pipelines and sluices [NESD]	15	26.44	13.91 (Note 5)	12.53

Notes:

1. 'Buildings' includes roads, bridges, culverts, wells and tubewells; 'factory buildings' does not include offices, godowns, officers and employees' quarters, roads, bridges, culverts, wells and tubewells according to the

Schedule XIV of the Companies Act, 1956. Hence the corresponding Schedule XIV rates considered for comparison for the following categories prescribed in Schedule II to the Companies Act, 2013 are those of *'buildings (other than factory buildings) NESD'* specified in Schedule XIV:

(a) 'Fences, wells and tubewells' under the head 'Buildings (NESD)'

(b) Bridges, culverts, bunders, etc (NESD)

(c) Roads (NESD)

2. Corresponding Schedule XIV rate considered for comparison for the sub-category 'others (including temporary structure etc)' under the category 'buildings (NESD)' prescribed in Schedule II to the Companies Act, 2013 is that of 'Purely temporary erections such as wooden structures' prescribed in Schedule XIV of the Companies Act, 1956.

3. Corresponding Schedule XIV rate considered for comparison for the following sub-categories are those of sub-category 'other ships (NESD)' under the category 'Ships' prescribed in the schedule XIV:

(a) Bulk Carriers and liner vessels

(b) Crude tankers, product carriers and easy chemical carriers with or without conventional tank coatings

(c) Chemicals and Acid Carriers

(d) Liquefied gas carriers

(e) Conventional large passenger vessels which are used for cruise purpose also

(f) Coastal service ships of all categories

(g) Offshore supply and support vessels

(h) Catamarans and other high speed passenger for ships or boats

(i) Drill ships

(j) Hovercrafts

4. Corresponding Schedule XIV rate considered for comparison for the item 'plant and machinery used in salt works' are those of general plant and machinery (other than continuous process plant and ship) for which no specific rates have been prescribed.

5. There are various items which were clubbed earlier under general plant and machinery category and now separate useful life has been prescribed for them after the introduction of Schedule II. For such items, Schedule XIV rate for comparison is taken to be the rate prescribed in Schedule XIV for the general category, ie, 'other than continuous process plant for which no special rate has been prescribed'.

4.5 ITEM-BY-ITEM COMPARISON AND ASCERTAINMENT OF IMPACT IN DOUBLE SHIFT (ASSUMING 1% RESIDUAL VALUE)

(*Note: The useful lives of assets working on shift basis have been specified in the Schedule II of the Companies Act, 2013, based on their single shift working. Except for assets in respect of which no extra shift depreciation is permitted (indicated by NESD), if an asset is used for any time during the year for double shift, the depreciation will increase by 50% for that period. Accordingly, the double shift WDV rate is computed by adding an increase of 50% in the single shift WDV rate.*)

		WDV BASIS		
Nature of Assets	*Useful Life for Single shift (Co. Act, 2013)*	*Double Shift rate (Co. Act, 2013) (1)*	*Double Shift rate (Co. Act, 1956) (2)*	*Impact Increase/ (decrease) (1)-(2)*
	(Years)	*(%)*	*(%)*	*(%)*
Plant and Machinery				
General rate applicable to plant and machinery not covered under special plant and machinery				
(a) Plant and Machinery other than continuous process plant not covered under specific industries	15	39.65	20.87	18.78
Special Plant and Machinery				
(a) Plant and Machinery related to production and exhibition of Motion Picture Films				
1. Cinematograph films—Machinery used in the production and exhibition of cinematograph films, recording and equipments, developing machines, printing machines, editing reproducing machines, synchronizers and studio lights except bulbs	13	44.74	20.00 *(NESD)*	24.74
2. Projecting equipment for exhibition of films	13	44.74	20.00 *(NESD)*	24.74
(b) Plant and Machinery used in				

Nature of Assets	Useful Life for Single shift (Co. Act, 2013)	WDV BASIS Double Shift rate (Co. Act, 2013) (1)	Double Shift rate (Co. Act, 1956) (2)	Impact Increase/ (decrease) (1)-(2)
	(Years)	(%)	(%)	(%)
glass manufacturing				
1. Plant and Machinery except direct fire glass melting furnaces Recuperative and regenerative glass melting furnaces	13	44.74	30	14.74
(c) Plant and Machinery used in manufacture of steel				
1. Sinter Plant	20	30.85	20.87	9.98
2. Blast Furnace	20	30.85	20.87	9.98
3. Coke ovens	20	30.85	20.87	9.98
4. Rolling mill in steel plant	20	30.85	20.87	9.98
5. Basic oxygen Furnace Converter	25	25.24	20.87	4.37
(d) Plant and Machinery used in civil construction				
1. Concreting, Crushing, Piling Equipments and Road Making Equipments	12	47.81	20.87	26.94
2. Heavy Lift Equipments				
Cranes with capacity of more than 100 tons	20	30.85	20.87	9.98
Cranes with capacity of less than 100 tons	15	39.65	20.87	18.78
3. Transmission line, Tunneling Equipments [NESD]	10	36.90 *(NESD)*	20.87	16.03
4. Earth-moving equipments	9	60.08	30.00 *(NESD)*	30.08
5. Others including Material Handling / Pipeline/Welding Equipments [NESD]	12	31.87 *(NESD)*	20.87	11.00
(e) Plant and Machinery used in				

		WDV BASIS		
Nature of Assets	***Useful Life for Single shift (Co. Act, 2013)***	***Double Shift rate (Co. Act, 2013) (1)***	***Double Shift rate (Co. Act, 1956) (2)***	***Impact Increase/ (decrease) (1)-(2)***
	(Years)	*(%)*	*(%)*	*(%)*
Telecommunications [NESD]				
1. Towers	18	22.57 *(NESD)*	20.87	1.70
2. Telecom transceivers, switching centres, transmission and other network equipment	13	29.83 *(NESD)*	20.87	8.96
3. Telecom—Ducts, Cab-les and optical fibre	18	22.57 *(NESD)*	20.87	1.70
4. Satellites	18	22.57 *(NESD)*	20.87	1.70
(f) Plant and Machinery used in exploration, production and refining oil and gas [NESD]				
1. Refineries	25	16.82 *(NESD)*	20.87	(4.05)
2. Oil and gas assets (including wells), processing plant and facilities	25	16.82 *(NESD)*	20.87	(4.05)
3. Petrochemical Plant	25	16.82 *(NESD)*	20.87	(4.05)
4. Storage tanks and related equipment	25	16.82 *(NESD)*	20.87	(4.05)
5. Pipelines	30	14.23 *(NESD)*	20.87	(6.64)
6. Loggers	8	43.77 *(NESD)*	20.87	22.90
(g) Plant and Machinery used in generation, transmit-ssion and distribution of power [NESD]				
1. Thermal/ Gas/ Combined Cycle Power Generation Plant	40	10.87 *(NESD)*	20.87	(10.00)
2. Hydro Power Generation	40	10.87	20.87	(10.00)

Nature of Assets	Useful Life for Single shift (Co. Act, 2013)	WDV BASIS Double Shift rate (Co. Act, 2013) (1)	Double Shift rate (Co. Act, 1956) (2)	Impact Increase/ (decrease) (1)-(2)
	(Years)	(%)	(%)	(%)
Plant		(NESD)		
3. Nuclear Power Generation Plant	40	10.87 (NESD)	20.87	(10.00)
4. Transmission lines, cables and other network assets	40	10.87 (NESD)	20.87	(10.00)
5. Wind Power Generation Plant	22	18.89 (NESD)	20.87	(1.98)
6. Electric Distribution Plant	35	12.33 (NESD)	20.87	(8.54)
7. Gas Storage and Distribution Plant	30	14.23 (NESD)	20.87	(6.64)
8. Water Distribution Plant including pipelines	30	14.23 (NESD)	20.87	(6.64)
(h) Plant and Machinery used in manufacture of non-ferrous metals				
1. Metal pot line [NESD]	40	10.87 (NESD)	20.87	(10.00)
2. Bauxite crushing and grinding section [NESD]	40	10.87 (NESD)	20.87	(10.00)
3. Digester Section [NESD]	40	10.87 (NESD)	20.87	(10.00)
4. Turbine [NESD]	40	10.87 (NESD)	20.87	(10.00)
5. Equipments for Calcin-ation [NESD]	40	10.87 (NESD)	20.87	(10.00)
6. Copper Smelter [NESD]	40	10.87 (NESD)	20.87	(10.00)
7. Roll Grinder	40	16.31	20.87	(4.56)
8. Soaking Pit	30	21.35	20.87	0.48
9. Annealing Furnace	30	21.35	20.87	0.48
10. Rolling Mills	30	21.35	20.87	0.48
11. Equipments for Sca-lping, Slitting, etc. [NESD]	30	14.23 (NESD)	20.87	(6.64)

		WDV BASIS		
Nature of Assets	***Useful Life for Single shift (Co. Act, 2013)***	***Double Shift rate (Co. Act, 2013) (1)***	***Double Shift rate (Co. Act, 1956) (2)***	***Impact Increase/ (decrease) (1)-(2)***
	(Years)	*(%)*	*(%)*	*(%)*
12. Surface Miner, Ripper Dozer, etc., used in mines	25	25.24	20.87	4.37
13. Copper refining plant [NESD]	25	16.82 *(NESD)*	20.87	(4.05)
(i) Plant and Machinery used in medical and surgical operations [NESD]				
1. Other Equipments.	15	26.44 *(NESD)*	20.87	5.57
(j) Plant and Machinery used in manufacture of pha-rmaceuticals and chemicals [NESD]				
1. Reactors	20	20.57 *(NESD)*	20.87	(0.30)
2. Distillation Columns	20	20.57 *(NESD)*	20.87	(0.30)
3. Drying equipments/ Centrifuges and Decanters	20	20.57 *(NESD)*	20.87	(0.30)
4. Vessel/storage tanks	20	20.57 *(NESD)*	20.87	(0.30)
(k) Plant and Machinery used in salt works [NESD]	15	26.44 *(NESD)*	20.87	5.57
Laboratory equipment [NESD]				
(i) General laboratory equipment	10	36.90 *(NESD)*	20.87	16.03
(ii) Laboratory equipments used in educational institutions	5	60.19 *(NESD)*	20.87	39.32

4.6 ITEM-BY-ITEM COMPARISON AND ASCERTAINMENT OF IMPACT IN TRIPLE SHIFT (ASSUMING 1% RESIDUAL VALUE)

(***Note:*** *The useful lives of assets working on shift basis have been specified in the Schedule II of the Companies Act, 2013, based on their single shift working. Except* *for assets in respect of which no extra shift depreciation is permitted (indicated by NESD), if an asset is used for any time during the year for triple shift, the depreciation should be calculated on the basis of 100% for that period. Accordingly, the triple shift WDV rate below is taken as 200% of the single shift WDV rate*).

		WDV BASIS		
Nature of Assets	**Useful Life for Single shift (Co. Act, 2013)**	**Triple Shift rate (Co. Act, 2013) (1)**	**Triple Shift rate (Co. Act, 1956) (2)**	**Impact Increase/ (decrease) (1)-(2)**
	(*Years*)	(%)	(%)	(%)
Plant and Machinery				
General rate applicable to plant and machinery not covered under special plant and machinery				
(a) Plant and Machinery other than continuous process plant not covered under specific industries	15	52.87	27.82	25.05
Special Plant and Machinery				
(a) Plant and Machinery related to production and exhibition of Motion Picture Films				
1. Cinematograph films—Machinery used in the production and exhibition of cinematograph films, recording and equipments, developing machines, printing machines, editing reproducing machines, synchronizers and studio lights except bulbs	13	59.66	20.00 (*NESD*)	39.66
2. Projecting equipment for exhibition of films	13	59.66	20.00 (*NESD*)	39.66
(b) Plant and Machinery used in glass manufacturing				
1. Plant and Machinery except direct fire glass melting furnaces	13	59.66	40	19.66

		WDV BASIS		
Nature of Assets	**Useful Life for Single shift (Co. Act, 2013)**	**Triple Shift rate (Co. Act, 2013) (1)**	**Triple Shift rate (Co. Act, 1956) (2)**	**Impact Increase/ (decrease) (1)-(2)**
	(*Years*)	(%)	(%)	(%)
Recuperative and regenerative glass melting furnaces				
(c) Plant and Machinery used in manufacture of steel				
1. Sinter Plant	20	41.13	27.82	13.31
2. Blast Furnace	20	41.13	27.82	13.31
3. Coke ovens	20	41.13	27.82	13.31
4. Rolling mill in steel plant	20	41.13	27.82	13.31
5. Basic oxygen Furnace Converter	25	33.65	27.82	5.83
(d) Plant and Machinery used in civil construction				
1. Concreting, Crushing, Piling Equipments and Road Making Equipments	12	63.74	27.82	35.92
2. Heavy Lift Equipments				
Cranes with capacity of more than 100 tons	20	41.13	27.82	13.31
Cranes with capacity of less than 100 tons	15	52.87	27.82	25.05
3. Transmission line, Tunneling Equipments [NESD]	10	36.90 *(NESD)*	27.82	9.08
4. Earth-moving equipments	9	80.10	30.00 *(NESD)*	50.10
5. Others including Material Handling /Pipeline/ Welding Equipments [NESD]	12	31.87 *(NESD)*	27.82	4.05
(e) Plant and Machinery used in Telecommunications [NESD]				
1. Towers	18	22.57	27.82	(5.25)

Nature of Assets	Useful Life for Single shift (Co. Act, 2013)	WDV BASIS Triple Shift rate (Co. Act, 2013) (1)	Triple Shift rate (Co. Act, 1956) (2)	Impact Increase/ (decrease) (1)-(2)
	(*Years*)	(%)	(%)	(%)
		(NESD)		
2. Telecom transceivers, switching centres, transmission and other network equipment	13	29.83 *(NESD)*	27.82	2.01
3. Telecom—Ducts, Cables and optical fibre	18	22.57 *(NESD)*	27.82	(5.25)
4. Satellites	18	22.57 *(NESD)*	27.82	(5.25)
(f) Plant and Machinery used in exploration, production and refining oil and gas [NESD]				
1. Refineries	25	16.82 *(NESD)*	27.82	(11.00)
2. Oil and gas assets (including wells), processing plant and facilities	25	16.82 *(NESD)*	27.82	(11.00)
3. Petrochemical Plant	25	16.82 *(NESD)*	27.82	(11.00)
4. Storage tanks and related equipment	25	16.82 *(NESD)*	27.82	(11.00)
5. Pipelines	30	14.23 *(NESD)*	27.82	(13.59)
6. Loggers	8	43.77 *(NESD)*	27.82	15.95
(g) Plant and Machinery used in generation, transmission and distribution of power [NESD]				
1. Thermal/ Gas/ Combined Cycle Power Generation Plant	40	10.87 *(NESD)*	27.82	(16.95)
2. Hydro Power Generation Plant	40	10.87 *(NESD)*	27.82	(16.95)

Nature of Assets	Useful Life for Single shift (Co. Act, 2013)	WDV BASIS Triple Shift rate (Co. Act, 2013) (1)	WDV BASIS Triple Shift rate (Co. Act, 1956) (2)	Impact Increase/ (decrease) (1)-(2)
	(*Years*)	(%)	(%)	(%)
3. Nuclear Power Generation Plant	40	10.87 *(NESD)*	27.82	(16.95)
4. Transmission lines, cables and other network assets	40	10.87 *(NESD)*	27.82	(16.95)
5. Wind Power Generation Plant	22	18.89 *(NESD)*	27.82	(8.93)
6. Electric Distribution Plant	35	12.33 *(NESD)*	27.82	(15.49)
7. Gas Storage and Distribution Plant	30	14.23 *(NESD)*	27.82	(13.59)
8. Water Distribution Plant including pipelines	30	14.23 *(NESD)*	27.82	(13.59)
(h) Plant and Machinery used in manufacture of non-ferrous metals				
1. Metal pot line [NESD]	40	10.87 *(NESD)*	27.82	(16.95)
2. Bauxite crushing and grinding section [NESD]	40	10.87 *(NESD)*	27.82	(16.95)
3. Digester Section [NESD]	40	10.87 *(NESD)*	27.82	(16.95)
4. Turbine [NESD]	40	10.87 *(NESD)*	27.82	(16.95)
5. Equipments for Calcination [NESD]	40	10.87 *(NESD)*	27.82	(16.95)
6. Copper Smelter [NESD]	40	10.87 *(NESD)*	27.82	(16.95)
7. Roll Grinder	40	21.75	27.82	(6.07)
8. Soaking Pit	30	28.46	27.82	0.64
9. Annealing Furnace	30	28.46	27.82	0.64
10. Rolling Mills	30	28.46	27.82	0.64
11. Equipments for Scalping,	30	14.23	27.82	(13.59)

Nature of Assets	Useful Life for Single shift (Co. Act, 2013)	WDV BASIS Triple Shift rate (Co. Act, 2013) (1)	Triple Shift rate (Co. Act, 1956) (2)	Impact Increase/ (decrease) (1)-(2)
	(*Years*)	(%)	(%)	(%)
Slitting , etc. [NESD]		*(NESD)*		
12. Surface Miner, Ripper Dozer, etc., used in mines	25	33.65	27.82	5.83
13. Copper refining plant [NESD]	25	16.82 *(NESD)*	27.82	(11.00)
(i) Plant and Machinery used in medical and surgical operations [NESD]				
1. Other Equipments.	15	26.44 *(NESD)*	27.82	(1.38)
(j) Plant and Machinery used in manufacture of pharmaceuticals and chemicals [NESD]				
1. Reactors	20	20.57 *(NESD)*	27.82	(7.25)
2. Distillation Columns	20	20.57 *(NESD)*	27.82	(7.25)
3. Drying equipments/Centrifuges and Decanters	20	20.57 *(NESD)*	27.82	(7.25)
4. Vessel/storage tanks	20	20.57 *(NESD)*	27.82	(7.25)
(k) Plant and Machinery used in salt works [NESD]	15	26.44 *(NESD)*	27.82	(1.38)
Laboratory equipment [NESD]				
(i) General laboratory equipment	10	36.90 *(NESD)*	27.82	9.08
(ii) Laboratory equipments used in educational institutions	5	60.19 *(NESD)*	27.82	32.37

4.7 ITEM-BY-ITEM COMPARISON AND ASCERTAINMENT OF IMPACT IN SINGLE SHIFT (ASSUMING 0.01% RESIDUAL VALUE)

		WDV BASIS		
Nature of Assets	**Useful Life (Co. Act, 2013)**	**Single Shift rate (Co. Act, 2013) (1)**	**Single Shift rate (Co. Act, 1956) (2)**	**Impact Increase/ (decrease) (1)-(2)**
	(*Years*)	(%)	(%)	(%)
I. Buildings [NESD]				
(a) Buildings (other than factory buildings) RCC Frame Structure	60	14.23	5	9.23
(b) Buildings (other than factory buildings) other than RCC Frame Structure	30	26.44	5	21.44
(c) Factory buildings	30	26.44	10	16.44
(d) Fences, wells, tube wells	5	84.15	5 (Note 1)	79.15
(e) Others (including temporary structure, etc.)	3	95.36	100 (Note 2)	(4.64)
II. Bridges, culverts, bunders, etc. [NESD]	30	26.44	5 (Note 1)	21.44
III. Roads [NESD]				
(a) Carpeted roads				
(i) Carpeted Roads-RCC	10	60.19	5 (Note 1)	55.19
(ii) Carpeted Roads-other than RCC	5	84.15	5 (Note 1)	79.15
(b) Non-carpeted roads	3	95.36	5 (Note 1)	90.36
IV. Plant and Machinery				
(i) General rate applicable to plant and machinery not covered under special plant and machinery				
(a) Plant and Machinery other than continuous process plant not covered under specific industries	15	45.88	13.91	31.97

Nature of Assets	Useful Life (Co. Act, 2013)	WDV BASIS Single Shift rate (Co. Act, 2013) (1)	Single Shift rate (Co. Act, 1956) (2)	Impact Increase/ (decrease) (1)-(2)
	(*Years*)	(%)	(%)	(%)
(b) continuous process plant for which no special rate has been prescribed under (ii) below [NESD]	25	30.82	15.33	15.49
(ii) Special Plant and Machinery				
(a) Plant and Machinery related to production and exhibition of Motion Picture Films				
Cinematograph films—Machinery used in the production and exhibition of cinematograph films, recording and equipments, developing machines, printing machines, editing reproducing machines, synchronizers and studio lights except bulbs	13	50.76	20	30.76
Projecting equipment for exhibition of films	13	50.76	20	30.76
(b) Plant and Machinery used in glass manufacturing				
1. Plant and Machinery except direct fire glass melting furnaces Recuperative and regenerative glass melting furnaces	13	50.76	20	30.76
2. Plant and Machinery except direct fire glass melting furnaces Moulds [NESD]	8	68.38	30	38.38
3. Float Glass Melting Furnaces [NESD]	10	60.19	27	33.19
(c) Plant and Machinery used in mines and quarries—Portable	8	68.38	30	38.38

		WDV BASIS		
Nature of Assets	**Useful Life (Co. Act, 2013)**	**Single Shift rate (Co. Act, 2013) (1)**	**Single Shift rate (Co. Act, 1956) (2)**	**Impact Increase/ (decrease) (1)-(2)**
	(*Years*)	(%)	(%)	(%)
underground machinery and earth moving machinery used in open cast mining [NESD]				
(d) Plant and Machinery used in Telecommunications [NESD]				
1. Towers	18	40.05	13.91 (Note 5)	26.14
2. Telecom transceivers, switching centres, transmission and other network equipment	13	50.76	13.91 (Note 5)	36.85
3. Telecom—Ducts, Cables and optical fibre	18	40.05	13.91 (Note 5)	26.14
4. Satellites	18	40.05	13.91 (Note 5)	26.14
(e) Plant and Machinery used in exploration, production and refining oil and gas [NESD]				
1. Refineries	25	30.82	13.91 (Note 5)	16.91
2. Oil and gas assets (including wells), processing plant and facilities	25	30.82	13.91 (Note 5)	16.91
3. Petrochemical Plant	25	30.82	13.91 (Note 5)	16.91
4. Storage tanks and related equipment	25	30.82	13.91 (Note 5)	16.91
5. Pipelines	30	26.44	13.91 (Note 5)	12.53
6. Drilling Rig	30	26.44	30	(3.56)
7. Field operations (above ground) Portable boilers, drilling tools, well-head tanks, etc.	8	68.38	30	38.38

Nature of Assets	Useful Life (Co. Act, 2013)	WDV BASIS Single Shift rate (Co. Act, 2013) (1)	Single Shift rate (Co. Act, 1956) (2)	Impact Increase/ (decrease) (1)-(2)
	(*Years*)	(%)	(%)	(%)
8. Loggers	8	68.38	13.91 (Note 5)	54.47
(f) Plant and Machinery used in generation, trans-mission and distribution of power [NESD]				
1. Thermal/ Gas/ Combined Cycle Power Generation Plant	40	20.57	13.91 (Note 5)	6.66
2. Hydro Power Generation Plant	40	20.57	13.91 (Note 5)	6.66
3. Nuclear Power Generation Plant	40	20.57	13.91 (Note 5)	6.66
4. Transmission lines, cables and other network assets	40	20.57	13.91 (Note 5)	6.66
5. Wind Power Generation Plant	22	34.21	13.91 (Note 5)	20.30
6. Electric Distribution Plant	35	23.14	13.91 (Note 5)	9.23
7. Gas Storage and Distribution Plant	30	26.44	13.91 (Note 5)	12.53
8. Water Distribution Plant including pipelines	30	26.44	13.91 (Note 5)	12.53
(g) Plant and Machinery used in manufacture of steel				
1. Sinter Plant	20	36.90	13.91 (Note 5)	22.99
2. Blast Furnace	20	36.90	13.91 (Note 5)	22.99
3. Coke ovens	20	36.90	13.91 (Note 5)	22.99
4. Rolling mill in steel plant	20	36.90	13.91 (Note 5)	22.99
5. Basic oxygen Furnace Converter	25	30.82	13.91 (Note 5)	16.91

Nature of Assets	Useful Life (Co. Act, 2013)	WDV BASIS		Impact Increase/ (decrease) (1)-(2)
		Single Shift rate (Co. Act, 2013) (1)	Single Shift rate (Co. Act, 1956) (2)	
	(*Years*)	(%)	(%)	(%)
(h) Plant and Machinery used in manufacture of non-ferrous metals				
1. Metal pot line [NESD]	40	20.57	13.91 (Note 5)	6.66
2. Bauxite crushing and grinding section [NESD]	40	20.57	13.91 (Note 5)	6.66
3. Digester Section [NESD]	40	20.57	13.91 (Note 5)	6.66
4. Turbine [NESD]	40	20.57	13.91 (Note 5)	6.66
5. Equipments for Calcination [NESD]	40	20.57	13.91 (Note 5)	6.66
6. Copper Smelter [NESD]	40	20.57	13.91 (Note 5)	6.66
7. Roll Grinder	40	20.57	13.91 (Note 5)	6.66
8. Soaking Pit	30	26.44	13.91 (Note 5)	12.53
9. Annealing Furnace	30	26.44	13.91 (Note 5)	12.53
10. Rolling Mills	30	26.44	13.91 (Note 5)	12.53
11. Equipments for Scalping, Slitting , etc. [NESD]	30	26.44	13.91 (Note 5)	12.53
12. Surface Miner, Ripper Dozer, etc., used in mines	25	30.82	13.91 (Note 5)	16.91
13. Copper refining plant [NESD]	25	30.82	13.91 (Note 5)	16.91
(i) Plant and Machinery used in medical and surgical operations [NESD]				
1. Electrical Machinery, X-ray and electrotherapeutic	13	50.76	20	30.76

Nature of Assets	Useful Life (Co. Act, 2013)	WDV BASIS Single Shift rate (Co. Act, 2013) (1)	Single Shift rate (Co. Act, 1956) (2)	Impact Increase/ (decrease) (1)-(2)
	(*Years*)	(%)	(%)	(%)
apparatus and accessories thereto, medical, diagnostic equipments, namely, Cat-scan, Ultrasound Machines, ECG Monitors, etc.				
2. Other Equipments.	15	45.88	13.91 (Note 5)	31.97
(j) Plant and Machinery used in manufacture of pharmaceuticals and chemicals [NESD]				
1. Reactors	20	36.90	13.91 (Note 5)	22.99
2. Distillation Columns	20	36.90	13.91 (Note 5)	22.99
3. Drying equipments/ Centrifuges and Decanters	20	36.90	13.91 (Note 5)	22.99
4. Vessel/storage tanks	20	36.90	13.91 (Note 5)	22.99
(k) Plant and Machinery used in civil construction				
1. Concreting, Crushing, Piling Equipments and Road Making Equipments	12	53.58	13.91 (Note 5)	39.67
2. Heavy Lift Equipments				
Cranes with capacity of more than 100 tons	20	36.90	13.91 (Note 5)	22.99
Cranes with capacity of less than 100 tons	15	45.88	13.91 (Note 5)	31.97
3. Transmission line, Tunneling Equipments [NESD]	10	60.19	13.91 (Note 5)	46.28
4. Earth-moving equipm-ents	9	64.06	30	34.06

Nature of Assets	Useful Life (Co. Act, 2013)	WDV BASIS Single Shift rate (Co. Act, 2013) (1)	Single Shift rate (Co. Act, 1956) (2)	Impact Increase/ (decrease) (1)-(2)
	(*Years*)	(%)	(%)	(%)
5. Others including Material Handling / Pipeline/Welding Equipments [NESD]	12	53.58	13.91 (Note 5)	39.67
(l) Plant and Machinery used in salt works [NESD]	15	45.88	13.91 (Note 4)	31.97
V. Furniture and fittings [NESD]				
(i) General furniture and fittings	10	60.19	18.1	42.09
(ii) Furniture and fittings used in hotels, restaurants and boarding houses, schools, colleges and other educational institutions, libraries; welfare centres; meeting halls, cinema houses; theatres and circuses; and furniture and fittings let out on hire for use on the occasion of marriages and similar functions.	8	68.38	25.88	42.50
VI. Motor Vehicles [NESD]				
1. Motor cycles, scooters and other mopeds	10	60.19	25.89	34.30
2. Motor buses, motor lorries, motor cars and motor taxies used in a business of running them on hire	6	78.46	40	38.46
3. Motor buses, motor lorries and motor cars other than those used in a business of running them on hire	8	68.38	30	38.38
4. Motor tractors, harvesting combines and heavy vehicles	8	68.38	30	38.38
5. Electrically operated vehicles including battery powered or fuel cell powered vehicles	8	68.38	20	48.38
VII. Ships [NESD]				

Nature of Assets	Useful Life (Co. Act, 2013)	WDV BASIS Single Shift rate (Co. Act, 2013) (1)	WDV BASIS Single Shift rate (Co. Act, 1956) (2)	Impact Increase/ (decrease) (1)-(2)
	(*Years*)	(%)	(%)	(%)
1. Ocean-going ships				
(i) Bulk Carriers and liner vessels	25	30.82	14.6 (Note 3)	16.22
(ii) Crude tankers, product carriers and easy chemical carriers with or without conventional tank coatings	20	36.90	14.6 (Note 3)	22.30
(iii) Chemicals and Acid Carriers:				
(a) With Stainless steel tanks	25	30.82	14.6 (Note 3)	16.22
(b) With other tanks	20	36.90	14.6 (Note 3)	22.30
(iv) Liquified gas carriers	30	26.44	14.6 (Note 3)	11.84
(v) Conventional large passenger vessels which are used for cruise purpose also	30	26.44	14.6 (Note 3)	11.84
(vi) Coastal service ships of all categories	30	26.44	14.6 (Note 3)	11.84
(vii) Offshore supply and support vessels	20	36.90	14.6 (Note 3)	22.30
(viii) Catamarans and other high speed passenger for ships or boats	20	36.90	14.6 (Note 3)	22.30
(ix) Drill ships	25	30.82	14.6 (Note 3)	16.22
(x) Hovercrafts	15	45.88	14.6 (Note 3)	31.28
(xi) Fishing vessels with wooden hull	10	60.19	27.05	33.14
(xii) Dredgers, tugs, barges, survey launches and other similar ships used mainly for dredging purposes	14	48.21	19.8	28.41

Nature of Assets	Useful Life (Co. Act, 2013)	WDV BASIS Single Shift rate (Co. Act, 2013) (1)	Single Shift rate (Co. Act, 1956) (2)	Impact Increase/ (decrease) (1)-(2)
	(*Years*)	(%)	(%)	(%)
2. Vessels ordinarily operating on inland waters				
(i) Speed boats	13	50.76	20	30.76
(ii) Other vessels	28	28.03	10	18.03
VIII. Aircrafts or Helicopters [NESD]	20	36.90	16.2	20.70
IX. Railways sidings, locomotives, rolling stocks, tramways and railways used by concerns, excluding railway concerns [NESD]	15	45.88	13.91 (Note 5)	31.97
X. Ropeway structures [NESD]	15	45.88	30	15.88
XI. Office equipment [NESD]	5	84.15	13.91 (Note 5)	70.24
XII. Computers and data processing units [NESD]				
(i) Servers and networks	6	78.46	40	38.46
(ii) End user devices, such as, desktops, laptops, etc.	3	95.36	40	55.36
XIII. Laboratory equipment [NESD]				
(i) General laboratory equipment	10	60.19	13.91 (Note 5)	46.28
(ii) Laboratory equipments used in educational institutions	5	84.15	13.91 (Note 5)	70.24
XIV. Electrical Installations and Equipment [NESD]	10	60.19	13.91 (Note 5)	46.28
XV. Hydraulic works, pipelines and sluices [NESD]	15	45.88	13.91 (Note 5)	31.97

Notes:

1. 'Buildings' includes roads, bridges, culverts, wells and tubewells; 'factory buildings' does not include offices, godowns, officers and employees'

quarters, roads, bridges, culverts, wells and tubewells according to the Schedule XIV of the Companies Act, 1956. Hence the corresponding Schedule XIV rates considered for comparison for the following categories prescribed in Schedule II to the Companies Act, 2013 are those of *'buildings (other than factory buildings) NESD'* specified in Schedule XIV:

(g) 'Fences, wells and tubewells' under the head 'Buildings (NESD)'

(h) Bridges, culverts, bunders, etc (NESD)

(i) Roads (NESD)

2. Corresponding Schedule XIV rate considered for comparison for the sub-category 'others (including temporary structure etc)' under the category 'buildings (NESD)' prescribed in Schedule II to the Companies Act, 2013 is that of 'Purely temporary erections such as wooden structures' prescribed in Schedule XIV of the Companies Act, 1956.

3. Corresponding Schedule XIV rate considered for comparison for the following sub-categories are those of sub-category 'other ships (NESD)' under the category 'Ships' prescribed in the schedule XIV:

(u) Bulk Carriers and liner vessels

(v) Crude tankers, product carriers and easy chemical carriers with or without conventional tank coatings

(w) Chemicals and Acid Carriers

(x) Liquefied gas carriers

(y) Conventional large passenger vessels which are used for cruise purpose also

(z) Coastal service ships of all categories

(aa) Offshore supply and support vessels

(bb) Catamarans and other high speed passenger for ships or boats

(cc) Drill ships

(dd) Hovercrafts

4. Corresponding Schedule XIV rate considered for comparison for the item 'plant and machinery used in salt works' are those of general plant and machinery (other than continuous process plant and ship) for which no specific rates have been prescribed.

5. There are various items which were clubbed earlier under general plant and machinery category and now separate useful life has been prescribed for them after the introduction of Schedule II. For such items, Schedule XIV rate for comparison is taken to be the rate prescribed in Schedule XIV for the general category, ie, 'other than continuous process plant for which no special rate has been prescribed'.

4.8 ITEM-BY-ITEM COMPARISON AND ASCERTAINMENT OF IMPACT IN DOUBLE SHIFT (ASSUMING 0.01% RESIDUAL VALUE)

(***Note:*** *The useful lives of assets working on shift basis have been specified in the Schedule II of the Companies Act, 2013, based on their single shift working. Except for assets in respect of which no extra shift depreciation is permitted (indicated by NESD), if an asset is used for any time during the year for double shift, the depreciation will increase by 50% for that period. Accordingly, the double shift WDV rate is computed by adding an increase of 50% in the single shift WDV rate.*)

Nature of Assets	Useful Life for Single shift (Co. Act, 2013)	WDV BASIS		
		Double Shift rate (Co. Act, 2013) (1)	Double Shift rate (Co. Act, 1956) (2)	Impact Increase/ (decrease) (1)-(2)
	(Years)	(%)	(%)	(%)
Plant and Machinery				
General rate applicable to plant and machinery not covered under special plant and machinery				
(a) Plant and Machinery other than continuous process plant not covered under specific industries	15	68.82	20.87	47.95
Special Plant and Machinery				
(a) Plant and Machinery related to production and exhibition of Motion Picture Films				
1. Cinematograph films—Machinery used in the production and exhibition of cinematograph films, recording and equipments, developing machines, printing machines, editing reproducing machines, synchronizers and studio lights except bulbs	13	76.14	20.00 *(NESD)*	56.14
2. Projecting equipment for exhibition of films	13	76.14	20.00 *(NESD)*	56.14

Nature of Assets	Useful Life for Single shift (Co. Act, 2013)	WDV BASIS Double Shift rate (Co. Act, 2013) (1)	Double Shift rate (Co. Act, 1956) (2)	Impact Increase/ (decrease) (1)-(2)
	(Years)	(%)	(%)	(%)
(b) Plant and Machinery used in glass manufacturing				
1. Plant and Machinery except direct fire glass melting furnaces Recuperative and regenerative glass melting furnaces	13	76.14	30	46.14
(c) Plant and Machinery used in manufacture of steel				
1. Sinter Plant	20	55.36	20.87	34.49
2. Blast Furnace	20	55.36	20.87	34.49
3. Coke ovens	20	55.36	20.87	34.49
4. Rolling mill in steel plant	20	55.36	20.87	34.49
5. Basic oxygen Furnace Converter	25	46.23	20.87	25.36
(d) Plant and Machinery used in civil construction				
1. Concreting, Crushing, Piling Equipments and Road Making Equipments	12	80.38	20.87	59.51
2. Heavy Lift Equipments				
Cranes with capacity of more than 100 tons	20	55.36	20.87	34.49
Cranes with capacity of less than 100 tons	15	68.82	20.87	47.95
3. Transmission line, Tunneling Equipments [NESD]	10	60.19 *(NESD)*	20.87	39.32
4. Earth-moving equipments	9	96.09	30.00 *(NESD)*	66.09
5. Others including Material Handling	12	53.58 *(NESD)*	20.87	32.71

		WDV BASIS		
Nature of Assets	**Useful Life for Single shift (Co. Act, 2013)**	**Double Shift rate (Co. Act, 2013) (1)**	**Double Shift rate (Co. Act, 1956) (2)**	**Impact Increase/ (decrease) (1)-(2)**
	(*Years*)	(%)	(%)	(%)
/Pipeline/Welding Equipments [NESD]				
(e) Plant and Machinery used in Telecommunications [NESD]				
1. Towers	18	40.05 *(NESD)*	20.87	19.18
2. Telecom transceivers, switching centres, transmission and other network equipment	13	50.76 *(NESD)*	20.87	29.89
3. Telecom—Ducts, Cables and optical fibre	18	40.05 *(NESD)*	20.87	19.18
4. Satellites	18	40.05 *(NESD)*	20.87	19.18
(f) Plant and Machinery used in exploration, production and refining oil and gas [NESD]				
1. Refineries	25	30.82 *(NESD)*	20.87	9.95
2. Oil and gas assets (including wells), processing plant and facilities	25	30.82 *(NESD)*	20.87	9.95
3. Petrochemical Plant	25	30.82 *(NESD)*	20.87	9.95
4. Storage tanks and related equipment	25	30.82 *(NESD)*	20.87	9.95
5. Pipelines	30	26.44 *(NESD)*	20.87	5.57
6. Loggers	8	68.38 *(NESD)*	20.87	47.51
(g) Plant and Machinery used in generation, transmission and distribution of power [NESD]				

Nature of Assets	Useful Life for Single shift (Co. Act, 2013)	WDV BASIS		
		Double Shift rate (Co. Act, 2013) (1)	Double Shift rate (Co. Act, 1956) (2)	Impact Increase/ (decrease) (1)-(2)
	(*Years*)	(%)	(%)	(%)
1. Thermal/ Gas/ Combined Cycle Power Generation Plant	40	20.57 *(NESD)*	20.87	(0.30)
2. Hydro Power Generation Plant	40	20.57 *(NESD)*	20.87	(0.30)
3. Nuclear Power Generation Plant	40	20.57 *(NESD)*	20.87	(0.30)
4. Transmission lines, cables and other network assets	40	20.57 *(NESD)*	20.87	(0.30)
5. Wind Power Generation Plant	22	34.21 *(NESD)*	20.87	13.34
6. Electric Distribution Plant	35	23.14 *(NESD)*	20.87	2.27
7. Gas Storage and Distribution Plant	30	26.44 *(NESD)*	20.87	5.57
8. Water Distribution Plant including pipelines	30	26.44 *(NESD)*	20.87	5.57
(h) Plant and Machinery used in manufacture of non-ferrous metals				
1. Metal pot line [NESD]	40	20.57 *(NESD)*	20.87	(0.30)
2. Bauxite crushing and grinding section [NESD]	40	20.57 *(NESD)*	20.87	(0.30)
3. Digester Section [NESD]	40	20.57 *(NESD)*	20.87	(0.30)
4. Turbine [NESD]	40	20.57 *(NESD)*	20.87	(0.30)
5. Equipments for Calcination [NESD]	40	20.57 *(NESD)*	20.87	(0.30)
6. Copper Smelter [NESD]	40	20.57 *(NESD)*	20.87	(0.30)
7. Roll Grinder	40	30.85	20.87	9.98

		WDV BASIS		
Nature of Assets	**Useful Life for Single shift (Co. Act, 2013)**	**Double Shift rate (Co. Act, 2013) (1)**	**Double Shift rate (Co. Act, 1956) (2)**	**Impact Increase/ (decrease) (1)-(2)**
	(*Years*)	(%)	(%)	(%)
8. Soaking Pit	30	39.65	20.87	18.78
9. Annealing Furnace	30	39.65	20.87	18.78
10. Rolling Mills	30	39.65	20.87	18.78
11. Equipments for Scalping, Slitting , etc. [NESD]	30	26.44 *(NESD)*	20.87	5.57
12. Surface Miner, Ripper Dozer, etc., used in mines	25	46.23	20.87	25.36
13. Copper refining plant [NESD]	25	30.82 *(NESD)*	20.87	9.95
(i) Plant and Machinery used in medical and surgical operations [NESD]				
1. Other Equipments.	15	45.88 *(NESD)*	20.87	25.01
(j) Plant and Machinery used in manufacture of pharmaceuticals and chemicals [NESD]				
1. Reactors	20	36.90 *(NESD)*	20.87	16.03
2. Distillation Columns	20	36.90 *(NESD)*	20.87	16.03
3. Drying equipments/Centrifuges and Decanters	20	36.90 *(NESD)*	20.87	16.03
4. Vessel/storage tanks	20	36.90 *(NESD)*	20.87	16.03
(k) Plant and Machinery used in salt works [NESD]	15	45.88 *(NESD)*	20.87	25.01
Laboratory equipment [NESD]				
(i) General laboratory equipment	10	60.19 *(NESD)*	20.87	39.32

Nature of Assets	Useful Life for Single shift (Co. Act, 2013)	WDV BASIS Double Shift rate (Co. Act, 2013) (1)	Double Shift rate (Co. Act, 1956) (2)	Impact Increase/ (decrease) (1)-(2)
	(Years)	(%)	(%)	(%)
(ii) Laboratory equipments used in educational institutions	5	84.15 *(NESD)*	20.87	63.28

4.9 ITEM-BY-ITEM COMPARISON AND ASCERTAINMENT OF IMPACT IN TRIPLE SHIFT (ASSUMING 0.01% RESIDUAL VALUE)

(***Note:*** *The useful lives of assets working on shift basis have been specified in the Schedule II of the Companies Act, 2013, based on their single shift working. Except for assets in respect of which no extra shift depreciation is permitted (indicated by NESD), if an asset is used for any time during the year for triple shift, the depreciation should be calculated on the basis of 100% for that period. Accordingly, the triple shift WDV rate below is taken as 200% of the single shift WDV rate*)

Nature of Assets	Useful Life for Single shift (Co. Act, 2013)	WDV BASIS Triple Shift rate (Co. Act, 2013) (1)	Triple Shift rate (Co. Act, 1956) (2)	Impact Increase/ (decrease) (1)-(2)
	(Years)	(%)	(%)	(%)
Plant and Machinery				
General rate applicable to plant and machinery not covered under special plant and machinery				
(a) Plant and Machinery other than continuous process plant not covered under specific industries	15	91.77	27.82	63.95
Special Plant and Machinery				
(a) Plant and Machinery related to production and exhibition of Motion Picture Films				

Nature of Assets	Useful Life for Single shift (Co. Act, 2013)	WDV BASIS Triple Shift rate (Co. Act, 2013) (1)	Triple Shift rate (Co. Act, 1956) (2)	Impact Increase/ (decrease) (1)-(2)
	(Years)	(%)	(%)	(%)
1. Cinematograph films—Machinery used in the production and exhibition of cinematograph films, recording and equipments, developing machines, printing machines, editing reproducing machines, synchronizers and studio lights except bulbs	13	101.52	20.00 *(NESD)*	81.52
2. Projecting equipment for exhibition of films	13	101.52	20.00 *(NESD)*	81.52
(b) Plant and Machinery used in glass manufacturing				
1. Plant and Machinery except direct fire glass melting furnaces Recuperative and regenerative glass melting furnaces	13	101.52	40	61.52
(c) Plant and Machinery used in manufacture of steel				
1. Sinter Plant	20	73.81	27.82	45.99
2. Blast Furnace	20	73.81	27.82	45.99
3. Coke ovens	20	73.81	27.82	45.99
4. Rolling mill in steel plant	20	73.81	27.82	45.99
5. Basic oxygen Furnace Converter	25	61.63	27.82	33.81
(d) Plant and Machinery used in civil construction				
1. Concreting, Crushing, Piling Equipments and Road Making Equipments	12	107.17	27.82	79.35

Nature of Assets	Useful Life for Single shift (Co. Act, 2013)	WDV BASIS		Impact Increase/ (decrease) (1)-(2)
		Triple Shift rate (Co. Act, 2013) (1)	Triple Shift rate (Co. Act, 1956) (2)	
	(Years)	(%)	(%)	(%)
2. Heavy Lift Equipments				
Cranes with capacity of more than 100 tons	20	73.81	27.82	45.99
Cranes with capacity of less than 100 tons	15	91.77	27.82	63.95
3. Transmission line, Tunneling Equipments [NESD]	10	60.19 *(NESD)*	27.82	32.37
4. Earth-moving equipments	9	128.12	30.00 *(NESD)*	98.12
5. Others including Material Handling /Pipeline/Welding Equipments [NESD]	12	53.58 *(NESD)*	27.82	25.76
(e) Plant and Machinery used in Telecommunications [NESD]				
1. Towers	18	40.05 *(NESD)*	27.82	12.23
2. Telecom transceivers, switching centres, transmission and other network equipment	13	50.76 *(NESD)*	27.82	22.94
3. Telecom—Ducts, Cables and optical fibre	18	40.05 *(NESD)*	27.82	12.23
4. Satellites	18	40.05 *(NESD)*	27.82	12.23
(f) Plant and Machinery used in exploration, production and refining oil and gas [NESD]				
1. Refineries	25	30.82 *(NESD)*	27.82	3.00
2. Oil and gas assets (including wells), processing plant and	25	30.82 *(NESD)*	27.82	3.00

Nature of Assets	Useful Life for Single shift (Co. Act, 2013)	WDV BASIS Triple Shift rate (Co. Act, 2013) (1)	Triple Shift rate (Co. Act, 1956) (2)	Impact Increase/ (decrease) (1)-(2)
	(Years)	(%)	(%)	(%)
facilities				
3. Petrochemical Plant	25	30.82 *(NESD)*	27.82	3.00
4. Storage tanks and related equipment	25	30.82 *(NESD)*	27.82	3.00
5. Pipelines	30	26.44 *(NESD)*	27.82	(1.38)
6. Loggers	8	68.38 *(NESD)*	27.82	40.56
(g) Plant and Machinery used in generation, transmission and distribution of power [NESD]				
1. Thermal/ Gas/ Combined Cycle Power Generation Plant	40	20.57 *(NESD)*	27.82	(7.25)
2. Hydro Power Generation Plant	40	20.57 *(NESD)*	27.82	(7.25)
3. Nuclear Power Generation Plant	40	20.57 *(NESD)*	27.82	(7.25)
4. Transmission lines, cables and other network assets	40	20.57 *(NESD)*	27.82	(7.25)
5. Wind Power Generation Plant	22	34.21 *(NESD)*	27.82	6.39
6. Electric Distribution Plant	35	23.14 *(NESD)*	27.82	(4.68)
7. Gas Storage and Distribution Plant	30	26.44 *(NESD)*	27.82	(1.38)
8. Water Distribution Plant including pipelines	30	26.44 *(NESD)*	27.82	(1.38)
(h) Plant and Machinery used in manufacture of non-ferrous metals				
1. Metal pot line [NESD]	40	20.57	27.82	(7.25)

Nature of Assets	Useful Life for Single shift (Co. Act, 2013)	WDV BASIS Triple Shift rate (Co. Act, 2013) (1)	Triple Shift rate (Co. Act, 1956) (2)	Impact Increase/ (decrease) (1)-(2)
	(Years)	(%)	(%)	(%)
		(NESD)		
2. Bauxite crushing and grinding section [NESD]	40	20.57 *(NESD)*	27.82	(7.25)
3. Digester Section [NESD]	40	20.57 *(NESD)*	27.82	(7.25)
4. Turbine [NESD]	40	20.57 *(NESD)*	27.82	(7.25)
5. Equipments for Calcination [NESD]	40	20.57 *(NESD)*	27.82	(7.25)
6. Copper Smelter [NESD]	40	20.57 *(NESD)*	27.82	(7.25)
7. Roll Grinder	40	41.13	27.82	13.31
8. Soaking Pit	30	52.87	27.82	25.05
9. Annealing Furnace	30	52.87	27.82	25.05
10. Rolling Mills	30	52.87	27.82	25.05
11. Equipments for Scalping, Slitting , etc. [NESD]	30	26.44 *(NESD)*	27.82	(1.38)
12. Surface Miner, Ripper Dozer, etc., used in mines	25	61.63	27.82	33.81
13. Copper refining plant [NESD]	25	30.82 *(NESD)*	27.82	3.00
(i) Plant and Machinery used in medical and surgical operations [NESD]				
1. Other Equipments.	15	45.88 *(NESD)*	27.82	18.06
(j) Plant and Machinery used in manufacture of pharmaceuticals and chemicals [NESD]				
1. Reactors	20	36.90 *(NESD)*	27.82	9.08

Nature of Assets	Useful Life for Single shift (Co. Act, 2013)	WDV BASIS Triple Shift rate (Co. Act, 2013) (1)	Triple Shift rate (Co. Act, 1956) (2)	Impact Increase/ (decrease) (1)-(2)
	(Years)	(%)	(%)	(%)
2. Distillation Columns	20	36.90 (NESD)	27.82	9.08
3. Drying equipments/Centrifuges and Decanters	20	36.90 (NESD)	27.82	9.08
4. Vessel/storage tanks	20	36.90 (NESD)	27.82	9.08
(k) Plant and Machinery used in salt works [NESD]	15	45.88 (NESD)	27.82	(18.06)
Laboratory equipment [NESD]				
(i) General laboratory equipment	10	60.19 (NESD)	27.82	32.37
(ii) Laboratory equipments used in educational institutions	5	84.15 (NESD)	27.82	56.33

4.10 ITEMS AGAINST WHICH NESD IS PRESCRIBED IN BOTH THE COMPANIES ACT, 2013 AS WELL AS COMPANIES ACT, 1956

It may be noted that the following categories of assets prescribed under Schedule II of the Companies Act, 2013 against which NESD is mentioned in the Schedule are also the items to which no extra shift depreciation is applicable under Schedule XIV to the Companies Act, 1956.

I. Buildings

II. Bridges, culverts, bunders, etc

III. Roads

Note: Bridges, culverts, bunders, fences, wells, tubewells etc, and roads are covered in 'Buildings' as per the Note 1 to the Schedule XIV of the Companies Act, 1956; ie 'Buildings' include roads, bridges, culverts, wells and tubewells.

IV. General rate applicable to plant and machinery not covered under special plant and machinery

(a) Continuous process plant for which no special rate has been prescribed under special plant and machinery category

V. Following categories of special plant and machinery

(a) Plant and Machinery used in glass manufacturing

(i) Plant and Machinery except direct fire glass melting furnaces-Moulds

(ii) Float Glass Melting Furnaces

(b) Plant and Machinery used in exploration, production and refining oil and gas:

(i) Drilling Rig

(ii) Field operations (above ground) Portable boilers, drilling tools, well-head tanks, etc.

(c) Plant and Machinery used in mines and quarries-

Portable underground machinery and earth moving machinery used in open cast mining

(d) Plant and Machinery used in medical and surgical operations:

Electrical Machinery, X-ray and electrotherapeutic apparatus and accessories thereto, medical, diagnostic equipments, namely, Cat-scan, Ultrasound Machines, ECG Monitors, etc.

VI. Furniture and fittings

VII. Motor Vehicles

VIII. Ships

IX. Aircrafts or Helicopters

X. Railways sidings, locomotives, rolling stocks, tramways and railways used by concerns, excluding railway concerns

XI. Ropeway structures

XII. Office equipment

XIII. Computers and data processing units

XIV. Electrical Installations and Equipment

XV. Hydraulic works, pipelines and sluices

Chapter 5

Industry Specific Examples on Depreciation Computation

In this chapter, a complete table showing the rates of depreciation as per SLM and WDV for single shift, double shift and triple shift are given for the Companies Act, 2013. This table is based on the same assumptions and computations as discussed in Chapters 3 and 4 of this book.

Further, examples from various industries have been given showing the computation of depreciation under the Schedule II to the Companies Act, 2013 and Schedule XIV to the Companies Act, 1956 as well as the difference in the depreciation amount arising on Schedule II to the Companies Act, 2013 becoming effective.

5.1 TABLE SHOWING SLM AND WDV RATES UNDER THE COMPANIES ACT, 2013 FOR ALL SHIFTS (ASSUMING 5% RESIDUAL VALUE)

Nature of Assets	SINGLE SHIFT		DOUBLE SHIFT		TRIPLE SHIFT	
	SLM (%)	WDV (%)	SLM (%)	WDV (%)	SLM (%)	WDV (%)
I. Buildings [NESD]						
(a) Buildings (other than factory buildings) RCC Frame Structure	1.58	4.87	1.58	4.87	1.58	4.87
(b) Buildings (other than factory buildings) other than RCC Frame Structure	3.17	9.50	3.17	9.50	3.17	9.50
(c) Factory buildings	3.17	9.50	3.17	9.50	3.17	9.50
(d) Fences, wells, tube wells	19.00	45.07	19.00	45.07	19.00	45.07
(e) Others (including temporary structure, etc.)	31.67	63.16	31.67	63.16	31.67	63.16
II. Bridges, culverts, bunders, etc. [NESD]	3.17	9.50	3.17	9.50	3.17	9.50
III. Roads [NESD]						
(a) Carpeted roads						
(i) Carpeted Roads-RCC	9.50	25.89	9.50	25.89	9.50	25.89

Nature of Assets	SINGLE SHIFT		DOUBLE SHIFT		TRIPLE SHIFT	
	SLM (%)	WDV (%)	SLM (%)	WDV (%)	SLM (%)	WDV (%)
(ii) Carpeted Roads-other than RCC	19.00	45.07	19.00	45.07	19.00	45.07
(b) Non-carpeted roads	31.67	63.16	31.67	63.16	31.67	63.16
IV. Plant and Machinery						
(i) General rate applicable to plant and machinery not covered under special plant and machinery						
(a) Plant and Machinery other than continuous process plant not covered under specific industries	6.33	18.10	9.50	27.16	12.67	36.21
(b) continuous process plant for which no special rate has been prescribed under (ii) below [NESD]	3.80	11.29	3.80	11.29	3.80	11.29
(ii) Special Plant and Machinery						
(a) Plant and Machinery related to production and exhibition of Motion Picture Films						
Cinematograph films—Machinery used in the production and exhibition of cinematograph films, recording and equipments, developing machines, printing machines, editing reproducing machines, synchronizers and studio lights except bulbs	7.31	20.58	10.96	30.87	14.62	41.16
Projecting equipment for exhibition of films	7.31	20.58	10.96	30.87	14.62	41.16
(b) Plant and Machinery used in glass manufacturing						
1. Plant and Machinery except direct fire glass melting furnaces Recuperative and regenerative glass melting furnaces	7.31	20.58	10.96	30.87	14.62	41.16
2. Plant and Machinery except direct fire glass melting furnaces Moulds [NESD]	11.88	31.23	11.88	31.23	11.88	31.23
3. Float Glass Melting Furnaces [NESD]	9.50	25.89	9.50	25.89	9.50	25.89
(c) Plant and Machinery used in mines and quarries—Portable underground machinery and earth moving machinery used in open cast mining [NESD]	11.88	31.23	11.88	31.23	11.88	31.23

Nature of Assets	SINGLE SHIFT		DOUBLE SHIFT		TRIPLE SHIFT	
	SLM (%)	WDV (%)	SLM (%)	WDV (%)	SLM (%)	WDV (%)
(d) Plant and Machinery used in Telecommunications [NESD]						
1. Towers	5.28	15.33	5.28	15.33	5.28	15.33
2. Telecom transceivers, switching centres, transmission and other network equipment	7.31	20.58	7.31	20.58	7.31	20.58
3. Telecom—Ducts, Cables and optical fibre	5.28	15.33	5.28	15.33	5.28	15.33
4. Satellites	5.28	15.33	5.28	15.33	5.28	15.33
(e) Plant and Machinery used in exploration, production and refining oil and gas [NESD]						
1. Refineries	3.80	11.29	3.80	11.29	3.80	11.29
2. Oil and gas assets (including wells), processing plant and facilities	3.80	11.29	3.80	11.29	3.80	11.29
3. Petrochemical Plant	3.80	11.29	3.80	11.29	3.80	11.29
4. Storage tanks and related equipment	3.80	11.29	3.80	11.29	3.80	11.29
5. Pipelines	3.17	9.50	3.17	9.50	3.17	9.50
6. Drilling Rig	3.17	9.50	3.17	9.50	3.17	9.50
7. Field operations (above ground) Portable boilers, drilling tools, well-head tanks, etc.	11.88	31.23	11.88	31.23	11.88	31.23
8. Loggers	11.88	31.23		31.23	11.88	31.23
(f) Plant and Machinery used in generation, transmission and distribution of power [NESD]						
1. Thermal/ Gas/ Combined Cycle Power Generation Plant	2.38	7.22	2.38	7.22	2.38	7.22
2. Hydro Power Generation Plant	2.38	7.22	2.38	7.22	2.38	7.22
3. Nuclear Power Generation Plant	2.38	7.22	2.38	7.22	2.38	7.22
4. Transmission lines, cables and other network assets	2.38	7.22	2.38	7.22	2.38	7.22
5. Wind Power Generation Plant	4.32	12.73	4.32	12.73	4.32	12.73
6. Electric Distribution Plant	2.71	8.20	2.71	8.20	2.71	8.20
7. Gas Storage and Distribution Plant	3.17	9.50	3.17	9.50	3.17	9.50
8. Water Distribution Plant including pipelines	3.17	9.50	3.17	9.50	3.17	9.50

Nature of Assets	SINGLE SHIFT		DOUBLE SHIFT		TRIPLE SHIFT	
	SLM (%)	WDV (%)	SLM (%)	WDV (%)	SLM (%)	WDV (%)
(g) Plant and Machinery used in manufacture of steel						
1. Sinter Plant	4.75	13.91	7.13	20.87	9.50	27.82
2. Blast Furnace	4.75	13.91	7.13	20.87	9.50	27.82
3. Coke ovens	4.75	13.91	7.13	20.87	9.50	27.82
4. Rolling mill in steel plant	4.75	13.91	7.13	20.87	9.50	27.82
5. Basic oxygen Furnace Converter	3.8	11.29	5.70	16.94	7.60	22.59
(h) Plant and Machinery used in manufacture of non-ferrous metals						
1. Metal pot line [NESD]	2.38	7.22	2.38	7.22	2.38	7.22
2. Bauxite crushing and grinding section [NESD]	2.38	7.22	2.38	7.22	2.38	7.22
3. Digester Section [NESD]	2.38	7.22	2.38	7.22	2.38	7.22
4. Turbine [NESD]	2.38	7.22	2.38	7.22	2.38	7.22
5. Equipments for Calcination [NESD]	2.38	7.22	2.38	7.22	2.38	7.22
6. Copper Smelter [NESD]	2.38	7.22	2.38	7.22	2.38	7.22
7. Roll Grinder	2.38	7.22	3.56	10.82	4.75	14.43
8. Soaking Pit	3.17	9.50	4.75	14.26	6.33	19.01
9. Annealing Furnace	3.17	9.50	4.75	14.26	6.33	19.01
10. Rolling Mills	3.17	9.50	4.75	14.26	6.33	19.01
11. Equipments for Scalping, Slitting, etc. [NESD]	3.17	9.50	3.17	9.50	3.17	9.50
12. Surface Miner, Ripper Dozer, etc., used in mines	3.80	11.29	5.70	16.94	7.60	22.59
13. Copper refining plant [NESD]	3.80	11.29	3.80	11.29	3.80	11.29
(i) Plant and Machinery used in medical and surgical operations [NESD]						
1. Electrical Machinery, X-ray and electrotherapeutic apparatus and accessories thereto, medical, diagnostic equipments, namely, Cat-scan, Ultrasound Machines, ECG Monitors, etc.	7.31	20.58	7.31	20.58	7.31	20.58
2. Other Equipments.	6.33	18.10	6.33	18.10	6.33	18.10
(j) Plant and Machinery used in manufacture of pharmaceuticals and chemicals [NESD]						
1. Reactors	4.75	13.91	4.75	13.91	4.75	13.91
2. Distillation Columns	4.75	13.91	4.75	13.91	4.75	13.91

Nature of Assets	SINGLE SHIFT		DOUBLE SHIFT		TRIPLE SHIFT	
	SLM (%)	WDV (%)	SLM (%)	WDV (%)	SLM (%)	WDV (%)
3. Drying equipments/Centrifuges and Decanters	4.75	13.91	4.75	13.91	4.75	13.91
4. Vessel/storage tanks	4.75	13.91	4.75	13.91	4.75	13.91
(k) Plant and Machinery used in civil construction						
1. Concreting, Crushing, Piling Equipments and Road Making Equipments	7.92	22.09	11.88	33.14	15.83	44.18
2. Heavy Lift Equipments						
Cranes with capacity of more than 100 tons	4.75	13.91	7.13	20.87	9.50	27.82
Cranes with capacity of less than 100 tons	6.33	18.10	9.50	27.16	12.67	36.21
3. Transmission line, Tunneling Equipments [NESD]	9.50	25.89	9.50	25.89	9.50	25.89
4. Earth-moving equipments	10.56	28.31	15.83	42.47	21.11	56.63
5. Others including Material Handling/Pipeline/Welding Equipments [NESD]	7.92	22.09	7.92	22.09	7.92	22.09
(l) Plant and Machinery used in salt works [NESD]	6.33	18.10	6.33	18.10	6.33	18.10
V. Furniture and fittings [NESD]						
(i) General furniture and fittings	9.50	25.89	9.50	25.89	9.50	25.89
(ii) Furniture and fittings used in hotels, restaurants and boarding houses, schools, colleges and other educational institutions, libraries; welfare centres; meeting halls, cinema houses; theatres and circuses; and furniture and fittings let out on hire for use on the occasion of marriages and similar functions.	11.88	31.23	11.88	31.23	11.88	31.23
VI. Motor Vehicles [NESD]						
1. Motor cycles, scooters and other mopeds	9.50	25.89	9.50	25.89	9.50	25.89
2. Motor buses, motor lorries, motor cars and motor taxies used in a business of running them on hire	15.83	39.30	15.83	39.30	15.83	39.30
3. Motor buses, motor lorries and motor cars other than those used in a business of running them on hire	11.88	31.23	11.88	31.23	11.88	31.23

Nature of Assets	SINGLE SHIFT		DOUBLE SHIFT		TRIPLE SHIFT	
	SLM (%)	WDV (%)	SLM (%)	WDV (%)	SLM (%)	WDV (%)
4. Motor tractors, harvesting combines and heavy vehicles	11.88	31.23	11.88	31.23	11.88	31.23
5. Electrically operated vehicles including battery powered or fuel cell powered vehicles	11.88	31.23	11.88	31.23	11.88	31.23
VII. Ships [NESD]						
1. Ocean-going ships						
(i) Bulk Carriers and liner vessels	3.80	11.29	3.80	11.29	3.80	11.29
(ii) Crude tankers, product carriers and easy chemical carriers with or without conventional tank coatings	4.75	13.91	4.75	13.91	4.75	13.91
(iii) Chemicals and Acid Carriers:						
(a) With Stainless steel tanks	3.80	11.29	3.80	11.29	3.80	11.29
(b) With other tanks	4.75	13.91	4.75	13.91	4.75	13.91
(iv) Liquified gas carriers	3.17	9.50	3.17	9.50	3.17	9.50
(v) Conventional large passenger vessels which are used for cruise purpose also	3.17	9.50	3.17	9.50	3.17	9.50
(vi) Coastal service ships of all categories	3.17	9.50	3.17	9.50	3.17	9.50
(vii) Offshore supply and support vessels	4.75	13.91	4.75	13.91	4.75	13.91
(viii) Catamarans and other high speed passenger for ships or boats	4.75	13.91	4.75	13.91	4.75	13.91
(ix) Drill ships	3.80	11.29	3.80	11.29	3.80	11.29
(x) Hovercrafts	6.33	18.10	6.33	18.10	6.33	18.10
(xi) Fishing vessels with wooden hull	9.50	25.89	9.50	25.89	9.50	25.89
(xii) Dredgers, tugs, barges, survey launches and other similar ships used mainly for dredging purposes	6.79	19.26	6.79	19.26	6.79	19.26
2. Vessels ordinarily operating on inland waters						
(i) Speed boats	7.31	20.58	7.31	20.58	7.31	20.58
(ii) Other vessels	3.39	10.15	3.39	10.15	3.39	10.15
VIII. Aircrafts or Helicopters [NESD]	4.75	13.91	4.75	13.91	4.75	13.91
IX. Railways sidings, locomotives, rolling stocks, tramways and railways used by concerns, excluding railway concerns [NESD]	6.33	18.10	6.33	18.10	6.33	18.10
X. Ropeway structures [NESD]	6.33	18.10	6.33	18.10	6.33	18.10
XI. Office equipment [NESD]	19.00	45.07	19.00	45.07	19.00	45.07

Nature of Assets	SINGLE SHIFT		DOUBLE SHIFT		TRIPLE SHIFT	
	SLM (%)	WDV (%)	SLM (%)	WDV (%)	SLM (%)	WDV (%)
XII. Computers and data processing units [NESD]						
(i) Servers and networks	15.83	39.30	15.83	39.30	15.83	39.30
(ii) End user devices, such as, desktops, laptops, etc.	31.67	63.16	31.67	63.16	31.67	63.16
XIII. Laboratory equipment [NESD]						
(i) General laboratory equipment	9.50	25.89	9.50	25.89	9.50	25.89
(ii) Laboratory equipments used in educational institutions	19.00	45.07	19.00	45.07	19.00	45.07
XIV. Electrical Installations and Equipment [NESD]	9.50	25.89	9.50	25.89	9.50	25.89
XV. Hydraulic works, pipelines and sluices [NESD]	6.33	18.10	6.33	18.10	6.33	18.10

5.2 INDUSTRY SPECIFIC EXAMPLES

A. Cinema Industry (Motion Pictures)

EXAMPLE 1

From the following information, compute the depreciation as per the provisions of Schedule XIV of the Companies Act, 1956 and Schedule II of the Companies Act, 2013 and show the difference in both.

Cost of the Machinery used in the production of cinematograph films	***INR 1,00,000***
Erection charges	***INR 10,000***
Residual Value of the Machine	***INR 5000***
Estimated Useful Life	***20 Years***
Useful Life prescribed in Schedule II	***13 years***

SOLUTION

COMPARISON BASED ON SLM RATES

Statement showing computation of depreciation

Particulars	Single shift Depreciation	Double Shift Depreciation	Triple Shift Depreciation
Under Schedule XIV (1956)			
(INR 100,000+INR 10,000) × 7.07% As per the minimum rate	INR 7,777	INR 7,777 *(NESD)*	INR 7,777 *(NESD)*

Particulars	Single shift Depreciation	Double Shift Depreciation	Triple Shift Depreciation
Under Schedule II (2013)			
(INR 100,000 + INR 10,000 – INR 5,000) × 7.69%	INR 8,075		
(INR 100,000 + INR 10,000 – INR 5,000) × 11.54%		INR 12,117	
(INR100,000 + INR 10,000 – INR 5,000) × 15.38%			INR 16,149
Difference (Extra Depreciation under Schedule II)	INR 298	INR 4,340	INR 8,372

Notes:

(a) Prescribed rates have been used for computation of depreciation under Schedule XIV of the Companies Act, 1956.

(b) The rates prescribed in the Schedule XIV of the Companies Act, 1956 have the inbuilt effect of residual value, ie, the rates are prescribed such that 5% of residual value remains after depreciating 95% of the cost over the specified period. Accordingly, the residual value is not deducted in the example in computing the depreciation under Schedule XIV.

(c) Useful life considered for computation of depreciation under Schedule II of the Companies Act, 2013 is the one prescribed in Part C of the schedule.

(d) According to the Schedule XIV of the Companies Act, 1956, lower rate of depreciation than prescribed cannot be used.

(e) According to the Schedule II of the Companies Act, 2013, entities may charge a lower depreciation than the rate envisaged in Schedule II on disclosing justification for the difference. In case the entity goes with the option of charging depreciation at the rates lower than the prescribed rates, the rates will be as follows:

Single shift: (1 × 100/20 = 5%)

Double Shift: (5% × 1.5 = 7.5%)

Triple Shift: (5% × 2 = 10%)

In this case, the difference would be as follows:

Particulars	Single shift Depreciation	Double Shift Depreciation	Triple Shift Depreciation
Under Schedule XIV (1956)			
(INR 100,000 + INR 10,000) × 7.07% As per the minimum rate	INR 7,777	INR 7,777 (*NESD*)	INR 7,777 (*NESD*)
Under Schedule II (2013)			
(INR 100,000 + INR 10,000 – INR 5,000) × 5%	INR 5,250		

Particulars	Single shift Depreciation	Double Shift Depreciation	Triple Shift Depreciation
(INR 100,000 + INR 10,000 – INR 5,000) × 7.5%		INR 7,875	
(INR 100,000 + INR 10,000 – INR 5,000) × 10%			INR 10,500
Difference (Extra Depreciation under Schedule II)	(INR 2,527)	INR 98	INR 2,723

COMPARISON BASED ON WDV RATES

Statement showing computation of depreciation

Particulars	Single shift Depreciation	Double Shift Depreciation	Triple Shift Depreciation
Under Schedule XIV (1956)			
(INR 100,000+INR 10,000) × 20% As per the minimum rate	INR 22,000	INR 22,000 (*NESD*)	INR 22,000 (*NESD*)
Under Schedule II (2013)			
(INR 100,000 + INR 10,000) × 20.58%	INR 22,638		
(INR100,000 + INR 10,000) × 30.87%		INR 33,957	
(INR 100,000 + INR 10,000) × 41.16%			INR 45,276
Difference (Extra Depreciation under Schedule II)	INR 638	INR 11,957	INR 23,276

Notes:

(a) Prescribed rates have been used for computation of depreciation under Schedule XIV of the Companies Act, 1956.

(b) The rates prescribed in the Schedule XIV of the Companies Act, 1956 have the inbuilt effect of residual value, ie, the rates are prescribed such that 5% of residual value remains after depreciating 95% of the cost over the specified period. Accordingly, the residual value is not deducted in the example in computing the depreciation under Schedule XIV.

(c) Under Schedule II, WDV rate of depreciation is computed after considering 5% residual value, hence, the residual value is not deducted separately.

(d) Useful life considered for computation of depreciation under Schedule II of the Companies Act, 2013 is the one prescribed in Part C of the schedule.

(e) According to the Schedule XIV of the Companies Act, 1956, lower rate of depreciation than prescribed cannot be used.

(f) According to the Schedule II of the Companies Act, 2013, entities may charge a lower depreciation than the rate envisaged in Schedule II on disclosing justification for the difference. In case the entity goes with the option of charging depreciation at the rates lower than the prescribed rates, the rates will be as follows:

Single shift: 13.91%

Double Shift: (13.91% × 1.5) = 20.87%

Triple Shift: (13.91% × 2) = 27.82%

In this case, the difference would be as follows:

Particulars	Single shift Depreciation	Double Shift Depreciation	Triple Shift Depreciation
Under Schedule XIV (1956)			
(INR 100,000 + INR 10,000) × 20% As per the minimum rate	INR 22,000	INR 22,000 *(NESD)*	INR 22,000 *(NESD)*
Under Schedule II (2013)			
(INR 100,000 + INR 10,000) × 13.91% (INR 100,000 + INR 10,000) × 20.87% (INR 100,000 + INR 10,000) × 27.82%	INR 15,301	INR 22,957	INR 30,602
Difference (Extra Depreciation under Schedule II)	(INR 6,699)	INR 957	INR 8,602

B. Telecommunication Industry

EXAMPLE 2

From the following information, compute the depreciation as per the provisions of Schedule XIV of the Companies Act, 1956 and Schedule II of the Companies Act, 2013 and show the difference in both.

Cost of the Telecom transceivers	***INR 3,00,000***
Installation charges	***INR 10,000***
Residual Value	***INR 5000***
Estimated Useful Life	***23 Years***
Useful Life prescribed in Schedule II	***13 years***

SOLUTION

COMPARISON BASED ON SLM RATES

Statement showing computation of depreciation

Particulars	Single shift Depreciation	Double shift Depreciation	Triple shift Depreciation
Under Schedule XIV (1956)			
(INR 300,000 + INR 10,000) × 4.75% (INR 300,000 + INR 10,000) × 7.42% (INR 300,000 + INR 10,000) × 10.34% As per the minimum rate	INR 14,725	INR 23,002	INR 32,054

Particulars	Single shift Depreciation	Double shift Depreciation	Triple shift Depreciation
Under Schedule II (2013)			
(INR 300,000 + INR 10,000 – INR 5,000) × 7.69%	INR 23,455	INR 23,455 (*NESD*)	INR 23,455 (*NESD*)
Difference (Extra Depreciation under Schedule II)	INR 8,730	INR 453	(INR 8,599)

Notes:

(a) Prescribed rates have been used for computation of depreciation under Schedule XIV of the Companies Act, 1956.

(b) The rates prescribed in the Schedule XIV of the Companies Act, 1956 have the inbuilt effect of residual value, ie, the rates are prescribed such that 5% of residual value remains after depreciating 95% of the cost. Accordingly, the residual value is not deducted in the example in computing the depreciation under Schedule XIV. But it is deducted for depreciation computed under the Schedule II of the Companies Act, 2013.

(c) Useful life considered for computation of depreciation under Schedule II of the Companies Act, 2013 is the one prescribed in Part C of the schedule.

(d) According to the Schedule XIV of the Companies Act, 1956, lower rate of depreciation than prescribed cannot be used.

(e) According to the Schedule II of the Companies Act, 2013, entities may charge a lower depreciation than the rate envisaged in Schedule II on disclosing justification for the difference in the financial statements. In case the entity goes with the option of charging depreciation at the rates lower than the prescribed rates, the rates will be as follows:
Single shift: (1*100/23= 4.35%)

In this case, the difference would be as follows:

Particulars	Single shift Depreciation	Double shift Depreciation	Triple shift Depreciation
Under Schedule XIV (1956)			
(INR 300,000 + INR 10,000) × 4.75%	INR 14,725		
(INR 300,000 + INR 10,000) × 7.42%		INR 23,002	
(INR 300,000 + INR 10,000) × 10.34% As per the minimum rate			INR 32,054
Under Schedule II (2013)			
(INR300,000 + INR 10,000 – INR 5,000) × 4.35%	INR 13,268	INR 13,268 (*NESD*)	INR 13,268 (*NESD*)
Difference (Extra Depreciation under Schedule II) (New-Old)	(INR 1,457)	(INR 9,734)	(INR 18,786)

COMPARISON BASED ON WDV RATES

Statement showing computation of depreciation

Particulars	Single shift Depreciation	Double shift Depreciation	Triple shift Depreciation
Under Schedule XIV (1956)			
(INR 300,000 + INR 10,000) × 13.91%	INR 43,121		
(INR 300,000 + INR 10,000) × 20.87%		INR 64,697	
(INR 300,000 + INR 10,000) × 27.82%			INR 86,242
As per the minimum rate			
Under Schedule II (2013)			
(INR 300,000 + INR 10,000) × 27.02%	INR 83,762	INR 83,762 (*NESD*)	INR 83,762 (*NESD*)
Difference (Extra Depreciation under Schedule II)	INR 40,641	INR 19,065	(INR 2,480)

Notes:

(a) Prescribed rates have been used for computation of depreciation under Schedule XIV of the Companies Act, 1956.

(b) The rates prescribed in the Schedule XIV of the Companies Act, 1956 have the inbuilt effect of residual value, ie, the rates are prescribed such that 5% of residual value remains after depreciating 95% of the cost. Accordingly, the residual value is not deducted in the example in computing the depreciation under Schedule XIV. But it is deducted for depreciation computed under the Schedule II of the Companies Act, 2013.

(c) Under Schedule II, WDV rate of depreciation is computed after considering 1.667% residual value, hence, the residual value is not deducted separately.

(d) Useful life considered for computation of depreciation under Schedule II of the Companies Act, 2013 is the one prescribed in Part C of the schedule.

(e) According to the Schedule XIV of the Companies Act, 1956, lower rate of depreciation than prescribed cannot be used.

(f) According to the Schedule II of the Companies Act, 2013, entities may charge a lower depreciation than the rate envisaged in Schedule II on disclosing justification for the difference in the financial statements. In case the entity goes with the option of charging depreciation at the rates lower than the prescribed rates, the rates will be as follows:

Single shift: 16.31%

In this case, the difference would be as follows:

Particulars	Single shift Depreciation	Double shift Depreciation	Triple shift Depreciation
Under Schedule XIV (1956)			
(INR 300,000 + INR 10,000) × 13.91%	INR 43,121		
(INR 300,000 + INR 10,000) × 20.87%		INR 64,697	
(INR 300,000 + INR 10,000) × 27.82% As per the minimum rate			INR 86,242
Under Schedule II (2013)			
(INR 300,000 + INR 10,000) × 16.31%	INR 50,561	INR 50,561 *(NESD)*	INR 50,561 *(NESD)*
Difference (Extra Depreciation under Schedule II) (New-Old)	INR 7,440	(INR 14,136)	(INR 35,681)

C. Oil and Gas Industry

EXAMPLE 3

From the following information, compute the depreciation as per the provisions of Schedule XIV of the Companies Act, 1956 and Schedule II of the Companies Act, 2013 and show the difference in both.

Cost of the Oil Storage tank	***INR 50,00,000***
Erection charges	***INR 5,00,000***
Residual Value	***INR 1,00,000***
Estimated Useful Life	***25Years***
Useful Life prescribed in Schedule II	***25 years***

SOLUTION

COMPARISON BASED ON SLM RATES

Statement showing computation of depreciation

Particulars	Single shift Depreciation (NESD)
Under Schedule XIV (1956)	
(INR 50,00,000 + INR 500,000) × 4.75% As per the minimum rate	INR 2,61,250
Under Schedule II (2013)	
(INR 50,00,000 + INR 500,000 – INR 1,00,000) × 4.00%	INR 2,16,000
Difference (Extra Depreciation under Schedule II) (New-Old)	(INR 45,250)

Notes:

(a) Prescribed rates have been used for computation of depreciation under Schedule XIV of the Companies Act, 1956.

(b) The rates prescribed in the Schedule XIV of the Companies Act, 1956 have the inbuilt effect of residual value, ie, the rates are prescribed such that 5% of residual value remains after depreciating 95% of the cost. Accordingly, the residual value is not deducted in the example in computing the depreciation under Schedule XIV. But it is deducted for depreciation computed under the Schedule II of the Companies Act, 2013.

(c) According to the Schedule XIV of the Companies Act, 1956, lower rate of depreciation (based on higher estimated useful life of 25 years) than prescribed cannot be used.

(d) Above asset is a NESD item in both Companies Act, 2013 as well as Companies Act, 1956, hence, double shift and triple shift depreciation calculations has not been carried out.

COMPARISON BASED ON WDV RATES

Statement showing computation of depreciation

Particulars	Single shift Depreciation (NESD)
Under Schedule XIV (1956)	
(INR 50,00,000 + INR 5,00,000) × 13.91% As per the minimum rate	INR 7,65,050
Under Schedule II (2013)	
(INR 50,00,000 + INR 500,000) × 14.49%	INR 7,96,950
Extra Depreciation under Schedule II (New-Old)	INR 31,900

It may be noted that under Schedule II, WDV rate of depreciation is computed after considering 2% residual value, hence, the residual value is not deducted separately.

D. Power Industry

EXAMPLE 4

From the following information, compute the depreciation as per the provisions of Schedule XIV of the Companies Act, 1956 and Schedule II of the Companies Act, 2013 and show the difference in both.

Capitalised value of Hydro Power Generation Plant	*INR 80,00,000*
Residual Value	*INR 3,00,000*
Estimated Useful Life	*40 Years*
Useful Life prescribed in Schedule II	*40 years*

SOLUTION

COMPARISON BASED ON SLM RATES

Statement showing computation of depreciation

Particulars	Single shift Depreciation	Double shift Depreciation	Triple shift Depreciation
Under Schedule XIV (1956)			
(INR 80,00,000) × 4.75% (INR 80,00,000) × 7.42% (INR 80,00,000) × 10.34% As per the minimum rate	INR 3,80,000	INR 5,93,600	INR 8,27,200
Under Schedule II (2013)			
(INR 80,00,000 – INR 3,00,000) × 2.50%	INR 1,92,500	INR 1,92,500 (*NESD*)	INR 1,92,500 (*NESD*)
Difference (Extra Depreciation under Schedule II) (New-Old)	(INR 1,87,500)	(INR 4,01,100)	(INR 6,34,700)

Notes:

(a) Prescribed rates have been used for computation of depreciation under Schedule XIV of the Companies Act, 1956.

(b) The rates prescribed in the Schedule XIV of the Companies Act, 1956 have the inbuilt effect of residual value, ie, the rates are prescribed such that 5% of residual value remains after depreciating 95% of the cost. Accordingly, the residual value is not deducted in the example in computing the depreciation under Schedule XIV. But it is deducted for depreciation computed under the Schedule II of the Companies Act, 2013.

(c) According to the Schedule XIV of the Companies Act, 1956, lower rate (based on higher estimated useful life of 40 years) of depreciation than prescribed cannot be used.

COMPARISON BASED ON WDV RATES

Statement showing computation of depreciation

Particulars	Single shift Depreciation	Double shift Depreciation	Triple shift Depreciation
Under Schedule XIV (1956)			
(INR 80,00,000) × 13.91% (INR 80,00,000) × 20.87% (INR 80,00,000) × 27.82% As per the minimum rate	INR 11,12,800	INR 16,69,600	INR 22,25,600
Under Schedule II (2013)			
(INR 80,00,000× 7.88%	INR 6,30,400	INR 6,30,400 (*NESD*)	INR 6,30,400 (*NESD*)
Difference (Extra Depreciation under Schedule II) (New-Old)	(INR 4,82,400)	(INR 10,39,200)	(INR 15,95,200)

It may be noted that under Schedule II, WDV rate of depreciation is computed after considering 3.75% residual value, hence, the residual value is not deducted separately.

E. Steel Industry

EXAMPLE 5

From the following information, compute the depreciation as per the provisions of Schedule XIV of the Companies Act, 1956 and Schedule II of the Companies Act, 2013 and show the difference in both.

Purchase price of the Blast Furnace	***INR 10,00,000***
Cost of Erection	***INR 1,50,000***
Residual Value of the Machine	***Nil***
Estimated Useful Life	***25 Years***
Useful Life prescribed in the Schedule II	***20 Years***

SOLUTION

COMPARISON BASED ON SLM RATES

Statement showing computation of depreciation

Particulars	Single shift Depreciation	Double Shift Depreciation	Triple Shift Depreciation
1. Under Schedule XIV (1956)			
(INR 10,00,000 + INR 1,50,000) × 4.75%	INR 54,625		
(INR 10,00,000 + INR 1,50,000) × 7.42%		INR 85,330	
(INR 10,00,000 + INR 1,50,000) × 10.34%			INR 1,18,910
As per the minimum rate			
2. Under Schedule II (2013)			
(INR 10,00,000 + INR 1,50,000) × 5.00%	INR 57,500		
(INR 10,00,000 + INR 1,50,000) × 7.50%		INR 86,250	
(INR 10,00,000 + INR 1,50,000) × 10.00%			INR 1,15,000
Difference (Extra Depreciation under Schedule II)	INR 2,875	INR 920	INR (3,910)

Notes:

(a) Prescribed rates have been used for computation of depreciation under Schedule XIV of the Companies Act, 1956.

(b) The rates prescribed in the Schedule XIV of the Companies Act, 1956 have the inbuilt effect of residual value, ie, the rates are prescribed such that 5% of residual value remains after depreciating 95% of the cost. Accordingly, the residual value is not deducted in the example in computing the depreciation under Schedule XIV. But it is deducted for depreciation computed under the Schedule II of the Companies Act, 2013.

(c) Useful life considered for computation of depreciation under Schedule II of the Companies Act, 2013 is the one prescribed in Part C of the schedule.

(d) According to the Schedule XIV of the Companies Act, 1956, lower rate (based on higher estimated useful life of 25 years) of depreciation than prescribed cannot be used.

(e) According to the Schedule II of the Companies Act, 2013, entities may charge a lower depreciation than the rate envisaged in Schedule II on disclosing justification for the difference in the financial statements. In case the entity goes with the option of charging depreciation at the rates lower than the prescribed rates, the rates will be as follows:

Single shift: (1 × 100/25 = 4%)

Double Shift: (4% × 1.5 = 6%)

Triple Shift: (4% × 2 = 8%)

In this case, the difference would be as follows:

Particulars	Single shift Depreciation	Double Shift Depreciation	Triple Shift Depreciation
Under Schedule XIV (1956)			
(INR 10,00,000 + INR 1,50,000) × 4.75%	INR 54,625		
(INR 10,00,000 + INR 1,50,000) × 7.42%		INR 85,330	
(INR 10,00,000 + INR 1,50,000) × 10.34%			INR 1,18,910
As per the minimum rate			
Under Schedule II (2013)			
(INR 10,00,000 + INR 1,50,000) × 4.00%	INR 46,000		
(INR 10,00,000 + INR 1,50,000) × 6.00%		INR 69,000	
(INR 10,00,000 + INR 1,50,000) × 8.00%			INR 92,000
Difference (Extra Depreciation under Schedule II) (New-Old)	(INR 8,625)	(INR 16,330)	(INR 26,910)

F. Non-ferrous metals Industry

EXAMPLE 6

A Ltd. is using Roll Grinder (falling in category of Plant and Machinery used in manufacture of non-ferrous metals in schedule II) in its operation process. From the following information, calculate depreciation as per the provisions of schedule XIV of the Companies Act, 1956 and Schedule II of the Companies Act, 2013 and show the difference in both.

Capitalised value of the Roll Grinder	***INR 5,00,000***
Useful Life	***40 Years***

Residual Value	***INR 25,000***
Useful Life prescribed in Schedule II	***40 years***

SOLUTION

COMPARISON BASED ON SLM RATES

Statement showing computation of depreciation

Particulars	Single shift Depreciation	Double Shift Depreciation	Triple Shift Depreciation
Under Schedule XIV (1956)			
(INR 5,00,000) × 4.75% (INR 5,00,000) × 7.42% (INR 5,00,000) × 10.34% As per the minimum rate	INR 23,750	INR 37,100	INR 51,700
Under Schedule II (2013)			
(INR 5,00,000 - INR 25,000) × 2.50% (INR 5,00,000 - INR 25,000) × 3.75% (INR 5,00,000 - INR 25,000) × 5.00%	INR 11,875	INR 17,813	INR 23,750
Difference in Depreciation under Schedule II (New-Old)	(INR 11,875)	(INR 19,287)	(INR 27,950)

Notes:

(a) Prescribed rates have been used for computation of depreciation under Schedule XIV of the Companies Act, 1956.

(b) The rates prescribed in the Schedule XIV of the Companies Act, 1956 have the inbuilt effect of residual value, ie, the rates are prescribed such that 5% of residual value remains after depreciating 95% of the cost. Accordingly, the residual value is not deducted in the example in computing the depreciation under Schedule XIV. But it is deducted for depreciation computed under the Schedule II of the Companies Act, 2013.

(c) According to the Schedule XIV of the Companies Act, 1956, lower rate (based on higher estimated useful life of 40 years) of depreciation than prescribed cannot be used.

COMPARISON BASED ON WDV RATES

Statement showing computation of depreciation

Particulars	Single shift Depreciation	Double Shift Depreciation	Triple Shift Depreciation
Under Schedule XIV (1956)			
(INR 5,00,000) × 13.91% (INR 5,00,000) × 20.87% (INR 5,00,000) × 27.82% As per the minimum rate	INR 69,550	INR 1,04,350	INR 1,39,100

Particulars	Single shift Depreciation	Double Shift Depreciation	Triple Shift Depreciation
Under Schedule II (2013)			
(INR 5,00,000) × 7.22% (INR 5,00,000) × 10.83% (INR 5,00,000) × 14.44%	INR 36,100	INR 54,150	INR 72,200
Difference (Extra Depreciation under Schedule II) (New-Old)	(INR 33,450)	(INR 50,200)	(INR 66,900)

It may be noted that under Schedule II, WDV rate of depreciation is computed after considering 5% residual value, hence, the residual value is not deducted separately.

G. Pharma and Chemical industry

EXAMPLE 7

From the following information, compute the depreciation as per the provisions of Schedule XIV of the Companies Act, 1956 and Schedule II of the Companies Act, 2013 and show the difference in both.

Purchase cost of the Reactors	***INR 40,00,000***
Cost of installation	***INR 1,50,000***
Residual Value	***Nil***
Estimated Useful Life	***25 Years***
Useful Life prescribed in Schedule II	***20 years***

SOLUTION

COMPARISON BASED ON WDV RATES

Statement showing computation of depreciation

Particulars	Single shift Depreciation	Double shift Depreciation	Triple shift Depreciation
Under Schedule XIV (1956)			
(INR 40,00,000 + INR 150,000) × 4.75% (INR 40,00,000 + INR 150,000) × 7.42% (INR 40,00,000 + INR 150,000) × 10.34% As per the minimum rate	INR 1,97,125	INR 3,07,930	INR 4,29,110
Under Schedule II (2013)			
(INR 40,00,000 + INR 150,000) × 5.00%	INR 2,07,500	INR 2,07,500 (NESD)	INR 2,07,500 (NESD)
Difference (Extra Depreciation under Schedule II)	INR 10,375	(INR 1,00,430)	(INR 2,21,610)

Notes:

(a) Prescribed rates have been used for computation of depreciation under Schedule XIV of the Companies Act, 1956.

(b) The rates prescribed in the Schedule XIV of the Companies Act, 1956 have the inbuilt effect of residual value, ie, the rates are prescribed such that 5% of residual value remains after depreciating 95% of the cost. Accordingly, the residual value is not deducted in the example in computing the depreciation under Schedule XIV. But it is deducted for depreciation computed under the Schedule II of the Companies Act, 2013.

(c) Useful life considered for computation of depreciation under Schedule II of the Companies Act, 2013 is the one that is prescribed in Part C of the Schedule.

(d) According to the Schedule XIV of the Companies Act, 1956, lower rate of depreciation (based on higher estimated useful life of 25 years) than prescribed cannot be used.

(e) According to the Schedule II of the Companies Act, 2013, entities may charge a lower depreciation than the rate envisaged in Schedule II on disclosing justification for the difference in the financial statements. In case the entity goes with the option of charging depreciation at the rates lower than the prescribed rates, the rates will be as follows: Single shift: (1 × 100/25= 4%)

In this case, the difference would be as follows:

Particulars	Single shift Depreciation	Double shift Depreciation	Triple shift Depreciation
Under Schedule XIV (1956)			
(INR 40,00,000 + INR 150,000) × 4.75%	INR 1,97,125		
(INR 40,00,000 + INR 150,000) × 7.42%		INR 3,07,930	
(INR 40,00,000 + INR 150,000) × 10.34%			INR 4,29,110
As per the minimum rate			
Under Schedule II (2013)			
(INR 40,00,000 + INR 150,000) × 4.00%	INR 1,66,000	INR 1,66,000 (NESD)	INR 1,66,000 (NESD)
Difference in Depreciation under Schedule II (New-Old)	(INR 31,125)	(INR 1,41,930)	(INR 2,63,110)

Chapter 6

Amortisation under the Companies Act, 2013

6.1 POSITION BEFORE THE COMPANIES ACT, 2013

Amortisation of intangible assets was hitherto, dealt only by AS 26, '*Intangible Assets*'. However, recently an amendment was made in Schedule XIV of the Companies Act, 1956 to deal with the manner in which toll roads should be amortised. Before discussing amortisation in detail, let us first discuss this aspect of amendment in Schedule XIV.

6.1.1 Amendment in Schedule XIV that deals with Intangible assets in the form of toll roads

"V-Intangible Assets

1. Intangible Assets (Toll Road) created under Build, Operate and Transfer, Build, Own, Operate and Transfer or any other form of Public Private Partnership Route."

$$\text{Amortisation rate} = \frac{\text{Amortisation Amount} \times 100}{\text{Cost of Intangible Assets (A)}}$$

Amortisation Amount

$$\text{Cost of Intangible Asset (A)} \times \frac{\text{Actual revenue for the year (B)}}{\text{Projected Revenue from Intangible Asset (till the end of the concession period) (C)}}$$

Cost of Intangible Asset (A) = Cost incurred by the Company in accordance with the Accounting Standards.

Actual Revenue for the year (B) = Actual Revenue (Toll Charges) received during the accounting year.

Projected Revenue from Intangible Asset (C) = Total Projected Revenue from the Intangible Asset as provided to the Project Lender at the time of financial closure/agreement.

The amortisation amount or rate should ensure that the whole of the cost of the intangible asset is amortised over the concession period.

Total Revenue would be reviewed at the end of each financial year and the projected revenue will be adjusted to reflect any changes in the estimate which would lead to the actual collection at the end of the concession period.

6.2 POSITION UNDER THE COMPANIES ACT, 2013

No separate depreciation rate has been prescribed for intangible assets in Schedule II of the Companies Act, 2013. Rather, the same will be governed by the notified Accounting Standard (i.e., Accounting Standard 26 on *'Intangible Assets'*).

In case of intangible assets (Toll Roads) created under 'Build, Operate and Transfer', 'Build, Own, Operate and Transfer' or any other form of Public Private Partnership route, in case of road projects, the amortization basis will be the same as what was applicable under the Companies Act, 1956. *(Amendment to Schedule II vide notification by MCA dated 31st March, 2014).*

The words 'may be' used in clause (ii) of paragraph 3 of Schedule II indicates that revenue-based amortisation as provided in Schedule II is optional and not mandatory. Moreover, the option is available only for intangible assets arising from toll road projects. Therefore, a company can follow a basis other than revenue-based amortisation for intangible assets arising from toll road projects. Intangible assets other than those arising from toll-roads should be amortised in accordance with AS 26.

Example

Facts: B Limited is a company engaged in various projects of infrastructure development. B's basic business model is to enter into various infrastructure development projects with the Central and State Governments controlled enterprises under Public Private Partnership (PPP) Model. During the year 2011-12, B Limited entered into a contract with the State Government of Haryana for developing a coal-fired thermal power plant serving the states of Haryana, Delhi, Rajasthan and Punjab.

Issue: At the year-end, i.e., 31st March, 2016, for providing amortisation on the intangible assets arising from the above mentioned projects for developing thermal power plant, B Limited is of the view that the revenue-based amortisation methodology as permitted by the Schedule II may be applied. Whether the view taken by B Limited is appropriate?

Response: In this case, use of revenue-based amortisation is inappropriate as Schedule II permits revenue based amortisation only for intangible assets arising from toll road projects and not from any other infrastructure projects even though they are entered into through PPP model, BOT or BOOT.

The authors would like to mention here that AS 26 does not support amortization based on revenue.

In practice, we do not expect a change in the amortization amount in respect of intangible assets, pursuant to the applicability of the Companies Act, 2013.

Position under Ind AS

Issue

Paragraph 7AA of Ind 38, Intangible Assets read with paragraph D22 of Ind AS 101, First-time Adoption of Indian Accounting Standards permits revenue based amortisation for the intangible assets arising from service concession arrangements in respect of toll roads recognised in the financial statements for the period ending immediately before the beginning of the first Ind AS reporting period. However, Schedule II to the Companies Act, 2013, permits revenue based amortisation for such intangible asset without any reference to any financial year. Whether a company is permitted to follow revenue based amortisation even for such new arrangements entered into after Ind AS become applicable?

Response

Paragraph D22 of Ind AS 101, *inter alia,* states as follows:

> *"D22 A first-time adopter may apply the following provisions while applying the Appendix A to Ind AS 11:*
>
> *(i) Subject to paragraph (ii), changes in accounting policies are accounted for in accordance with Ind AS 8, i.e. retrospectively, except for the policy adopted for amortization of intangible assets arising from service concession arrangements related to toll roads recognised in the financial statements for the period ending immediately before the beginning of the first Ind AS financial reporting period as per the previous GAAP................"*

Paragraph D7AA of Ind AS 38, *Intangible Assets,* states as follows:

> *"7AA The amortisation method specified in this Standard does not apply to an entity that opts to amortise the intangible assets arising from service concession arrangements in respect of toll roads recognised in the financial statements for the period ending immediately before the beginning of the first Ind AS reporting period as per the exception given in paragraph D22 of Appendix D to Ind AS 101."*

Schedule II to the Companies Act, 2013, provides that for intangible assets, the provisions of the accounting standards applicable for the time being in force shall apply, except in case of intangible assets (Toll Roads) created under 'Build, Operate and Transfer', 'Build, Own, Operate and Transfer' or any other form of public private partnership route in case of road projects. Amortisation in such cases may be done on the basis of revenue as specified Schedule II.

Paragraph 7AA of Ind 38 read with paragraph D22 of Ind AS 101, specifically provides exemption for service concession arrangements in respect of toll roads recognised in the financial statements for the period ending immediately before the beginning of the first Ind AS reporting period as per the previous GAAP, i.e., as per Schedule II to the Companies Act, 2013, considering the requirements contained in that Schedule. Companies (Accounts) Rules, 2014 prescribes to follow Ind AS in preparation of financial statements.

Hence, in view of Rules and Ind AS 38 read with Ind AS 101, principles of Ind AS 38 should be followed for all service concession arrangements including roll roads once Ind AS is applicable to an entity.

(*Issue13 of Ind AS Transition Facilitation Group (ITFG) Clarification Bulletin 3*)

6.2.1 Amortisation: Meaning

Para 2 of Part A of Schedule II of the Companies Act, 2013 provides that the term 'depreciation' includes 'amortisation'.

AS 26, '*Intangible Assets*' defines amortisation as the systematic allocation of the depreciable amount of an intangible asset over its useful life.

6.2.2 What is an Intangible Asset?

An asset is said to be an 'intangible asset' if it satisfies the following criteria:

(i) It is identifiable

- To be identifiable, it should be possible to clearly distinguish the asset, in terms of the consideration made, from the 'goodwill'. An 'intangible asset' can be clearly distinguished from 'goodwill', if the asset is separable.
- An asset is separable if the enterprise can rent, sell, exchange or distribute the specific future economic benefits which are attributable to the asset, without also disposing of the future economic benefits that flow from other assets used in the same revenue earning activity.
- Apart from separability, if an intangible asset is acquired with a group of assets, the transaction may involve the transfer of legal rights that enable an enterprise to identify the intangible asset.
- Similarly, if an internal project aims to create legal rights for the enterprise, the nature of these rights may assist the enterprise in identifying an underlying internally generated intangible asset.

- Also, even if an asset generates future economic benefits only in combination with other assets, the asset is identifiable if the enterprise can identify the future economic benefits that will flow from the asset.

(ii) It is a non-monetary asset

- An asset is said to be a non-monetary asset, if the value to be received against such an asset is not fixed by any contract or otherwise, for example, 'goodwill'; as in case of goodwill, the value that an enterprise will be able to draw, cannot be fixed by a contract or otherwise. Similarly, patents, trademarks, franchises, etc., are non-monetary assets.
- As against a non-monetary asset, the value to be received against an asset can be fixed in case of a monetary asset, for example, debtors.

(iii) It should be without physical substance

- However, in some cases, intangible assets may have a physical substance, for example, a compact disk (in the case of computer software), legal documentation (in the case of a licence or patent) or film (in the case of a motion picture).
- In such cases, what needs to be seen is whether, the cost of the physical substance is insignificant or not. In case the cost of the physical substance is insignificant, in relation to the total cost of the asset, the entire asset is treated as an intangible asset (including the physical substance).
- Similarly in some cases, an asset may incorporate both intangible and tangible elements, that are, in practice, inseparable, for example, computer software for a computer-controlled machine tool, that cannot operate without that specific software, is an integral part of the related hardware.
- Now, tangible assets, i.e. 'fixed assets' are covered by AS 10 and intangible assets are covered by AS 26. The question that arises is whether, to treat the asset as per AS 10 or as per AS 26. In such cases, a judgment is required to assess as to which element is predominant. If the tangible element is predominant, then, the asset is to be treated as per AS 10, else, as per AS 26, for example, in the case of a computer software for a computer controlled machine tool, that cannot operate without that specific software, the computer software is treated as a 'fixed asset', as the predominant element in this case is tangible.

(iv) It is held for use in the production or supply of goods or services, for rental to others, or for administrative purposes.

6.2.3 Recognition of intangible assets

- An intangible asset should be recognised if, and only if:
  - (a) it is probable that the future economic benefits that are attributable to the asset, will flow to the enterprise; and
  - (b) the cost of the asset can be measured reliably.
- An enterprise should assess the probability of future economic benefits, using reasonable and supportable assumptions that represent the best estimate of the set of economic conditions, which will exist over the useful life of the asset.
- An intangible asset should be measured initially at cost.

6.2.4 Calculation of the depreciable amount of an intangible asset

The depreciable amount of an intangible asset should be allocated over the best estimate of the useful life of the intangible asset, on a systematic basis.

6.2.5 Normal useful life of an intangible asset

The useful life of an intangible asset depends on various factors, such as, expected usage, product life-cycle, technical factors, etc. However, AS 26 provides that, normally the useful life of an intangible asset should not be taken as more than **10 years**. However, **this presumption is rebuttable**. If there is a persuasive evidence that the useful life of an intangible asset will be longer than 10 years, then, the asset should be amortised over that period, for example, if X Ltd. purchases exclusive rights to operate a toll bridge for 40 years and it is expected that the toll bridge will be used for 40 years, then, the intangible asset should be amortised over a period of 40 years. However, X Ltd. should estimate the recoverable amount of the intangible asset at least annually, in order to identify any impairment loss; and disclose the reasons why the presumption is rebutted and the factor(s) that played a significant role in determining the useful life of the asset.

6.2.5.1 Estimation of the useful life of an intangible asset

If control over the future economic benefits from an intangible asset is achieved through legal rights that have been granted for a finite period, the useful life of the intangible asset should not exceed the period of the legal rights unless:

(i) the legal rights are renewable, and

(ii) renewal is virtually certain.

***Note* - Amortisation of Land Right of Way**

Paragraphs 68 of AS 26, specifically envisages that, the useful life of an intangible asset is always finite, howsoever long and indefinite it may be. AS 26 does not justify non-amortisation; it only requires disclosures where the useful life is considered more than 10 years. It stipulates that the life has to be determined on a prudent and rational basis.

The view that the useful life of land right of way is infinite is not correct. The useful life of the land right of way may be determined considering various technical, legal and economic factors, such as, useful life of petroleum reserves from which the petroleum products are being produced and then transported, technological changes in the transportation modes, alternative resources of energy, etc. As per AS 26, the useful life of the land right of way may be indefinite, but, it is not infinite and, accordingly, the depreciable amount should be allocated on a systematic basis over the best estimate of its useful life. Therefore, the practice of the company not to amortise the land right of way, is not correct.

In case useful life of the intangible assets is determined to exceed more than 10 years, the company should provide reasons for such presumption as per the requirements of paragraph 94 of AS 26. *(Recent Opinion 3 of The Expert Advisory Committee on ICAI Website)*

6.2.6 Commencement of amortisation of an intangible asset

Amortisation of an intangible asset should commence when the asset is available for use.

6.2.7 Choice of amortisation method

The amortisation method used should reflect the pattern in which the asset's economic benefits are consumed by the enterprise. These methods include the 'straight-line method', the 'diminishing balance method' and the 'unit of production method'. If a pattern cannot be determined reliably, the 'straight-line method' should be used.

The amortisation charge for each period should be recognised as an expense, unless, another Accounting Standard permits or requires it to be included in the carrying amount of another asset, for example, amortisation of intangible asset, which is used in a production process, is included in the carrying amount of inventories.

6.2.8 Estimation of residual value of an intangible asset

The residual value of an intangible asset should normally be taken as 'zero'. However, in the following cases this will not hold good:

(*i*) when there is a commitment by a third party to purchase the asset at the end of its useful life; or

(*ii*) when there is an active market for the asset, and

 (*a*) residual value can be determined by reference to that market, and (*b*) it is probable that such a market will exist at the end of the asset's useful life.

6.2.9 Review of amortisation period and method

The amortisation period and the amortisation method should be reviewed at least at the end of each financial year. If the expected useful life of the asset is significantly different from previous estimates, the amortisation period should be changed accordingly. If there has been a significant change in the expected pattern of economic benefits from the asset, the amortisation method should be changed to reflect the changed pattern. Such changes should be accounted for in accordance with AS 5, *'Net Profit or Loss for the Period, Prior Period Items and Changes in Accounting Policies'*.

6.2.10 Examples

EXAMPLE 1

X Ltd. acquired a patent at a cost of INR 80,00,000 for a period of 5 years and the product life-cycle is also 5 years.. After two years it was found that the product life-cycle may continue for another 5 years from then. The net cash flows from the product during these 5 years were expected to be INR 36,00,000, INR 46,00,000, INR 44,00,000, INR 40,00,000 and INR 34,00,000. Find out the amortisation cost of the patent for each of the years.

SOLUTION:

The Standard requires that depreciable amount of an intangible asset should be allocated over the best estimate of the useful life of the intangible asset, on a systematic basis.

So far as useful life is concerned, the Standard provides that if control over the future economic benefits from an intangible asset is achieved through legal rights that have been granted for a finite period, the useful life of the intangible asset should not exceed the period of the legal rights unless:

(*i*) the legal rights are renewable; and

(*ii*) renewal is virtually certain.

In the present case, the patents have been granted for 5 years and the product life cycle is also 5 years. Hence, the useful life of the patents should be taken to be 5 years.

The next question to be examined relates to the amortisation method. The amortisation method used should reflect the pattern in which the asset's economic benefits are consumed by the enterprise. If that pattern cannot be determined reliably, the straight-line method should be used.

In this case, the pattern in which the economic benefits have been consumed by X Ltd. in first 2 years has not been given. Therefore, we assume that initially the benefits were expected to accrue evenly for the entire useful life of 5 years. Based on this, the amortisation cost of the patent for year 1 and year 2 would be INR 16,00,000 each (being INR 8,00,000/5).

AS 26 also requires that the amortisation period and the amortisation method should be reviewed at least at each financial year end. If the expected useful life of the asset is significantly different from previous estimates, the amortisation period should be changed accordingly. If there has been a significant change in the expected pattern of economic benefits from the asset, the amortisation method should be changed to reflect the changed pattern. Assuming that the patents are renewable for two more years (so that they can be used by the company for the extended product life cycle), the unamortised cost of INR 48,00,000 (being INR 80,00,000 – INR 32,00,000) would be amortised in the following manner:

Year	Net cash Flows INR in lakhs	Amortisation Cost INR in lakhs
3	36	48 × 36/200 = 8.64
4	46	48 × 46/200 = 11.04
5	44	48 × 44/200 = 10.56
6	40	48 × 40/200 = 9.60
7	34	48 × 34/200 = 8.16
	200	48

EXAMPLE 2

Suresh Ltd. purchased a trademark from Trilok Ltd. on 1 May, 2013 for a price of INR 50 lakh. It is well established in the industry that the expected useful life of such a trademark is 22 years. Trilok Ltd. acquired this trademark two years age. Suresh Ltd. wants to amortise the trademark over its remaining useful life of 20 years whereas a consultant has advised that having regard to AS 26, the remaining amortisation period is 8 years only as the total period allowed for amortisation of intangible assets under this Standard is 10 years only. Comment.

SOLUTION:

Trademark can be written off over a period of 20 years, presumption of 10 years of useful life is rebuttable.

EXAMPLE 3

The cost of creation of a toll road was INR 500 crore. The total period of agreement was 20 years and the time used for creation of Intangible asset was 2 years. Toll road is to be amortised in a period of 18 years. Total revenue to be generated out of toll road over the period is estimated to be INR 600 crore.

Year No.	Revenue (INR in Crores)
Year 1	5
Year 2	7.5
Year 3	10
Year 4	12.5
Year 5	17.5
Year 6	20
Year 7	23
Year 8	27
Year 9	31
Year 10	34
Year 11	38
Year 12	41
Year 13	46
Year 14	50
Year 15	53
Year 16	57
Year 17	60
Year 18	67.5
Total	600

The actual revenue for first 4 years was as under:

Year	Revenue (INR Crores)
1	5
2	8
3	10
4	12

There was no change in the overall estimated revenue during the life of the toll road.

Compute the amortisation amount to be charged in years 1 to 4.

SOLUTION

The charge for first year would be INR 4.16 crore (approximately) (i.e., INR 5/INR 600 × INR 500 crore) which would be charged to the profit and loss account and 0.83% (i.e., INR 4.16 crore /500 crore × 100) is the amortisation rate for the first year.

Similarly, charge for further years is as follows:

Year	Revenue (INR in Crores)	Computation (INR in Crores)	Charge (amount to be debited to the Statement of Profit and Loss) (INR in Cr.)	Amortisation rate (%)	
Year 2	8	INR 8/INR 600 × INR 500	6.67	6.67 × 100/500	1.33%
Year 3	10	INR 10/INR 600 × INR 500	8.33	8.33 × 100/500	1.67%
Year 4	12	INR 12/INR 600 × INR 500	10	10 × 100/500	2.00%

EXAMPLE 4

A Ltd. purchased a trademark from B Ltd. on 1 May, 2014 for a price of INR 50 lakhs. It is well established in the industry that the expected useful life of such a trademark is 22 years. B Ltd. acquired this trademark two years ago. At the end of year 2012, A Ltd. has a contract with C Ltd. to sell this trademark for INR 15 lakhs. How much amount should be amortised by A Ltd. every year?

SOLUTION

For A Ltd., the useful life of the trademark is 10 years (12 years-2 years).

The amount to be amortised is INR 50 lakhs less INR 15 lakhs, i.e., INR 35 lakhs.

INR 35 lakhs would be amortised over a period of 10 years. INR 3.50 lakhs would be amortised in each year upto the 12th Year.

Chapter 7
Impact of Impairment on Depreciation

7.1 WHAT IS IMPAIRMENT?

An asset is carried at more than its recoverable amount, if its carrying amount exceeds the amount to be recovered through use or sale of the asset. If this is the case, the asset is described as 'impaired'.

7.2 IMPAIRMENT LOSS

An impairment loss is the amount by which the carrying amount of an asset exceeds its recoverable amount. (*Para 4.5 of AS 28, 'Impairment of assets'*)

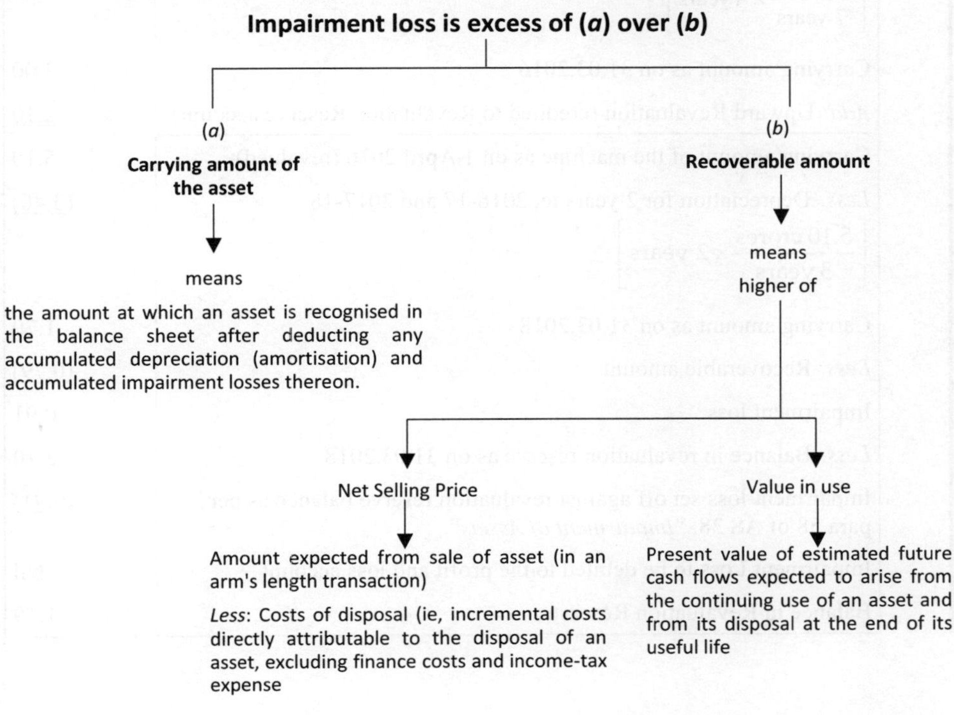

EXAMPLE 1

G Ltd. acquired a machine on 1 April, 2012 for INR 7 crore that had an estimated useful life of 7 years. The machine is depreciated on straight-line basis and does not carry any residual value. On 1 April, 2016, the carrying value of the machine was reassessed at INR 5.10 crore and the surplus arising out of the revaluation being credited to revaluation reserve. For the year ending in March, 2018, conditions indicating an impairment of the machine existed and the amount recoverable ascertained to be only INR 79 lakh.

You are required to calculate the loss on impairment of the machine and show how this loss is to be treated in the books of G Ltd.

SOLUTION

The computation of impairment loss is given as under:

Particulars	(INR in Crores)
Carrying amount of the machine as on 1 April 2012	7.00
Depreciation for 4 years ie, 2012-13 to 2015-16 $\left[\frac{7 \text{ crores}}{7 \text{ years}} \times 4 \text{ years}\right]$	(4.00)
Carrying amount as on 31.03.2016	3.00
Add: Upward Revaluation (credited to Revaluation Reserve account)	2.10
Carrying amount of the machine as on 1 April 2016 (revalued)	5.10
Less: Depreciation for 2 years ie, 2016-17 and 2017-18 $\left[\frac{5.10 \text{ crores}}{3 \text{ years}} \times 2 \text{ years}\right]$	(3.40)
Carrying amount as on 31.03.2018	1.70
Less: Recoverable amount	(0.79)
Impairment loss	0.91
Less: Balance in revaluation reserve as on 31.03.2018:	2.10
Impairment loss set off against revaluation reserve balance as per para 58 of AS 28, "*Impairment of Assets*"	(0.91)
Impairment Loss to be debited to the profit and loss account	Nil
Balance in Revaluation Reserve	1.19

EXAMPLE 2

In the above example, keeping all the facts same, except that, the carrying value of the machine was reassessed at INR 0.60 crore and the amount recoverable ascertained was INR 19 lakh, you are required to calculate the loss on impairment of the machine and show how this loss is to be treated in the books of G Ltd.

SOLUTION

The computation of impairment loss is given as under:

Particulars	(INR in Crores)
Carrying amount of the machine as on 1 April 2012	7.00
Depreciation for 4 years i.e., 2012-13 to 2015-16 $\left[\frac{7\text{ crores}}{7\text{ years}}\times 4\text{ years}\right]$	(4.00)
Carrying amount as on 31.03.2016	3.00
Add: Upward Revaluation (credited to Revaluation Reserve account)	0.60
Carrying amount of the machine as on 1 April 2016 (revalued)	3.60
Less: Depreciation for 2 years i.e., 2016-17 and 2017-18 $\left[\frac{3.60\text{ crores}}{3\text{ years}}\times 2\text{ years}\right]$	(2.40)
Carrying amount as on 31.03.2018	1.20
Less: Recoverable amount	(0.19)
Impairment loss	1.01
Less: Balance in revaluation reserve as on 31 March, 2018:	0.60
Impairment loss set off against revaluation reserve balance as per Para 58 of AS 28, "*Impairment of Assets*"	(0.60)
Impairment Loss to be debited to the profit and loss account	0.41
Balance in Revaluation Reserve	Nil

7.3 WHEN SHOULD AN ENTERPRISE ASSESS WHETHER ANY ASSET HAS BEEN IMPAIRED?

At each balance sheet date, an enterprise should assess whether, there is any indication that an asset has been impaired.

Some of the indications are as follows:

(*i*) External sources of information

(*a*) A significant decline in the market value of an asset (more than the normal decline) during the period under consideration;

(*b*) significant changes with an adverse effect on the enterprise have taken place during the period, or will take place in the near future, in the technological, market, economic or legal environment in which the enterprise operates or in the market to which an asset is dedicated;

(*c*) market interest rates or other market rates of return on investments have increased during the period, and are likely to affect the discount rate used in calculating an asset's value in use and decrease the asset's recoverable amount materially; and

(*d*) the carrying amount of the net assets of the reporting enterprise is more than its market capitalisation.

(*ii*) Internal sources of information

(*a*) Evidence relating to obsolescence or physical damage to an asset;

(*b*) significant changes with an adverse effect on the enterprise have taken place during the period, or are expected to take place in the near future, in the extent to which, or manner in which, an asset is used or is expected to be used;

(*c*) evidence on the basis of internal reporting indicating poor economic performance (than what is expected) of the asset.

7.4 SHOULD AN ENTERPRISE CONSIDER MATERIALITY IN IDENTIFYING WHETHER THE RECOVERABLE AMOUNT OF AN ASSET NEEDS TO BE ESTIMATED?

Yes, an enterprise should consider materiality in identifying the need to estimate the recoverable amount of an asset, for example, if in the previous reporting period, the recoverable amount of the asset was 30% higher than its carrying amount, and no events have occurred in the current reporting period that can eliminate this difference, then, in such a case, there is no need to estimate the recoverable amount of the asset in question in the current reporting period.

7.5 IF THERE IS AN INDICATION AS TO IMPAIRMENT OF AN ASSET, SHOULD THE REMAINING USEFUL LIFE, DEPRECIATION METHOD AND RESIDUAL VALUE BE ALSO REVIEWED?

Yes, if there is an indication that an asset may have been impaired, the remaining useful life, the 'depreciation method', as well as, the residual value may also have to be reviewed and adjusted according to the requirements of the other applicable Accounting Standards such as, AS 6 or AS 26. This is notwithstanding whether, any impairment loss has been recognised for the asset. Once the impairment loss is recognised, depreciation should be adjusted for future periods, so as to allocate the revised carrying amount *less* its residual value over the remaining useful life of the asset.

7.6 SHOULD THE RECOVERABLE AMOUNT BE DETERMINED FOR ASSETS INDIVIDUALLY OR FOR CASH GENERATING UNITS?

Recoverable amount is determined for an individual asset, unless the asset does not generate cash inflows from continuing use that are largely independent of those from the other assets or groups of assets. If that be the case, recoverable amount should be determined for the cash-generating unit to which the asset belongs, unless either:

(*a*) the asset's net selling price is higher than its carrying amount, or

(*b*) the asset's value in use, can be estimated to be close to its net selling price and the net selling price can be determined.

7.7 HOW TO MEASURE RECOVERABLE AMOUNT OF AN INDIVIDUAL ASSET?

Net Selling Price

is arrived at by

1st Preference
Ascertain the price in a binding sale agreement in an arm's length transaction. This price should be adjusted for incremental costs directly attributable to the disposal of the asset

2nd Preference
Market Price (current bid price or price or price at most recent transaction).
Less: Cost of disposal

3rd Preference
Price, based on the next best possible information available, at the balance sheet date.

Value in Use

apply following steps

Step 1: Estimate the future cash flows (both inflows and outflows) on account of continuing use of asset and from its ultimate disposal.

Step 2: Find the discounted cash flows by applying the suitable discount rate.

7.7.1 Net selling price: Some Key Points

1. Net selling price does not reflect price under a forced sale, unless, the management is under a compulsion to sell the asset immediately.
2. Costs of disposal, other than those that have already been recognised as liabilities, for example, legal costs, costs of removing the asset, etc., are deducted in determining the net selling price.
3. If the disposal of an asset requires the buyer to take over a liability and only a single net selling price is available for both, the asset and the liability, then, the net selling price will be the net amount (received or receivable) from disposal, after considering the liability taken over, *less* disposal costs.

EXAMPLE 3

A Ltd. is disposing of one of its assets. The buyer has agreed to take-over the asset for INR 50 lakh, with a stipulation that A Ltd. will have to take over a concerned liability. The costs of disposal are expected to be INR 2 lakh. The net selling price of the asset, in this case will be INR 48 lakh.

7.7.2 Value in use: Some Key Points

I. Estimation of future cash flows

(a) Composition of future cash flows

The following should be included in 'future cash flows':

(*i*) Cash inflows from the continuing use of the asset;

(*ii*) cash outflows necessary to generate the cash inflows from continuing use of the asset (including cash outflows to prepare the asset for use) and those can be directly attributed, or allocated on a reasonable and consistent basis, to the asset, and

(*iii*) net cash flows, if any, to be received (or paid) for the disposal of the asset at the end of its useful life.

(b) Cash flow projections

Cash flow projections should be based on reasonable and supportable assumptions that represent the management's best estimate of the set of economic conditions that will exist over the remaining useful life of the asset. Greater weight should be given to the external evidence.

Further, these projections should be based on the most recent financial budgets/forecasts approved by the management. Normally, these budgets/forecasts should be for a period not exceeding 5 years. Cash flow projections, beyond the period covered by the most recent budgets/forecasts, should be estimated by extrapolating the projections based on the budgets/forecasts, using a steady or declining growth rate for subsequent years, unless an increasing rate can be justified. This growth rate should not exceed the long-term average growth rate for the products, industries, or country or countries in which the enterprise operates, or for the market in which the asset is used, unless, a higher rate can be justified.

(c) For the purpose of estimation, cash flows should be the ones that are based on the current condition of the asset

Cash inflows or outflows expected to arise from a future restructuring, should not be included unless, the enterprise has committed itself to such restructuring. Similarly, future capital expenditure that will improve or enhance the asset in excess of its originally assessed standard of performance should also not be included. However, future capital expenditure necessary to maintain or sustain an asset at its originally assessed standard of performance should be included while estimating the future cash flows.

(d) *Future cash flow estimates should not include cash flows from financial activities or income-tax receipts/payments.*

(e) *Disposal value should be determined on the basis of price in an arm's length transaction.*

(f) *Foreign currency future cash flows should be estimated in the currency in which the cash flows will be generated.*

These should then, be discounted using an appropriate rate. An enterprise should translate the present values at the exchange rate prevailing on the balance sheet date, in accordance with AS 11.

II. Discount rate

(*a*) Rates permissible to be used as a discount rate:

(*i*) Weighted Average Cost of Capital for the enterprise; or

(*ii*) Incremental borrowing rate for the enterprise; or

(*iii*) Other market borrowing rates.

The above rates require adjustment to reflect the way that the market would assess the specific risks associated with the projected cash flows; and to exclude risks that are not relevant to the projected cash flows.

(*b*) It should be pre-tax rate.

(*c*) It should reflect current market assessments of the time, value of money and the risks specific to the asset. In other words, it should be the return that investors would require if they were to choose an investment that would generate cash flows of amounts, timing and risk profile similar to those that the enterprise in question expects to derive from the asset.

(*d*) If an asset's specific rate is not directly available from the market, some other suitable basis may also be used.

(*e*) Generally, a single discount rate should be used for estimating the 'value in use' of an asset. However, separate discount rates may also be used for different future periods where the value in use is sensitive to a difference in risks, for different periods or to the term structure of the interest rates.

(*f*) Discount rate should not reflect risks for which future cash flow estimates have been adjusted.

(*g*) Discount rate should be independent of the enterprise's capital structure and the way the enterprise financed the purchase of the asset.

***Note:* Determination of discount rate for calculating value in use for impairment of assets as per AS 28**

Discount rate to be applied should be an estimate of the rate of return that the market would expect, on an equally risky investment. This rate is estimated from the rate implicit in the current market transactions, for similar assets or from WACC of a listed enterprise, that has a single asset (or a portfolio of assets) similar in terms of service potential and risks to the asset under review. Thus, the determination of discount rate is a matter of estimation and judgement considering various factors related to the assessment of the time value of money and the risks specific to the asset under review. In the absence of the aforesaid rate, the company may use its WACC as the discount rate, as adjusted to reflect the way that the market would assess the specific risks associated with the projected cash flows and to exclude risks that are not relevant to the projected cash flows. While using the company's own WACC as the discount rate, there are certain considerations, including the following, which should also be kept in mind:

(i) WACC is a post-tax rate and AS 28 requires using a pre-tax rate for determining the value in use. Accordingly, it should be adjusted to a pre-tax basis.

(ii) Company's own WACC is based on its capital structure, which may be different from the typical capital structure of market participants.

(iii) Discount rate as per AS 28 should reflect the risks specific to the asset and not the risks relating to the entity as a whole.

As regards the adjustment of discount rate for various risks, such as, currency risk, price risk, country risk, cash flow risks, etc., as per the provisions of AS 28, the effect of the variability of cash flows can be reflected in either of the two ways:

(i) the expected value of cash flows can be adjusted for risk and the adjusted figure (the certainty equivalent) discounted at a risk-free rate, or

(ii) the expected value of cash flows can be discounted at a risk-adjusted rate.

Thus, the discount rate should not reflect risks for which future cash flow estimates have been adjusted.

Hence, determination of discount rate is a matter of estimation and judgement, considering various factors related to the assessment of the time value of money and risks specific to the asset under review. Therefore, the company should take into account all the factors related to the determination of discount rate. *(EAC Opinion, 34.2)*

III. Other important points

(*a*) If any of the two amounts, i.e., the net selling price or value in use, exceed the carrying amount of asset in question, the determination of the other amount is not required.

(*b*) If it is not possible to determine the net selling price, take the value in use as the recoverable amount.

(*c*) In case an asset is held for disposal, its net selling price may be taken as the recoverable amount, i.e., there is no need to ascertain its value in use.

7.8 IDENTIFYING A CASH GENERATING UNIT (CGU) TO WHICH AN ASSET BELONGS

Sometimes we need to identify CGU, to which the asset in question belongs to. Issues, such as, when does such need arise and, in such cases, how to identify the relevant CGU, have been discussed below:

7.8.1 When should the recoverable amount of a CGU need to be ascertained instead of an individual asset?

The recoverable amount of a CGU, need to be ascertained, if it is not possible to estimate the recoverable amount of an individual asset.

The recoverable amount of an individual asset cannot be determined if:

(i) If the value in use of an asset cannot be estimated to be close to its net selling price, and

(ii) If the asset does not generate cash inflows from continuing use that are largely independent of those from other assets. In such cases, the value in use and, therefore, the recoverable amount, can be determined only for the asset's cash-generating unit.

For example, the Food Corporation of India (FCI) site owns a private railway track to support its activities. The private railway track could be sold only for scrap value and it does not generate cash inflows from continuing use that are largely independent of the cash inflows from the other assets of the FCI. In such a case, the value in use of the private railway track cannot be said to be its scrap value and at the same time, it is not possible to estimate its recoverable amount by some other reasonable basis also. Thus, the FCI should estimate the recoverable amount of the cash generating unit to which the private railway track belongs, i.e., the site as a whole.

7.8.2 What is the criterion, on the basis of which a CGU may be identified?

If an active market exists for the output produced by an asset or a group of assets, such asset or group of assets should be identified as a separate CGU. It is immaterial, whether, the output is sold internally or externally.

7.8.3 Can an enterprise change CGU to which an asset belongs to in the later periods?

Preferably, CGU should be identified consistently from period to period, for the same asset or types of assets.

However, if a change can be justified, then in such a case, an enterprise can change the CGU by suitably disclosing the current and former way of aggregating the assets and the reasons for changing the way, the CGU is identified.

7.9 HOW TO ASCERTAIN RECOVERABLE AMOUNT AND CARRYING AMOUNT OF A CGU?

The recoverable amount of a CGU is the *higher of*:

(*i*) Net selling price, and

(*ii*) Value in use of the CGU in question.

The recoverable amount of a CGU should be determined in a manner similar to the one adopted for an individual asset. Regarding the determination of the carrying amount, the following points should be kept in mind:

(*a*) Carrying amount of only those assets should be included that can be attributed directly or allocated on a reasonable and consistent basis, to the CGU and that will generate the future cash inflows estimated in determining the CGU's value in use. However, it does not include the carrying amount of any recognised liability, unless the recoverable amount of the CGU cannot be determined without consideration of this liability.

(*b*) If any recognised liability has been considered in determination of the recoverable amount of a CGU, then, the carrying amount of the liability is deducted in determining both the CGU's value in use and its carrying amount, so as to facilitate a meaningful comparison between the carrying amount and the recoverable amount of CGU.

(*c*) If the recoverable amount of a CGU is determined after consideration of the assets that are not part of the CGU, for example, receivables or other financial assets or liabilities that have already been recognised in the financial statements, for example, payables, pensions and other provisions, the carrying amount of CGU should be increased by the carrying amount of those assets and decreased by the carrying amount of those liabilities.

7.10 HOW TO RECOGNISE AND MEASURE AN IMPAIRMENT LOSS?

Various issues relating to recognition and measurement of an impairment loss are as under:

7.10.1 How to determine impairment loss of an individual asset?

For this purpose, the following three-step approach should be adopted:

Step 1: Ascertain the recoverable amount of the asset.

Step 2: Compare the recoverable amount, with the carrying amount of the asset.

Step 3: If the recoverable amount is less than the carrying amount, then, the difference is treated as an 'impairment loss'.

7.10.2 How to determine impairment loss of a CGU?

An impairment loss should be recognised for a CGU, only if its recoverable amount is less than its carrying amount. The impairment loss should be allocated to reduce the carrying amount of the assets of the unit in the following order:

(*i*) to goodwill allocated to the cash-generating unit (if any), and

(*ii*) to the other assets of the unit on a pro rata basis, as based on the carrying amount of each asset in the unit.

Note.—For the purpose of allocation of the impairment loss, the carrying amount of an asset *should not be reduced below the highest of*:

(*a*) its net selling price (if determinable);

(*b*) its value in use (if determinable); and

(*c*) zero.

The amount of the impairment loss that would otherwise have been allocated to the asset should be allocated to the other assets of the unit on a pro rata basis. Thus, the carrying amount of any individual asset in the CGU can never be negative.

7.10.3 How to recognise impairment loss?

Impairment loss (whether of an individual asset of a CGU) is recognised in the following manner:

(a) *Impairment loss of a revalued asset*

It is recognised directly against any revaluation surplus for the asset to the extent, that, the impairment loss does not exceed the amount held in the revaluation surplus for that same asset. The balance, if any, is recognised as an expense in the profit and loss account.

(b) *Impairment loss of other assets*

Impairment loss of any other asset should be recognised as an expense in the profit and loss account.

7.10.4 When should an impairment loss be recognised as a liability?

An impairment loss should be recognised as a liability, only when the amount estimated for an impairment loss is greater than the carrying amount of the asset to which it relates. However, even in such a case, it can be recognised as a liability, only if, this is in accordance with some Accounting Standard.

7.11 DOES THE IMPAIRMENT LOSS AFFECT DEPRECIATION?

Yes, the depreciation charge does get affected by an impairment loss. The revised carrying amount, less the disposal value, should be allocated on a systematic basis over the remaining useful life of the asset.

EXAMPLE 4

From the following details of an asset:

(i) *Find out impairment loss*

(ii) *Treatment of impairment loss*

(iii) *Current year depreciation*

Particulars of assets:

Cost of asset	*INR 56 lakh*
Useful life	*10 years*
Salvage value	*Nil*
Current carrying value	*INR 27.30 lakh*

Remaining useful life *3 years*

Recoverable amount *INR 12 lakh*

Upward revaluation done in last year *INR 14 lakh*

SOLUTION

(i) *Impairment loss*

Impairment loss = Carrying amount of the asset – Recoverable amount

= INR 27.30 lakh – INR 12 lakh

= INR 15.30 lakh

(ii) *Treatment of impairment loss*

As per AS 28, *'Impairment of assets'*, impairment loss (whether of an individual asset of a CGU) is recognised in the following manner:

(*a*) *Impairment loss of a revalued asset*: It is recognised directly against any revaluation surplus for the asset to the extent that the impairment loss does not exceed the amount held in the revaluation surplus for that same asset. The balance, if any, is recognised as an expense in the profit and loss account.

(*b*) *Impairment loss of other assets*: Impairment loss of any other asset should be recognised as an expense in the profit and loss account.

Since, the asset in question has been revalued upwards, the impairment loss will be adjusted first against the revaluation surplus of INR 14 lakh. The balance amount of INR 1.30 lakh will be recognised as an expense in the profit and loss account.

(iii) *Current year depreciation*

	Amount (INR)
Revised carrying amount (after recognising impairment loss)	12 lakh
Remaining useful life	3 year
Salvage value	NIL
Annual depreciation	4 lakh (12/3)

Note: In case, there is no impairment, the depreciation would be simply INR 9.1 lakh per year (INR 27.30/3 years), (ie, Current carrying value / remaining useful life).

7.12 REVERSAL OF IMPAIRMENT LOSS

When an impairment loss, previously recognised, has decreased or ceased to exist, there is a need to reverse the impairment loss. However, an impairment loss recognised for goodwill should not be reversed in a subsequent period unless:

- the impairment loss was caused by a specific external event of an exceptional nature, that is not expected to recur; and
- Subsequent external events have occurred that reverse the effect of that event.

7.13 DOES THE DEPRECIATION CHARGE GET AFFECTED BY THE REVERSAL? IF YES, HOW?

Yes, the depreciation charge does get affected by the reversal of an impairment loss. The depreciation (amortisation) charge for the asset should be adjusted in future periods to allocate the asset's revised carrying amount, less its residual value (if any), on a systematic basis, over its remaining useful life.

EXAMPLE 5

A machine originally costing INR 5,00,000 and with a carrying amount of INR 3,00,000 on 31 March, 2016, was written off to recoverable amount of INR 1,20,000 on 31 March, 2016. Depreciation is provided for over the original estimated useful life of 5 years. On 31 March, 2017 information obtained by the company shows that recoverable amount of the machine has increased to INR 2,30,000.

Required:

Depreciation amount for the year ended on 31 March, 2018.

SOLUTION

Reversal of impairment loss:

Particulars	Before impairment (INR)	After impairment (INR)
Cost	5,00,000	
Accumulated depreciation on 31 March, 2016	2,00,000	
Carrying amount on 31 March, 2016	3,00,000	3,00,000
Impairment Loss (INR 3,00,000 – 1,20,000)		(1,80,000)
Recoverable amount on 31 March, 2016		1,20,000
Depreciation for 2016-17	(1,00,000)	(40,000)
Carrying amount on 31 March, 2017	2,00,000	80,000
Recoverable Amount on 31 March, 2017		2,30,000

Note: As per Para 101 of the AS 28, the increased carrying amount of an asset due to a reversal of an impairment loss should not exceed the carrying amount that would have been determined (net of amortisation or depreciation), had no impairment loss been recognised for the asset in the prior accounting periods. Thus, the increased carrying amount of the asset will be restricted to INR 2,00,000.

Effect on depreciation

Depreciation (31 March, 2017 – 31 March 2018)

Carrying amount as on 31 March, 2017	INR 2,00,000
Remaining useful life	2 Years
Depreciation for the year ended 31 March, 2018	INR 1,00,000 (INR 2,00,000/2)

In case, the impairment loss would not have been reversed, depreciation for 2017-18 would have been INR 40,000 (i.e., INR 1,20,000/3).

Chapter 8

Transitional Provisions under the Companies Act, 2013

In this Chapter, we have discussed the transitional provisions relating to depreciation. Essentially, these provisions deal with how the transition from Companies Act, 1956 to Companies Act, 2013 will be made in so far as it relates to depreciation.

8.1 TRANSITIONAL PROVISIONS

From the date Schedule II comes into effect, the carrying amount of the asset as on that date:

(a) shall be depreciated over the remaining useful life of the asset as per Schedule II;

(b) after retaining the residual value, may be recognised in the opening balance of retained earnings where the remaining useful life of an asset is Nil. (*Note 6 to Part C of Schedule II of the Companies Act, 2013 read with notification dated 29th August, 2014*).

If the company opts to adjust the carrying amount of the assets to the retained earnings in accordance with the transitional provisions of Schedule II, the tax effect of the same should also be adjusted directly against the retained earnings in accordance with the Announcement issued by the Institute of Chartered Accountants of India, *"Tax effect of expenses/income adjusted directly against the reserves and/or Securities Premium Account"*.

8.2 EXAMPLES

EXAMPLE 1

A company acquired a building (other than factory building and RCC Frame Structure) at a cost of INR. 10 crores. The company was depreciating the building according to Schedule XIV SLM rate, i.e., 1.63% (rate computed assuming useful life to be approximately 60 years). Now, in April 2014, Schedule II of the Companies Act, 2013 became effective, useful life specified in which is 30 years.

Explain how the transitional provision effect will be accounted for

A. If the building is acquired on 1st April, 2000

B. If the building is acquired on 1st April, 1980

SOLUTION

A. Transition effect in case the building is acquired on 1st April, 2000

Depreciation charged till FY 2013-14, i.e., depreciation on SLM for 14 years

INR. 10 crores*1.63%* 14yrs

INR. 2,28,20,000

Carrying Value as on 1st April, 2014

Cost less accumulated depreciation till FY 2013-14

INR. 10,00,00,000 – INR. 2,28,20,000

INR. 7,71,80,000

The carrying value as on 1st April, 2014 will be depreciated over the remaining useful life of the asset as per Schedule II of the Companies Act, 2013.

The remaining useful life as per new Schedule is (30-14) 16 years. Accordingly, depreciable amount of INR. 7,71,80,000 will be depreciated over 16 years.
So, annual depreciation to be charged to Profit and loss account from FY 2014-15 onwards would be INR. 7,71,80,000/16yrs , i.e., INR. 48,23,750.

Impact

(a) After 16 years from FY 2014-15, i.e., from FY 2030-31 onwards no depreciation would be charged

(b) For 16 years, i.e., from FY 2014-15 to FY 2029-30, higher depreciation would be charged. If Schedule II would not have been introduced, depreciation charged annually would have been INR. 10 cr. * 1.63% = INR. 16,30,000. After the introduction of Schedule II of the Companies Act, 2013, depreciation charged for these 16 years would be INR. 48,23,750 which is higher by INR. 31,93,750.

B. Transition effect in case the building is acquired on 1st April, 1980

If the building would have been purchased on 1st April, 1980, then as on 1st April, 2014, useful life of 30 years as per new Schedule has already expired.

(i) If the company exercises the option of recognizing the carrying value as on 1st April, 2014 in the opening balance of retained earnings:

Depreciation charged till FY 2013-14, i.e., depreciation on SLM for 34 years

INR. 10 crores*1.63%* 34yrs

INR. 5,54,20,000

Carrying Value as on 1st April, 2014

Cost less accumulated depreciation till FY 2013-14

INR. 10,00,00,000 – INR. 5,54,20,000

INR. 4,45,80,000

Carrying value as on 1st April, 2014 of INR. 4,45,80,000 would be recognized in the opening balance of retained earnings. (assuming residual value to be Nil)

Retained Earnings A/c Dr.	INR. 4,45,80,000
To Accumulated Depreciation on Building A/c	INR. 4,45,80,000

Impact

(a) Opening balance of retained earnings would be reduced by the carrying amount.

(b) No depreciation from FY 2014-15 onwards will be charged to the profit and loss account, which otherwise would have been charged if Schedule II would not have come into force.

Note: In case, there is a residual value, say, INR. 10,00,000 then INR. 4,35,80,000 would be recognized in the opening balance of retained earnings and INR. 10,00,000 will remain in the carrying amount of asset.

(ii) If the company does not exercise the option of recognizing the carrying value as on 1st April, 2014 in the opening balance of retained earnings:

Carrying value as on 1st April, 2014 of INR. 4,45,80,000 (computed in para (i) above) would be recognized in the statement of profit and loss. (Assuming residual value to be nil)

Profit and Loss A/c Dr.	INR. 4,45,80,000
To Accumulated Depreciation on Building A/c	INR. 4,45,80,000

Impact

(a) In the FY 2014-15, amount of carrying value reduced by the residual value would be recognized in the statement of profit and loss which otherwise would have not been charged if Schedule II would not have come into force.

(b) There would be no effect on retained earnings.

(c) No depreciation from FY 2014-15 onwards shall be charged to the profit and loss account, which otherwise would have been charged if Schedule II would not have come into force.

(d) Book profits will go down and consequently MAT liability will go down (unless there is a corresponding change in Income Tax Act,1961)

Note: *In case, there is a residual value, say, INR. 10,00,000 then INR. 4,35,80,000 would be recognized in the statement of profit and loss and INR. 10,00,000 will remain in the carrying amount of asset.*

EXAMPLE 2

A company constructed a non-carpeted road at a cost of INR. 40 crores. The company was depreciating the road according to Schedule XIV SLM rate, i.e., 1.63% (rate computed assuming useful life to be approximately 60 years). Now, in April 2014, Schedule II of the Companies Act, 2013 became effective, useful life specified in which is 3 years.

Explain how the transitional provision effect will be accounted for.

A. If the road is constructed on 1st April, 1995

B. If the road is constructed on 1st April, 2012

(***Note:*** *"Buildings" include 'roads' under schedule XIV of the Companies Act, 1956, so the rate for non-carpeted roads under schedule XIV is taken to be that of buildings (other than factory buildings)*)

SOLUTION

A. Transition effect in case the road is constructed on 1st April, 1995

Depreciation charged till FY 2013-14, i.e., depreciation on SLM for 19 years

INR. 40 crores*1.63%*19 yrs

INR. 12,38,80,000

Carrying Value as on 1st April, 2014

Cost less accumulated depreciation till FY 2013-14

INR. 40,00,00,000 – INR. 12,38,80,000

INR. 27,61,20,000

The useful life as per new Schedule is only 3 years which has already expired.

(i) If the company exercises the option of recognizing the carrying value of INR. 27,61,20,000 as on 1st April, 2014 in the opening balance of retained earnings:

Impact

(a) Opening balance of retained earnings would be reduced by the carrying amount.

(b) No depreciation from FY 2014-15 onwards will be charged to the profit and loss account, which otherwise would have been charged if Schedule II would not have come into force.

(ii) If the company does not exercise the option of recognizing the carrying value as on 1st April, 2014 in the opening balance of retained earnings:

Carrying value as on 1st April, 2014 of INR. 27,61,20,000 would be recognized in the statement of profit and loss. (Assuming residual value to be nil)

Impact

(a) In the FY 2014-15, amount of carrying value as reduced by the residual value would be recognized in the statement of profit and loss which otherwise would have not been charged if Schedule II would not have come into force.

(b) There would be no effect on retained earnings.

(c) No depreciation from FY 2014-15 onwards shall be charged to the profit and loss account, which otherwise would have been charged if Schedule II would not have come into force.

(d) Book profits will go down and consequently MAT liability will go down (unless there is a corresponding change in Income Tax Act, 1961)

B. Transition effect in case the road is constructed on 1st April, 2012

If the road would have been constructed on 1st April, 2012, then as on 1st April, 2014, useful life of 2 years as per new Schedule has already expired.

Depreciation charged till FY 2013-14, i.e., depreciation on SLM for 2 years

INR. 40 crores*1.63%*2 yrs

INR. 1,30,40,000

Carrying Value as on 1st April, 2014

Cost less accumulated depreciation till FY 2013-14

INR. 40,00,00,000 – INR. 1,30,40,000

INR. 38,69,60,000

Accordingly, depreciable amount of INR. 38,69,60,000 will be depreciated over 1 year.

Impact

(a) After 1 year from FY 2014-15, i.e., from FY 2015-16 onwards no depreciation would be charged

(b) For 1 year, i.e., FY 2014-15, higher depreciation would be charged. If Schedule II would not have been introduced, depreciation charged annually would have been INR. 40 cr. * 1.63% = INR. 65,20,000. After the introduction of Schedule II of the Companies Act, 2013, depreciation charged for FY 2014-15 would be INR. 38,69,60,000 which is higher by INR. 38,04,40,000.

EXAMPLE 3

A company acquired a reactor used in the manufacture of pharmaceuticals and chemicals at a cost of INR. 40 lakhs on 1st April, 2005. The reactor worked for triple shift. The company was depreciating the reactor according to Schedule XIV triple shift SLM rate, i.e., 10.34%. Now, in April 2014, Schedule II of the Companies Act, 2013 became effective, useful life specified in which is 20 years.

Explain how the transitional provision effect will be accounted for

A. If the reactor is acquired on 1st April, 2005

B. If the reactor is acquired on 1st April, 1993

SOLUTION

Notes:

(a) Reactor was not specifically covered under the Schedule XIV of the Companies Act, 1956, so rate is taken to be the rate applicable to 'general plant and machinery (not being a ship) other than a continuous process plant for which no specific rate has been prescribed'.

(b) Reactor is specified as NESD under the Schedule II of the Companies Act, 2013, i.e., under new schedule, no extra shift depreciation would be applicable. However, under old schedule extra shift depreciation was applicable as earlier it was covered under the category of 'general plant and machinery (not being a ship) other than a continuous process plant for which no specific rate has been prescribed' and it was not specified in the items of general plant and machinery (for which no specific rate has been prescribed) to which extra shift depreciation is not applicable.

A. If the reactor is acquired on 1st April, 2005

Depreciation charged till FY 2013-14, i.e., depreciation on SLM for 9 years

INR. 40 lakhs*10.34%*9 yrs

INR. 37,22,400

Carrying Value as on 1st April, 2014

Cost less accumulated depreciation till FY 2013-14

INR. 40,00,000 – INR. 37,22,400

INR. 2,77,600

The carrying value as on 1st April, 2014 will be depreciated over the remaining useful life of the asset as per Schedule II of the Companies Act, 2013.

The remaining useful life as per new Schedule is (20-9) 11 years.

Accordingly, depreciable amount of INR. 2,77,600 will be depreciated over 11 years.

So, annual depreciation to be charged to Profit and loss account from FY 2014-15 onwards would be INR. 2,77,600/11yrs, i.e., INR. 25,236. (assuming residual value to be nil)

Impact

(a) After 11 years from FY 2014-15, i.e., from FY 2025-26 onwards no depreciation would be charged

(b) If Schedule II would not have been introduced, the reactor would have been fully depreciated (except residual value) in 10th year itself. On the other hand, under Schedule II, depreciation will continue upto FY 2024-25.

B. If the reactor is acquired on 1st April, 1993

If the reactor would have been purchased on 1st April, 1993, then as on 1st April, 2014, useful life of 20 years as per new Schedule has already expired.

a. If the company exercises the option of recognizing the carrying value as on 1st April, 2014 in the opening balance of retained earnings:

Since, the reactor would have been fully depreciated by the end of 10th year from 1st April, 1993. Accordingly there would be no carrying value as on 1st April, 2014.

Impact

(a) There would be no effect on retained earnings.

(b) No depreciation from FY 2014-15 onwards shall be charged to the profit and loss account, which would have been the same if Schedule II would not have come into force. Hence, there would be no effect on the Statement of Profit and Loss as well.

b. If the company does not exercise the option of recognizing the carrying value as on 1st April, 2014 in the opening balance of retained earnings:

Carrying value as on 1st April, 2014 would be recognized in the statement of profit and loss. Since, the carrying value is nil, there would be no impact on the statement of profit and loss. (Assuming residual value to be nil)

Impact

(a) There would be no effect on retained earnings.

(b) No depreciation from FY 2014-15 onwards shall be charged to the profit and loss account, which would have been the same if Schedule II would not have come into force. Hence, there would be no effect on the Statement of Profit and Loss.

(c) There will be no impact on Book profits and MAT liability.

Chapter 9

Depreciation in Special Circumstances

In this chapter we have provided guidance on how to charge depreciation in special situations. This guidance is essentially based on various Expert Advisory Opinions and other literature of ICAI.

9.1 DEPRECIATION IN CASE OF USE OF AN ASSET FOR CONSTRUCTION

If a fixed asset (such as an office building) is used directly or indirectly for the purpose of construction (for example, it accommodates purchase department which, during construction period, performs the functions of purchasing various materials and supplies for the construction activity), depreciation on such a building would get charged to the other assets under construction (for example, the construction of the building, which would accommodate the plant and machinery). In such a situation, fixed assets (for example, office building), if fully used, directly or indirectly, for the purpose of carrying on various construction activities should be depreciated and the gross block of the fixed assets (for example, building), would be the depreciated amount on the commencement of commercial production. If such a fixed asset (for example, building), is partly used, only the relevant part of the depreciation would be charged to the construction cost of the other fixed assets. In such a case, the gross value of the fixed assets (for example, building), on the commencement of commercial production would be the depreciated amount, to the extent of the depreciation charged to the other assets under construction, i.e., original cost/ gross value of the fixed assets (for example, building) *minus* depreciation charged to other assets under construction. If such a fixed asset (for example, building) is not at all used for construction activity (for example, it is rented out to a third party pending the commencement of commercial production) such a fixed asset (for example, building), cannot be considered to be used for construction activity and in such a case, its gross block would be the original cost at which the fixed assets (for example, building) was acquired or constructed. Thus, the determining factor is whether or not, and the extent to which the fixed assets are actually used for construction activity, even though such fixed assets might have been purchased for regular use even after the commencement of commercial production. In other words, it is not necessary that such assets are especially purchased only for the construction activity. (*EAC Opinion, 23.7*)

9.2 DEPRECIATION IN CASE OF PART CAPITALISATION

Those parts, which are ready to commence commercial production or are ready for their intended use and can be operated independently of the remaining parts, should be considered to be ready for commencement of commercial production / intended use. The main packages should be capitalised pending the capitalisation of ancillary packages or *vice-versa*, when it is considered that the same are ready to commence commercial production independent of each other or are ready for their intended use. After part capitalisation, general overheads, administrative overheads, etc., should be segregated on an appropriate basis for charging the same to the profit and loss account and to the expenditure during construction account. Similarly, depreciation on infrastructural facilities like roads, buildings, etc., should be allocated to profit and loss account and expenditure during construction account on an appropriate basis. (*EAC Opinion, 22.24 and EAC Opinion, 23.10*)

9.3 DEPRECIATION OF INSURANCE / MACHINERY SPARES LYING IN STOCK

Insurance / machinery spares lying in stock (if not capitalised earlier), should be capitalised and depreciated retrospectively from the date of purchase over a period not exceeding the useful life of the asset to which they relate. The depreciation charge, pertaining to the prior periods, constitute a 'prior period item' in the current year and should be disclosed in the current year's profit and loss account in a manner that its impact on the current year's profit or loss can be perceived. (*EAC Opinion, 23.27 and EAC Opinion, 21.40*)

9.4 DEPRECIATION OF SPARES PURCHASED IN RELATION TO FIXED ASSETS WHICH HAS BEEN FULLY DEPRECIATED

Spares purchased subsequently in relation to fixed assets whose useful life has expired (i.e., the concerned principal items of fixed assets have been fully depreciated in the books of account) and they are of capital nature that can be used only in connection with the specific fixed assets, should be charged to the statement of profit and loss in the year of the purchase itself. Capital spare, in such a case, does not have a useful life of its own, as its useful life is linked to the useful life of the principal item. Thus, a capital spare does not depreciate as an independent item of 'plant and machinery' in terms of its own wear and tear. For instance, an item of capital spare may be totally new at the time when the principal item is discarded. Yet, it should be written off. In other words, the capital spare does not have any residual value. The cost of such machinery spares, lying in an inventory, should also be charged to the statement of profit and loss and a disclosure in the notes to accounts should be made in this regard. (*EAC Opinion, 25.16; EAC Opinion, 25.13; EAC Opinion, 23.3 and EAC Opinion, 24.33*)

9.5 TEST TO DETERMINE WHETHER A STRUCTURE IS 'FACTORY BUILDING' OR 'PLANT AND EQUIPMENT'

In the absence of the definitions of the terms 'Factory Buildings' and 'Plant and Equipment', under the Companies Act, 1956, a functional test has to be applied to determine whether a structure is 'plant' or not. The functional test requires to examine various aspects of the structure to determine whether it is an apparatus with which the activity or activities is/are carried on or it is a mere setting of or part of the premises in which the activity is/activities are carried on, for example, the civil works of Water Treatment Plant and Effluent Treatment Plant consisting of reservoirs, drains, lagoons, various clarifiers, neutralisation pit, aeration pond, and sludge thickener are directly involved in the process of treatment of water and effluent. The civil works involved in the Water Treatment Plant and Effluent Treatment Plant, excluding intake well sumps, de-mineralisation plant, softening plant and filter house building, are not merely the premises in which the work is carried on; these are rather the means with which and through which the activities of treatment of water and effluent are carried on. Hence, the civil works directly involved in the treatment of water and effluent should be capitalised as 'Plant and Equipment' instead of 'Factory Buildings'. Other civil works, i.e., which are not directly involved in the process of treatment of water and effluent, such as, intake well sumps, de-mineralisation plant, softening plant and filter house building is concerned, these civil works only act as the setting or structure containing various equipment and are not directly involved in the process of water treatment and effluent treatment. Hence, these civil works should be classified as 'Factory Buildings'. In case of reservoir, if the nature of the reservoir is such that it is not directly involved in the treatment of water and effluent, it should be treated as 'Factory Building'. Depreciation should be provided, keeping in view the rates applicable to 'Plant and Equipment' and 'Factory Buildings' under Schedule XIV. (*EAC Opinion, 26.4 and EAC Opinion, 24.25*)

9.6 NO DEPRECIATION ON PERPETUAL LEASE

No provision for depreciation should be made on the asset acquired under perpetual lease. The fact, that, no provision for depreciation in respect of the said asset has been made, should be indicated by way of a note to the accounts with the reason thereof. (*EAC Opinion, 8.26*)

9.7 DEPRECIATION ON ASSET UNDER LEASE

A **finance lease** is a lease that transfers substantially, all the risks and rewards incident to the ownership of an asset. *(Para 3.2 of AS 19)*

In case of a finance lease, depreciation is to be provided by the lessee, since the lessee is the real owner of the asset, irrespective of legal form. On the other hand, in case of an operating lease, depreciation is to be provided by the lessor.

In case of finance lease (in the financial statements of lessee)

(a) A finance lease gives rise to a depreciation expense for the asset, as well as, a finance expense for each accounting period. The depreciation policy for a leased asset should be consistent with that for depreciable assets which are owned, and the depreciation recognised should be calculated on the basis set out in AS 10, 'Property, Plant and Equipment'. (Para 18 of AS 19)

(b) The depreciable amount of a leased asset is allocated to each accounting period during the period of expected use on a systematic basis, consistent with the depreciation policy that the lessee adopts for depreciable assets that are owned. If there is reasonable certainty that the lessee will obtain ownership by the end of the lease term, the period of expected use is the useful life of the asset. If there is no reasonable certainty that the lessee will obtain ownership by the end of the lease term, the asset should be fully depreciated over the lease term or its useful life, whichever is shorter. (Para 18 and Para 19 of AS 19)

(c) The sum of the depreciation expense for the asset and the finance expense for the period is rarely the same as the lease payments payable for the period, and it is, thus, inappropriate simply to recognise the lease payments payable as an expense in the statement of profit and loss. Accordingly, the asset and the related liability are unlikely to be equal in amount after the inception of the lease. (Para 20 of AS 19)

(d) Leasehold improvements should be depreciated over the shorter of useful life of the leasehold improvement and the lease period.

In case of operating lease (in the financial statements of lessor)

The depreciation of leased assets should be on a basis which is consistent with the normal depreciation policy of the lessor for similar assets, and the depreciation charge should be calculated on the basis set out in AS 10 (Revised), 'Property, Plant and Equipment'. (Para 43 of AS 19)

9.8 USEFUL LIFE FOR THE PURPOSE OF DEPRECIATION ON LEASEHOLD LAND

Assessment of depreciation and the amount to be charged in respect thereof, in an accounting period, are usually based on the following three factors:

(i) historical cost or other amount substituted for the historical cost of the depreciable asset when the asset has been revalued;

(ii) expected useful life of the depreciable asset; and

(iii) estimated residual value of the depreciable asset.

The useful life of a depreciable asset is shorter than its physical life and is:

(i) pre-determined by legal or contractual limits, such as the expiry dates of related leases;

(ii) directly governed by extraction or consumption;

(iii) dependent on the extent of use and physical deterioration on account of wear and tear, which again depends on operational factors, such as, the number of shifts for which the asset is to be used, repair and maintenance policy of the enterprise, etc.; and

(iv) reduced by obsolescence arising from such factors as:

  (a) technological changes;

  (b) improvement in production methods;

  (c) change in market demand for the product or service output of the asset; or

  (d) legal or other restrictions.

The determination of the useful life of a depreciable asset is a matter of estimation and is normally based on various factors including experience with similar types of assets.

The Statute governing an enterprise may provide the basis for computation of the depreciation. If the management's estimate of the useful life of an asset of the enterprise is shorter than as envisaged under the provisions of the relevant Statute, then, depreciation provision is appropriately computed by applying a higher rate. If the management's estimate of the useful life of the asset, is longer than as envisaged under the Statute, then, the depreciation rate, lower than as envisaged by the Statute, can be applied only in accordance with the requirements of the Statute.

The management should estimate the useful lives of the relevant assets constructed on the leasehold land on the basis of the considerations discussed above. Thus, the useful life will be the expected period of the lease of the land, including the expected period of extension which is reasonably certain at the inception of the lease. The depreciation rate should be worked out on that basis. If the rate so worked out is lower than the rate specified in the Statute, the rate specified in the Statute should be adopted. (*EAC opinion, 27.2*)

9.9 DEPRECIATION ON ASSET ESCAPING DUTY

Depreciation should be charged on prospective basis, where the change in historical cost of the asset is due to change in liability on the account of the exchange fluctuations, price adjustments, changes in duties or similar factors. The aforesaid changes in historical cost are caused by factors which are basically beyond the control of the management at the time the change takes place as these are triggered by market forces, suppliers, government, etc. In other words, the changes in historical cost are not brought about by the actions or omissions to act on the part of the management. Thus, the nature of change in historical cost of the fixed asset as stated above is different from that of the revision of the historical cost, for example, an asset escaping duty is not of the nature of change in historical cost of the fixed asset on account of change in the duty. Accordingly, the depreciation should be worked out on retrospective basis, i.e., the depreciation in respect of the past years, since the acquisition of the asset, should be charged in the profit and loss account of the current year and should be disclosed as a prior period item in accordance with AS 5, '*Prior Period and Extraordinary Items and Changes in Accounting Policies*'. Prior period items should be separately disclosed in the current statement of profit and loss, together with their nature and amount, in a manner that their impact on current profit or loss can be perceived. (*EAC Opinion, 16.24*)

9.10 PERFORMANCE GUARANTEE

In case of performance guarantees invoked by an enterprise (where the supplier of fixed asset was subject to liquidated damages in case of performance failure), which is in dispute, the most appropriate course of action should be to keep the amount of guarantees invoked in a suspense account till such time, that, the dispute is settled. In case the dispute is settled in favour of the company, it should be appropriate to effect change in the historical cost of the fixed asset(s) concerned, to the extent the liquidated damages represents reduction in the standard of performance. The total guarantee amount received can be apportioned amongst the various items of plant and machinery concerned on a reasonable basis, for example, in proportion of gross value of the various items of plant and machinery concerned. The depreciation charge for future years would require to be suitably adjusted to take account of the change in the historical cost of fixed assets. That part of the liquidated damages which does not represent reduction in the standard of performance, should be treated as other income and should be disclosed as an 'Extraordinary Item' as recommended in AS 5, '*Prior Period and Extraordinary Items and Changes in Accounting Policies*'. However, if it is not possible to ascertain the extent of the amount of penalty (i.e., the amount not attributable to reduction in the standard of performance), the entire amount should be deducted from the cost of the assets concerned. (*EAC Opinion, 8.1.39*)

9.11 DEPRECIATION ON FREEHOLD LAND HAVING MINERAL RESERVES AND THE INTERNAL ROADS CONSTRUCTED IN THE MINE AREA

As per the GAAPs prevalent in India, freehold land is considered to have an unlimited life and, therefore, cost thereof, is not depreciated. In case of a land where after complete extraction of minerals, the land does not have any economic use to the company and if it is clearly evident that such land can never be put to any other use, such land should be considered to have limited useful life.

If the sole purpose of acquisition of land is to exploit it for extraction of mineral resources and extraction of such minerals is the only economic use of the land for the company, the useful life of the freehold land should be governed by the extractable minerals available on the land and extraction thereof. In other words, it should be more appropriate to depreciate the freehold land on the basis of units of minerals extracted, *viz.,* 'Units of Production' method. Accordingly, the cost of acquisition of freehold land, in the extant case, should be depreciated on the basis of the actual quantity of minerals extracted during a period as against the estimated quantity of extractable mineral reserves. At times, the estimated quantity of mineral reserves also undergoes changes due to subsequent developments, such as, information about the probability of finding additional reserves or information confirming the existence of the estimated quantity of reserves, etc. Accordingly, the company should periodically review the estimated unextracted quantity of reserves and it should be used prospectively as the basis of calculating the depreciation of the freehold land. In case the right to extract mineral reserves is also subject to the term of the mining lease, while calculating/reviewing the depreciation for a period, the remaining lease period and the reasonable certainty for its extension in the future should also be taken into account.

The internal said roads in the mine area have an independent useful life which would not only depend upon the minerals mined, but, even on other factors, such as, wear and tear due to weathering effect, etc. Accordingly, the application of the Units of Production method for depreciation of roads is not appropriate and the same should be depreciated separately, based on their useful life. (*EAC Opinion 31.5*)

9.12 ACCOUNTING FOR EXPENDITURE ON SHARED INFRASTRUCTURE FACILITIES AND DEPRECIATION THEREON

It is only an addition or extension which retains a separate identity and is capable of being used after the existing asset is disposed of, and is accounted for and depreciated independently on the basis of an estimate of its own useful life. However, in the present case, such expenditure is not creating any new asset which is separately identifiable, but, such asset will be used beyond useful life assessed for power plants at Stage 1. Accordingly, it should be capitalised with the cost of the existing assets concerned. Further, in case such expenditure results in the increase of the useful life of the concerned asset, the unamortised depreciable amount of the concerned assets, alongwith, the expenditure incurred, should be charged over the revised remaining useful life. Such depreciation should be charged with reference to the 'useful life' and not with reference to 'physical life' of the asset. Had such expenditure on infrastructure facility resulted into replacement of existing infrastructure facilities, then such expenditure would have been capitalised while derecognising the carrying amount of the assets that have been replaced. Further, the costs, thus capitalised would have been depreciated over the useful life of replaced asset.

As regards inclusion of the depreciation charged on the assets used in the construction activity of Stage 2 in the cost of the asset(s) capitalised under Stage 2, to the extent the asset is being used for construction activity, depreciation on the asset is a directly attributable cost of bringing the asset to its working condition for its intended use and accordingly, it should be capitalised with the cost of the asset(s) being constructed. However, the directly attributable cost can be capitalised if the same has been incurred for bringing the asset to its working condition for its intended use. Thus, the depreciation should be capitalised only to the extent to which an asset is actually used for construction activity and any further depreciation incurred after the date of commercial production of the asset(s) being constructed should be charged to the statement of profit and loss.

The company can capitalise the additional expenditure on common infrastructure facilities during Stage 2 as it will increase the future benefits from the existing asset beyond its previously assessed standard of performance. However, since such expenditure is not creating any new asset which is separately identifiable, it should be capitalised with the cost of the existing asset concerned. Further, in case such expenditure results into increase in the useful life of the concerned asset, the unamortised depreciable amount of the concerned asset along with the expenditure incurred should be charged over the revised remaining useful life. (*Recent Opinion 22 on ICAI Website*)

Chapter 10

Disclosure requirements under the Companies Act, 2013

10.1 DISCLOSURE CHECKLIST

Having regard to the fact that Schedule III of the Companies Act, 2013 provides that the disclosure requirements contained in Schedule III are in addition to and not in substitution of the disclosure requirements specified in accounting standards, the following checklist can be used for complying with depreciation related disclosure requirements:

Disclosure checklist as per AS 10 (Revised) read with Guidance Note on Accounting for Depreciation in companies in the context of Schedule II to the Companies Act, 2013) (relating to depreciation)

(*It may be noted that disclosure checklist as per AS 10 (Revised) is same as that of Ind AS 16*)

S. No.	Particulars	Yes	No	N/A
1.	Whether the enterprise has disclosed the following? (a) depreciation, whether recognised in profit or loss or as a part of the cost of other assets, during a period; and (b) accumulated depreciation at the end of the period. (c) depreciation methods used (d) The useful lives or the depreciation rates used- (AS 10 (Revised) on 'Property Plant and Equipment')- In case the useful lives or the depreciation rates used are different from those specified in the Statute governing the enterprise, it should make a specific mention of that fact (this requirement is specific to only AS 10 (Revised). Ind AS 16 doesn't require this disclosure). In this regard, following disclosures should be made: (i) Disclosure of assets alongwith their useful lives where different from those specified under Schedule II including where the useful life estimated as per			

S. No.	Particulars	Yes	No	N/A
	double/triple shift is different from that as would be estimated on the basis of increase in depreciation by 50% or 100% in case of double shift and triple shift respectively of single shift based depreciation. (ii) The fact that the said useful lives/residual values are supported by technical advice. **(Guidance Note on Accounting for Depreciation in companies in the context of Schedule II to the Companies Act, 2013)**			
2.	In case of changes in estimates with respect to: (a) residual values; (b) the estimated costs of dismantling, removing or restoring items of property, plant and equipment; (c) useful lives; and (d) depreciation methods Whether, an entity has disclosed the nature and effect of a change in an accounting estimate that has an effect in the current period or is expected to have an effect in subsequent periods in accordance with AS 5. (AS 10 (Revised) on 'Property Plant and Equipment')			

Disclosure checklist as per AS 26

S. No.	Particulars	Yes	No	N/A
Requirements as per AS 26				
1	Whether the financial statements have disclosed the following for each class of intangible assets, distinguishing between internally generated intangible assets and other intangible assets: (i) The useful lives or the amortisation rates used (ii) The amortisation methods used (iii) The gross carrying amount and the accumulated amortisation (aggregated with accumulated impairment losses) at the beginning and end of the period (iv) A reconciliation of the carrying amount at the beginning and the end of the period showing: (a) Additions, indicating separately those from internal development and through amalgamation (b) Retirements and disposals (c) Impairment losses recognised in the statement of profit and loss during the period			

S. No.	Particulars	Yes	No	N/A
	(if any) (d) Impairment losses reversed in the statement of profit and loss during the period (if any) (e) Amortisation recognised during the period (f) Other changes in the carrying amount during the period			
2	Whether the financial statements also disclosed the following: (i) (a) If an intangible asset is amortised over more than ten years, the reasons why it is presumed that the useful life of an intangible asset will exceed ten years from the date when the asset is available for use (b) In giving the reasons mentioned in (a) above, whether the enterprise has described the factor(s) that played a significant role in determining the useful life of the asset (i) A description, the carrying amount and remaining amortisation period of any individual intangible asset that is material to the financial statements of the enterprise as a whole			

Disclosure checklist as per the Companies Act, 2013

S. No.	Particulars	Yes	No	N/A
Requirements as per the Companies Act, 2013				
1	Whether depreciation methods used are disclosed in the financial statements?			
2	Whether the useful lives of the assets for computing depreciation, if they are different from the life specified in the Schedule have been disclosed?			

10.2 ILLUSTRATIVE DISCLOSURES ON DEPRECIATION

(*It may be noted that illustrative disclosures given in para 10.2.1 of this Chapter are based on the Companies Act, 1956. The purpose here is to give an idea of generally followed disclosure practices relating to depreciation.*

In para 10.2.2 of this Chapter, the illustrative disclosures based on the concept of useful life and component accounting under the Companies Act, 2013 have been given.)

10.2.1 Disclosures in practice under the regime of the Companies Act, 1956

1. A Limited

Depreciation/Amortisation

Leasehold land, leasehold buildings and improvements thereon, and other leased assets are amortised over the period of lease or their life, whichever is lower. Business and commercial rights are amortised at lower of the period during which the benefits arising out of these are expected to accrue and 10 years, while software products – others and goodwill arising on merger / acquired goodwill is amortised over a period of 5 years.

Software products (meant for sale) are amortized over a period of 10 years. Depreciation on other fixed assets is provided on straight-line method at the rates and in the manner prescribed in Schedule XIV to the Companies Act, 1956. In the case of some subsidiary companies, it is provided on straight-line basis over the estimated useful life of the assets given herein below:

Fixed Asset	Useful life in years
Leasehold improvements	1–5
Furniture, Fixtures and Equipment	3–8
Vehicles	3–8
Computers	1–6

2. B Limited

Depreciation is provided using the Straight-line method (SLM) rates as per the useful lives of the fixed assets as estimated by the management or those prescribed under the Schedule XIV to the Companies Act, 1956, whichever is higher. The company has used following rates to provide depreciation on its fixed assets:

Particulars	Rate of Depreciation (SLM)
Building	1.63%
Office equipment	4.75%
Plant and equipment	4.75–11.31%
Computers	4.75–16.21%
Furniture and fixtures	6.33%
Vehicles	9.50–11.31%
Leasehold land	Over the lease term on straight-line basis.
Assets costing less than INR 5,000	Fully depreciated in the year of acquisition

3. C Limited

All fixed assets are stated at cost of acquisition *less* accumulated depreciation / amortisation and impairment in value, if any. Cost comprises the purchase price and any other attributable cost of bringing the asset to its working condition for its intended use. Depreciation has been provided on the written down value (WDV) method at the rates specified in Schedule XIV of the Companies Act, 1956, except in respect of computers, photocopiers, facsimile machines, modems and appliances where depreciation has been provided at 80%, which are included in furniture, fittings and office equipment. Depreciation on addition/ deletion to fixed assets during the year is provided on a pro rata basis. Cost of purchased software and trademarks is amortised over a period of 3 to 5 years. Cost of leasehold land / improvement is amortised over the period of lease. Fixed Assets costing INR 5,000 or less are fully depreciated in the year of acquisition.

4. D LIMITED

Depreciation/Amortisation

(i) Depreciation is provided on straight-line method in accordance with Schedule XIV of the Companies Act, 1956.

(ii) Depreciation on addition/deletion from the assets during the year is provided on pro rata basis.

(iii) Depreciation on shuttering material is provided at 100 per cent on pro rata basis. Items costing below INR 5000 are provided at 100 per cent on pro rata basis / charged to the Statement of Profit and Loss.

(iv) Depreciation is charged on the historical cost of fixed assets (except for revalued assets) including taxes, duties and installation costs.

(v) Depreciation on revalued amount of fixed assets is being charged to the Revaluation Reserve Account.

(vi) Leasehold land is amortised over the period of lease.

5. E Limited

Depreciation and amortisation

Depreciation other than on capital work-in-progress is charged so as to write-off the cost of assets, on the following basis:

Type of asset	Method	Rate
Leasehold land	Straight line	1.63
Freehold and leasehold buildings	Straight line	1.63
Furniture and fixtures	Straight line	6.33
Computers and IT equipment	Straight line	16.21

Type of asset	Method	Rate
Motor Vehicles	Straight line	9.5
Office equipment	Straight line	4.75
Civil and plumbing work	Straight line	1.63

Depreciation is charged only from the date the asset concerned is put to use by the company. Fixed assets, individually costing INR 5,000 or less, have been fully depreciated in the year of purchase.

Intangible assets are amortised over the estimate useful life.

6. F Limited

Depreciation and Amortisation

Depreciation is charged on a pro rata basis at the straight-line method rates prescribed in Schedule XIV to the Companies Act, 1956, except in respect of the following, where the depreciation is charged based on the asset's estimated useful life: Computers - 4 years; Office equipment – 8 years; Moulds – 3 years. Individual assets, costing up to INR 5,000 each, are fully depreciated in the year of purchase.

Intangible assets, comprising expenditure on computer software, are amortised on a straight-line method over a period of 4 years.

7. G Limited

Depreciation and Amortisation

Depreciation on fixed assets is provided on straight-line method at the rates and in the manner specified in the Schedule XIV of the Indian Companies Act, 1956, except,:

(a) Certain items of plant and machinery (including computers) installed at and used in institutional projects, which are depreciated over the number of years till the completion of the period of the contract when the assets are transferred to those parties.

(b) Vehicles purchased under the 'Own Your Car' (OYC) scheme for the employees, which are depreciated over the period of the scheme.

(c) Goodwill arising on acquisition of business unit is amortised over a period of 10 years.

(d) Depreciation on buildings, computer hardware, software, courseware and furniture and fixtures acquired on or after 1 January 2006 is provided at the following rates based on estimated useful life:

Office premises	3.33%
Furniture and fixtures	20.00%
Computers Hardware, Software and Courseware	33.33%

(e) Depreciation on furniture and fixtures, which are installed at leasehold premises, are amortised over lease period

(f) Depreciation on the fixed assets added / disposed of / discarded during the year has been provided on pro rata basis with reference to the date of addition/disposition/discardation.

(g) Assets purchased during the year, whose acquisition cost is INR 5,000 or less, are depreciated fully in the month of purchase.

(h) The method/rates of depreciation which are different other than above, followed by any entities, if any, are disclosed by way of notes to accounts.

8. H Limited

Depreciation

Depreciation, other than on oil and gas producing properties, is provided on the written down value method at the rates prescribed in Schedule XIV to the Companies Act, 1956. Cost of certain fixed assets located in leasehold properties under the head 'Building and Furniture', as mentioned below, have been depreciated over their respective lease periods which is higher than the Schedule XIV rates.

Building and Furniture: Lease period - between 3 to 9 years.

Cost of certain fixed assets at estates under the head 'Buildings and Vehicles' are depreciated at rates based on the estimated life of each asset and the aggregate depreciation so calculated is higher than the Schedule XIV rates.

The following depreciation rates are considered and applied: Building 25% and 33.33% Vehicles 30%.

Capitalised software costs are amortised over its useful life of 5 years on a straight-line basis.

In respect of revalued assets the incremental depreciation on account of revaluation is recouped from Revaluation Reserve. Land and development, including leasehold land, are not depreciated.

Depreciation in respect of oil and gas producing assets is calculated on the capitalised cost according to the 'unit of production method', under which the oil and gas assets are written off at the same rate as the quantitative depletion of the related reserve. Unit of production depletion rates are revised when there is an indication of the need for revision based on revised reserve estimate, which is carried out once in a year. Such revisions are also accounted for prospectively to give effect in the books of account of the company.

Assets like buildings, plant and machinery, etc, included in oil and gas producing properties for which depreciation rates have been prescribed in Schedule XIV of the Companies Act, 1956 are depreciated on written down value method at the rates prescribed in Schedule XIV of the Companies Act, 1956. Other assets are depreciated according to the 'unit of production' method as prescribed by the Institute of Chartered Accountants of India in the 'Guidance Note on Accounting for Oil and Gas Producing Activities'.

9. I Pharma Limited

Depreciation is provided on the straight-line method, based on the useful life of the assets as estimated by the management which generally coincides with rates prescribed under Schedule XIV to the Companies Act, 1956, except assets acquired at the Bhiwadi unit in Rajasthan for which depreciation is provided on a straight-line basis, at the rates that are higher than those specified in Schedule XIV to the Companies Act, 1956 and are based on useful lives as estimated by management.

In these cases the rates are as under:

Leasehold buildings: 5%, Plant and machinery:20%

Assets costing below INR 5,000 are depreciated fully in the year of purchase.

10. J Logistics Limited

Depreciation and amortisation

Depreciation on fixed assets is provided under the straight-line method. The depreciation rates prescribed in Schedule XIV to the Companies Act, 1956 are considered as the minimum rates. Depreciation on additions to fixed assets has been calculated on pro rata basis. Individual low cost assets (acquired for INR 5,000 or less) are fully depreciated in the year of acquisition. The company has used the following rates to provide depreciation:

Rates (SLM):

Office premises	1.63%
Plant and machinery	4.75%
Office equipment	4.75%
Furniture and fixtures	6.33%
Vehicles:	
Motor cars	9.50 %
Motor trucks	11.31 %
Computer and software	16.21 %

11. K Bank Limited

Depreciation is provided on the straight-line method from the date of addition. The rates of depreciation, as prescribed in Schedule XIV to the Companies Act, 1956, are considered as the minimum rates. If the management's estimate of the useful life of a fixed asset at the time of acquisition of the asset or of the remaining useful life on a subsequent review is shorter, then depreciation is provided at a higher rate, based on the management's estimate of the useful life / remaining useful life. Pursuant to this policy, depreciation has been provided using the following estimated useful life:

Asset	Estimated useful life
Owned premises	61 years
Assets given on operating lease	20 years
Computer hardware including printers	3 years
Application software	5 years
Vehicles	4 years
EPABX, telephone instruments	8 years
CCTV and video conferencing equipment	3 years
Mobile phone	2 years
Locker cabinets/cash safe /strong room door	16 years
Modem, scanner, routers, hubs, switches, racks/cabinets for IT equipment	5 years
UPS, VSAT, fax machines	5 years
Cheque book/cheque encoder, currency counting machine, fake note detector	5 years
Assets at staff residence	3 years
All other fixed assets	10 years

All fixed assets individually costing less than INR 5,000 are fully depreciated in the year of installation.

Depreciation on assets sold during the year is recognised on a pro rata basis to the profit and loss account till the date of sale.

The carrying amounts of assets are reviewed at each balance sheet date to ascertain if there is any indication of impairment based on internal/external factors. An impairment loss is recognised wherever the carrying amount of an asset exceeds its recoverable amount. The recoverable amount is the greater of the asset's net selling price and value in use. In assessing value in use, the estimated future cash flows are discounted to their present value at the weighted average cost of capital. After impairment, depreciation is provided on the revised carrying amount of the asset over its remaining useful life.

Profit on sale of premises is appropriated to the capital reserve account in accordance with RBI's instructions.

12. L Auto Limited

Fixed assets

(i) Fixed assets are carried at cost of acquisition or construction cost and includes amount added on fair valuation, less accumulated depreciation (except freehold land), amortisation and impairment loss, if any.

(ii) Expenditure during construction period incurred on the projects under implementation is treated as pre-operative expenses pending allocation to the assets, and is included under 'capital work-in-progress'. These expenses are apportioned to fixed assets on commencement of commercial production. Capital work-in-progress is stated at the amount expended up to the date of balance sheet.

Depreciation

(i) Depreciation on fixed assets (including on revalued portion on fair value) has been provided as under:

(a) Plant & Machinery and Aircraft:

These are depreciated on straight-line method basis, at the rates and in the manner specified in Schedule XIV to the Companies Act, 1956.

(b) Other Assets (except clause 'c' below):

These are depreciated on written down value basis at the rates and in the manner specified in Schedule XIV to the Companies Act, 1956.

(c) Intangible assets, represented by computer software, are being amortised over a period of 5 years.

(d) Leasehold land is amortised over the lease period.

(ii) Depreciation on assets added, sold or discarded during the year has been provided on pro rata basis.

13. M Limited

Depreciation is provided following the straight-line method. Rates of depreciation are in accordance with the provisions of the Companies Act, 1956, as prevailing from time to time, except for items covered under paragraphs (g) and (h) below.

(g) The company reviews the depreciation policies followed for various items of assets, their useful life and circumstances prevailing in the business so as to make a more appropriate preparation or presentation of the financial statements. Necessary adjustment is made in the depreciation charge for the assets, if any significant variation is noticed in the pattern of economic benefits embodied in the assets.

Based on technical review, (i) certain items of electrical installations and equipment, furniture and fittings, and typewriter, accounting machine, and office equipment, are being depreciated at 15%, 20% and 20% per annum respectively; (ii) mobile phones at 50% per annum; (iii) motor cars at 20% per annum (iv) portable personal computers at 50% per annum; (v) items given to employees under the furniture equipment scheme at 25% per annum for computers and 15% per annum for other items; and (vi) assets whose actual cost does not exceed INR 5000, at the rate of 100% in the year of addition of the asset, irrespective of the date of addition.

(h) Machinery spares, which can be used only in connection with an item of fixed asset and whose use is expected to be irregular, are treated as fixed assets and depreciated over a period of 5 years (by charging depreciation at 20% per annum on straight-line basis) or the residual life of the principal asset, whichever is lower.

14. N Cropscience Limited

Depreciation on tangible assets is provided on straight-line method, based on the following useful lives of the assets, which are s of the rates prescribed in Schedule XIV to the Act.

Assets	Useful Lives in years
Buildings	20 to 29
Plant and equipment	9 to 12
Furniture and Fixtures	10
Vehicles	8
Office Equipment	10
Computers	5

Leasehold land and leasehold improvement are amortised over the period of lease. Depreciation on assets costing INR 5,000 or less is provided at the rate of 100% in the year of acquisition of the assets.

15. O Power Limited

Depreciation is provided on straight-line basis at the rates and in the manner prescribed in Schedule XIV to the Companies Act, 1956.

Leasehold land is stated at historical cost less amounts written off proportionate to expired lease period.

Spares of the nature of capital/insurance spares are added to the cost of the assets. The total cost of such spares is depreciated over a period not exceeding the useful life of the fixed asset to which they relate.

16. P Heavy Electrical Limited

Depreciation

(i) Depreciation on fixed assets (other than those used abroad under contract) is charged up to the total cost of the assets on straight-line method as per the rates prescribed in Schedule XIV of the Companies Act, 1956, except where depreciation is charged at rates determined on the basis of the technically assessed estimated useful lives shown hereunder:

	Single Shift	Double Shift	Triple Shift
General Plant & Machinery	8%	12%	16%
Automatic/Semi-Automatic Machines	10%	15%	20%
Erection Equipment, Capital Tools & Tackles	20%		
Township Buildings – Second Class	2.5%		
– Third Class	3.5%		
Railway Sidings	8%		
Locomotives & Wagons	8%		
Electrical Installations	8%		
Office & Other Equipment	8%		
Drainage, Sewerage & Water Supply	3.34%		
Electronic Data, Processing Equipment	20%		

In respect of additions to / deductions from the fixed assets, depreciation is charged on pro rata monthly basis.

(ii) Fixed assets used outside India pursuant to long-term contracts are depreciated over the duration of the initial contract.

(iii) Fixed assets costing INR 10,000 or less and those whose written down value as at the beginning of the year is INR 10,000 or less, are depreciated fully. In so far as township buildings are concerned, the cost per tenement is the basis for the limit of INR 10,000.

(iv) At erection/project sites: The cost of roads, bridges and culverts is fully amortised over the tenure of the contract, while sheds, railway sidings, electrical installations and other similar enabling works (other than purely temporary erections, wooden structures) are so depreciated after retaining 10% as residual value.

(v) Purely temporary erection, such as wooden structures, is fully depreciated in the year of construction.

(vi) Leasehold land and buildings are amortised over the period of lease. Buildings constructed on land taken on lease are depreciated over their useful life or the lease period, whichever is earlier.

17. Q Universal Limited

(a) Depreciation on fixed assets has been provided on straight-line method at the rates specified in Schedule XIV of the Companies Act, 1956, except that:

(i) Leased vehicles, which are depreciated over 4 years and Lease hold improvements are depreciated over 6 years, are depreciated at a rate higher than Schedule XIV rates.

(ii) In respect of assets held by Indian Subsidiaries and Overseas Subsidiaries, Joint Ventures and Associates, depreciation is provided based on the estimated useful life of those assets as estimated by the respective Companies.

(iii) Assets held by Ciria India Ltd (joint venture) are depreciated at Schedule XIV rates on written down value basis.

(iv) The difference between the depreciation for the year on the revalued assets and depreciation calculated on the original cost is recouped from the fixed assets revaluation reserve.

(b) Intangible assets are amortised over the estimated useful life of the assets on straight line basis.

18. R Oil Limited

Depreciation is provided pro rata to the period of use on straight-line method based on the estimated useful lives of the assets, which have been determined by management, as stated below. These rates of depreciation are higher than the rates specified under Schedule XIV of the Companies Act, 1956.

Fixed assets	Useful lives	Fixed assets	Useful lives
Residential and office building	25 years	Office equipment	10 years
Factory building	30 years	Computers	4 years
Plant and machinery	10 years to 21 years	Vehicles	4 years
Intangibles:		Workshop equipment	2to 4 years
Moulds	4 years		
Furniture and Fixtures	8 years	* Dealer Boards	3 years

*Workshop equipment, provided against sales agreements, is depreciated over the standard period of agreement. Assets, individually costing less than INR 5,000, are fully depreciated in the year of acquisition.

19. S Rating Agency Limited

Depreciation is provided using the straight-line method ('SLM'), as per the useful lives of the assets estimated by the management, or at the rates prescribed under Schedule XIV of the Companies Act, 1956, whichever is higher.

	Rates (SLM)	Schedule XIV Rates (SLM)
Assets	5.00%	1.63%
Buildings	10.00%	6.33%
Furniture and fixtures	10.00%	4.75%
Office Equipment	33.33%	16.21%
Computers	33.33%	9.50%
Vehicles	5.00%	1.63%

Leasehold improvements are amortised over the lease term or useful life of the asset, whichever is less. Leasehold improvements are amortised over the period of 8.5 years to 9 years in the current year.

Fixed assets, having original cost of less than INR 5,000 individually, are depreciated fully in the year/period of purchase.

20. T Shipping Company Limited

Depreciation/Amortisation

(i) Depreciation on fixed assets including assets created on leasehold land is provided on 'straight-line method' at the rates and in the manner prescribed in Schedule XIV of the Companies Act, 1956, except for roads, pavements, boundary wall, warehouses and electrical fittings of terminals on which depreciation has been provided at 3.34% and 10.34% respectively and for upgraded BFKI Wagons at 6.79%.

(ii) Leasehold land other than acquired on perpetual lease is amortised over the period of lease. Leasehold buildings are amortised over the period of lease or useful life of the building, whichever is less, as per rates prescribed under Schedule XIV.

(iii) Capital expenditure on enabling assets, like roads, culverts and electricity transmissions, etc, the ownership of which is not with the company, is charged off to revenue in the accounting period of incurrence of such expenditure. However, capital expenditure on enabling assets, ownership of which rests with the company and which have been created on land not belonging to the company, is written off to the P&L Account over its approximate period of utility or over a period of 5 years, whichever is less. For this purpose, land is not considered to be belonging to the company, if the same is not owned or leased/licensed to the company.

21. U Coal Company Limited

Depreciation

Depreciation on fixed assets is provided on straight-line method at the rates and manner specified in Schedule XIV of the Companies Act, 1956 (as amended) except for telecommunication equipment. Depreciation on such equipment is charged over the technically estimated life, at higher rates, viz.: at 15.83% p.a. and at 10.55% p.a.

Further, depreciation on certain equipment/HEMM is charged over the technically estimated life at higher rates, viz., at 11.88%; 13.57% and 15.83%, as applicable.

Depreciation on SDL and LHD (equipment) is charged at 19% p.a. and 15.83% p.a. respectively on the basis of technical estimation.

Depreciation on the assets added / disposed of during the year is provided on pro rata basis with reference to the month of addition/disposal, except on those assets attracting 100% depreciation p.a. (SLM basis), which are fully depreciated in the year of their addition.

Value of land acquired under Coal Bearing Area (Acquisition & Development) Act, 1957 is amortised on the basis of the balance life of the project. Value of leasehold land is amortised on the basis of lease period or balance life of the project, whichever is earlier.

Prospecting, boring and development expenditure are amortised from the year when the mine is brought under revenue in 20 years or working life of the project, whichever is less.

22. V Construction Company Limited

Depreciation on fixed assets is provided under written down value method at the rates specified in Schedule XIV to the Companies Act, 1956 except for the variations in respect of the following items:

- Office equipment - 40%
- Temporary structures / interiors - 20%

23. W Petroleum Company Limited

(a) Depreciation on fixed assets is provided in accordance with the rates as specified in Schedule XIV to the Companies Act, 1956, on straight-line method, up to 95% of the cost of the asset, other than insurance spares, which are depreciated up to 100%. Depreciation is charged pro rata on quarterly basis on assets, from/up to the quarter of capitalisation/sale, disposal and dismantled during the year.

(b) Assets costing not more than INR 5000 each are depreciated in full in the year of addition.

(c) Capital expenditure on assets, on which the ownership and control that does not vest with the company are charged to revenue in the year in which it is incurred.

(d) Cost of leasehold land (including premium) for 99 years or less is amortised during the lease period.

24. X Real Estate Company Limited

Depreciation on assets (including buildings and related equipment rented out and included under current assets as inventories) is provided on straight-line method at the rates and in the manner prescribed in Schedule XIV to the Companies Act, 1956.

(i) Capital work-in-progress (including intangible assets under development) represents expenditure incurred in respect of capital projects/intangible assets under development and are carried at cost. Cost includes land, related acquisition expenses, development/ construction costs, borrowing costs and other direct expenditure.

(ii) Leasehold land, under perpetual lease, is not amortised. Leasehold land, other than on perpetual lease, are being amortised on time-proportion basis over their respective lease periods.

25. Y Oil Company Limited

Depreciation on plant and machinery is provided as per straight-line method. All other assets are depreciated as per written down value method. Depreciation is computed at the rates based on the estimated useful lives of the assets or at the rates provided under Schedule XIV of the Companies Act, 1956, whichever is higher.

Depreciation on additions/deductions to fixed assets made during the year is provided on a pro-rata basis from/up to the date of such additions/deductions, as the case may be.

Cost of assets purchased and/or constructed by the company whose ownership vests with others by virtue of a contract or otherwise, are amortised at the higher of rates based on the estimated useful lives of the assets or the contract period, or at the rates provided under Schedule XIV of the Companies Act, 1956.

26. Z Engineering Company Limited

Depreciation on tangible fixed assets is provided, on straight-line method on plant and machinery and on written down value method on all other fixed assets, on the basis of the depreciation rates prescribed in Schedule XIV of the Companies Act, 1956 or based on useful life of the asset, whichever is higher.

Intangible assets are amortised using the straight-line method over their estimated useful life as under:

(i) Software and Licenses: over a period of 6 years

(ii) Technical know-how: over a period of 6 years from the date of actual production.

27. AB Banking Company Limited

Depreciation is charged over the estimated useful life of the fixed asset on a straight-line basis. The rates of depreciation for certain key fixed assets, which are not lower than the rates prescribed in Schedule XIV of the Companies Act, 1956, are given below:

Asset	Depreciation rate per annum
Owned premises	1.63%
VSATs	10.00%
ATMs	10.00%
Office equipment	16.21%
Computers	33.33%
Motor cars	25.00%
Software and system development expenditure	20.00%
Assets at residences of executives of the Bank	25.00%

Improvements to leasehold premises are charged off over the remaining primary period of lease.

Items (excluding staff assets), costing less than INR 5,000, and point-of-sale terminals are fully depreciated in the year of purchase.

All other assets are depreciated as per the rates specified in Schedule XIV of the Companies Act, 1956. For assets purchased and sold during the year, depreciation is provided on pro rata basis by the bank.

The bank undertakes assessment of the useful life of an asset at periodic intervals taking into account changes in environment, changes in technology, the utility and efficacy of the asset in use, etc. Whenever there is a revision of the estimated useful life of an asset, the unamortised depreciable amount is charged over the revised remaining useful life of the said asset.

28. AC Automation Company Limited

Depreciation on fixed assets is computed on straight-line method over their useful lives at rates which are higher than the rates prescribed under Schedule XIV of the

Companies Act, 1956. The estimated useful lives for various fixed assets are as follows:

Class of Asset	Useful Life
Buildings	30 years
Plant and Machinery	10 years
Demo Equipment	4 years
Computers	3 years
Office Equipment	5–6 years
Furniture and Fixtures	5–10 years
Vehicles	4–5 years
Intangible Assets (Software)	3 years

The following assets are depreciated/amortised on a straight-line method over the period of their estimated useful lives:

Product distribution rights – HSPL are amortised over a period of 10 years and the amount so amortised is included in depreciation.

Total Asset Management (TAM) assets are depreciated over the life of the respective contracts, or 7 years, whichever is earlier.

Assets installed in leased premises are depreciated over 4 years representing average life of the lease for such premises. Assets costing INR 5,000 or less are depreciated fully in the year of purchase.

If the useful life of an asset is ascertained to be lower than was previously determined, the carrying value of the asset is depreciated over the revised residual life of the asset.

29. AD Communication Limited

Depreciation, Amortisation and Impairment

(a) Depreciation is provided for on buildings (including buildings taken on lease) and plant and machinery on straight-line method and on other fixed assets on written down value method at the rates prescribed in the Schedule XIV of the Companies Act, 1956.

(b) Depreciation due to increase or decrease in the liability on account of exchange fluctuation or on account of rollover charges on forward exchange contract is provided prospectively over the residual life of the assets.

(c) On assets acquired on lease (including improvements to the leasehold premises), depreciation has been provided for on straight-line method at the rates as per Schedule XIV of the Companies Act, 1956 or at the rates worked out on the basis of remaining useful life of the assets, whichever is higher.

(d) Premium on leasehold land is amortised over the period of lease.

(e) The technical know-how fee is written off over a period of 6 years from the year of the commencement of commercial production of the respective projects. If the production has not commenced and the benefit of know-how is unlikely to accrue, the fee paid therefore is fully written off in the year in which it is so determined.

(f) Intangible assets are amortised over a period of 5 years or life of the product considered at the end of each financial year, whichever is earlier. Amortisation commences when the asset is available for use.

(g) At the balance sheet date, an impairment loss is recognised whenever the carrying amount of an asset exceeds its recoverable amount.

30. AE Chemical Company Limited

Depreciation on fixed assets situated at Liluah Unit – I (Howrah), Vapi and Vizag is provided on written down value method and on other fixed assets is provided on straight-line method at the rates and in the manner specified in Schedule XIV to the Companies Act, 1956.

(a) The carrying amounts of assets are reviewed at each balance sheet date if there is any indication of impairment based on internal/external factors. An impairment loss is recognised wherever the carrying amount of an asset exceeds its recoverable amount. The recoverable amount is the higher of the asset's net selling price and value in use, which is determined by the present value of the estimated future cash flows.

(b) Cost of the fixed assets that are not yet ready for their intended use at the balance sheet date together with all related expenses and advances paid to acquire fixed assets are shown under capital work-in-progress.

31. AF Media Company Limited

Depreciation on fixed assets is calculated on straight-line basis using the rates arrived at based on the useful lives estimated by management. The company has used following useful lives for the fixed assets:

Asset category	Useful life
Building	30 years
Ownership flats	62 years
Plant and equipment	2–21 years
Furniture and fixtures	2–16 years
Vehicles	3–11 years
Information technology and related equipment	2–7 years

Asset category	Useful life
Intangible assets:	
• Brands/trademarks	5 years
• Website costs	5 years
• Computer software	3–5 years
Leasehold improvements	Over the lease period or estimated useful life, whichever is shorter.

32. AG Media Company Limited

Depreciation on revalued buildings is recognised in profit or loss. On the subsequent sale or retirement of a revalued property, the attributable revaluation surplus remaining in the properties revaluation reserve is transferred directly to retained earnings.

Freehold land is not depreciated.

Fixtures and equipment are stated at cost less accumulated depreciation and accumulated impairment losses.

Depreciation is recognised so as to write off the cost or valuation of assets (other than freehold land and properties under construction) less their residual values over their useful lives, using the straight line method. The estimated useful lives, residual values and depreciation method are reviewed at the end of each reporting period, with the effect of any changes in estimate accounted for on a prospective basis.

Assets held under finance leases are depreciated over their expected useful lives on the same basis as owned assets. However, when there is no reasonable certainty that ownership will be obtained by the end of lease term, assets are depreciated over the shorter of the lease term and their useful lives.

33. AG Media Company Limited

Land is not depreciated. Depreciation on other assets is calculated using the straight line method to allocate their costs or revalued amounts to their residual values over their estimated useful lives, as follows:

Buildings 25-40 years

Machinery10-15 years

Vehicles3-5 years

Furniture, fittings and equipment3-8 years

The assets' residual values and useful lives are reviewed, and adjusted if appropriate, at the end of each reporting period.

An assets' carrying amount is written down immediately to its recoverable amount if the asset's carrying amount is greater than its estimated recoverable amount.

When revalued assets are sold, the amounts included in other reserves are transferred to retained earnings.

10.2.2 Disclosures incorporating the concept of useful life and component accounting

(a) A Limited

Land is assumed to have an indefinite useful life and is, therefore, not depreciated. Depreciation of wind turbines is undertaken on a straight-line basis down to the asset's estimated residual value and over the asset's expected useful life. The depreciation of wind turbines is initiated in conjunction with the takeover from the supplier. For the calculation of depreciation according to plan, the following useful lives are applied:

- Buildings: 20 years
- Wind turbines: 25 years
- Other equipment: 3–5 years

(b) B Limited

The Group's policy is to write off the difference between the cost of each item of property, plant and equipment and its residual value over its estimated useful life on a straight-line basis. Assets under construction are not depreciated.

Reviews are made annually of the estimated remaining lives and residual values of individual productive assets, taking account of commercial and technological obsolescence as well as normal wear and tear. Under this policy it becomes impractical to calculate average asset lives exactly. However, the total lives range from approximately 10 to 50 years for buildings, and 3 to 13 years for plant and equipment. All items of property, plant and equipment are tested for impairment when there are indications that the carrying value may not be recoverable. Any impairment losses are recognised immediately in profit.

(c) C Limited

If an item of property and equipment comprises major components with different useful lives, the components are accounted for as separate items of plant and equipment.

Stripping cost

Stripping costs incurred during the mining production phase are allocated between cost of inventory produced and the existing mine asset. Stripping costs are allocated as a component of the mine asset when they represent significantly improved access to ore. Stripping costs include such activities as removal of vegetation as well as digging the actual pit for mining the ore.

A component of an item of property, plant and equipment with a significantly differing useful life and a cost that is significant in relation to the item is depreciated separately.

(d) D Limited

Tangible fixed assets

The acquisition value of assets is divided into material components and each component must be amortised separately over its estimated useful life, ie component depreciation. This applies to buildings as well as to machines and equipment.

(e) E Limited

Depreciation is provided on components that have homogenous useful lives by using the straight-line method so as to depreciate the initial cost down to the residual value over the estimated useful lives.

(f) F Limited

To the extent that an asset consists of components which differ materially in respect of their useful lives, these are written off separately (component depreciation).

(g) G Limited

If the costs of certain components of an item of property, plant and equipment are significant in relation to the total cost of the item, they are accounted for and depreciated separately.

(h) H Limited

Depreciation is based on the cost of an asset less its residual value. Significant components of individual assets are assessed and if a component has a useful life, which is different from the remainder of that asset, then that component is depreciated separately.

Depreciation is recognised in the income statement on a straight-line basis over the estimated useful lives of each component of an item of property and equipment.

The estimated useful lives for the current and comparative periods are as follows:

- technology hardware: 3–5 years
- broadband networks: term of agreement up to 25 years
- computer software: 2–10 years
- furniture and fixtures: 3–10 years; and
- leasehold improvements: 10 years.

(i) I Limited

Passenger ships

For all passenger ships, hotel and catering components are depreciated on a straight-line basis over 10 years. For fast ferries, hull and machinery components are depreciated on a straight-line basis over an estimated useful life of 15 years. For conventional ferries, hull and machinery components are depreciated over an initial estimated useful life of 30 years but this is reviewed on a periodic basis for vessels remaining in service 25 years after original construction.

Dry docking

Costs incurred in renewing the vessel passenger certificate are capitalised as a separate component within passenger ships and depreciated over the period to expiry of certificate.

(j) J Limited

Property, plant and equipment

Property, plant and equipment are recorded at cost. Major components of heavy construction equipment in use such as engines and drive trains are recorded separately.

(k) K Limited

Tangible fixed assets

The determining factor whether an incremental expenditure is added to cost is whether it relates to the replacement of identifiable components, or parts thereof. If so, the cost is capitalised. Even in cases where a new component is created, the expenditure is added to cost. Any un-depreciated carrying amount of replaced components, or parts of components, is disposed of and expensed in connection with the replacement. Repairs are expensed as incurred.

(l) L Limited

Depreciation

The estimated useful lives are as follows:

Asset	Basis	Useful life
Land improvements	Straight line	30 years
Buildings and improvements	Straight line	10 to 25 years
Leasehold improvements	Straight line	Lesser of estimated useful life or lease term
Construction equipment	Straight line	10 to 20 years
Automotive equipment	Straight line	5 years

Asset	Basis	Useful life
Office furniture and equipment	Straight line	3 to 5 years
Computer hardware	Straight line	1 to 3 years
Equipment components	Straight line	1.5 to 3 years

(m) M Limited

Depreciation principles

Depreciation is reported on a straight-line basis in the income statement over the estimated useful life of the assets. The Group applies component depreciation, which means that the components' estimated useful life provides the basis for the straight-line depreciation. Estimated useful lives are unchanged compared with the preceding year for all property, plant and equipment. Estimated useful lives are described further in Note 24 to the consolidated accounts, property, plant and equipment.

(n) N Limited

Depreciation charges on property, plant and equipment are based on the expected useful lives of its components. In detail, the following useful lives are applied:

Useful life	Years
Residential, office, plant and other plant facilities	20–50
Hydroplant buildings	75
Machinery	6–75
Electrical installations	5–33
Power lines	50
Office and plant equipment	4–10

Chapter 11

Other Provisions in the Companies Act, 2013 involving the use of depreciation

11.1 NET WORTH

Meaning as per section 2(57) of the Companies Act, 2013:

'Net worth' means:

Aggregate value of the following:

- paid-up share capital;
- all reserves created out of the profits; and
- securities premium account

After *deducting* the aggregate value of the following:

- accumulated losses;
- deferred expenditure; and
- miscellaneous expenditure not written off, as per the audited balance sheet

Note: It does not include reserves created out of revaluation of assets, write-back of depreciation and amalgamation.

Section 2(29A) of the Companies Act, 1956 defined 'net worth' as the sum total of the paid-up capital and free reserves after deducting the provisions or expenses, as may be prescribed.

As per the Explanation to section 2(29A) of the Companies Act, 1956, 'free reserves' means all reserves created out of the profits and share premium account but does not include reserves created out of revaluation of assets, write-back of depreciation provisions and amalgamation.

Thus, now, it has been specifically prescribed that aggregate value of the accumulated losses, deferred expenditure and miscellaneous expenditure not written off as per the audited balance sheet should be deducted while calculating the net worth.

It may also be noted that the definition of 'free reserves' has significantly changed now. Section 2(43) of the Companies Act, 2013 defines 'free reserves' as such reserves which, as per the latest audited balance sheet of a company, are available for distribution as dividend, provided that,:

(i) any amount representing unrealised gains, notional gains or revaluation of assets, whether shown as a reserve or otherwise, or

(ii) any change in carrying amount of an asset or of a liability recognised in equity, including surplus in profit and loss account on measurement of the asset or the liability at fair value,

will not be treated as free reserves.

11.2 DECLARATION OF DIVIDEND

Section 123 of the Companies Act, 2013 provides that,

(1) No dividend should be declared or paid by a company for any financial year except:

(*a*) out of the profits of the company for that year arrived at after providing for depreciation in accordance with the provisions of sub-section (*2*), or out of the profits of the company for any previous financial year or years arrived at after providing for depreciation in accordance with the provisions of that sub-section and remaining undistributed, or out of both; or

(*b*) out of money provided by the Central Government or a State Government for the payment of dividend by the company in pursuance of a guarantee given by that Government.

(2) For the purposes of clause (*a*) of sub-section (*1*), depreciation should be provided in accordance with the provisions of Schedule II.

This section seeks to provide that dividend will be declared by a company for any financial year at a general meeting out of the profits for that year or any previous year or years arrived at after providing for depreciation or out of money provided by the Central or a State Government for the payment of dividend. No dividend will be declared or paid by the company from its reserves other than free reserves. The section also provides that the depreciation will be provided in accordance with Schedule II to the Act.

Declaration of dividend out of reserves

In the event of inadequacy or absence of profits in any year, a company may declare dividend out of surplus subject to the fulfillment of the following conditions, namely:

(1) The rate of dividend declared shall not exceed the average of the rates at which dividend was declared by it in the three years immediately preceding that year;

However, this will not apply to a company, which has not declared any dividend in each of the three preceding financial year.

(2) The total amount to be drawn from such accumulated profits should not exceed an amount equal to one-tenth of the sum of its paid-up share capital and free reserves as appearing in the latest audited financial statement;

(3) The amount so drawn should first be utilised to set off the losses incurred in the financial year in which dividend is declared before any dividend in respect of equity shares is declared.

(4) The balance of reserves after such withdrawal should not fall below fifteen per cent of its paid up share capital as appearing in the latest audited financial statement.

(Rule 3 of Companies (Declaration and Payment of Dividend) Rules, 2014) read with Companies (Declaration and Payment of Dividend) Amendment Rules, 2014 read with the Companies (Declaration and Payment of Dividend) Second Amendment Rules, 2015.)

EXAMPLE 1

X Limited wants to declare dividend for the FY 2014-15. Company has incurred a loss of INR 20 Crore during FY 2014-15 and has an accumulated profit of INR 100 Crore. It has a paid-up share capital of INR 100 Crore and free reserves of INR 200 Crore.. Dividend declared by the company during last three financial years is under:

Financial Year	Dividend Declared
2013-14	30% of paid-up Share Capital
2012-13	25% of paid-up Share Capital
2011-12	5% of paid-up Share Capital

What amount of dividend can be declared by X Limited?

SOLUTION

- As per Section 123(1) of the Companies Act, 2013, Dividend can be declared by a company for any financial year; out of the profits of the company for that year or out of the profits of the company for any previous financial year or years or out of both.
- X Limited has to utilize accumulated profit to declare divided as it has not earned profits during the current financial year 2014-15.
- According to Rule 3(1) of Companies (Declaration and Payment of Dividend) Rules, 2014), maximum dividend that can be declared is average of dividend paid during last three financial years i.e. 20%. {(30+25+5)/3}

- According to Rule 3(2) of Companies (Declaration and Payment of Dividend) Rules, 2014), maximum amount that can be withdrawn from accumulated profits for dividend declaration is 10% of paid-up share capital and free reserves.

(Amount in INR)

Paid-up Share Capital (A)	100 Crores
Add: Free Reserves (B)	200 Crores
Total C=(A+B)	**300 Crores**
Amount that can Be Withdrawn (C*10%)	**30 Crores**

- According to Rule 3(4) of Companies (Declaration and Payment of Dividend) Rules, balance of reserves after such withdrawal should not fall below fifteen per cent of its paid up share capital as appearing in the latest audited financial statement.
- Reserves after such withdrawal:

(Amount in INR)

Free Reserves (A)	200 crores
Add: Accumulated Profits (B)	100 crores
Less: Withdrawal (C)	30 Crores
Reserves after Withdrawal (A+B-C)	**270 Crores**

(Amount in INR)

Paid-up Share Capital (A)	100 Crores
15% of Paid-up Share Capital (A*15%)	15 Crores

- Thus, Reserves are above 15% of Paid-up Share Capital.
- According to Rule 3(3) of Companies (Declaration and Payment of Dividend) Rules, amount so drawn should first be utilised to set off the losses incurred in the financial year in which dividend is declared before any dividend is declared.
- Balance amount for dividend declaration after set off of current year losses:

(Amount in INR)

Amount Withdrawn (A)	30 Crores
Less: Losses for the FY 2014-15 (B)	20 Crores
Amount available for dividend declaration (A-B)	**10 Crores**

- Hence, X Limited can declare dividend upto INR 10 Crores which is 10% of Paid-up Share Capital.

Comparison with the Companies Act, 1956

With respect to the declaration of dividend, there were no express provisions in the Companies Act, 1956 that dividends will be declared only out of free reserves, however, the Companies Act, 2013 contains such express provision. As per the Companies Act, 2013, the Central Government cannot permit declaration of dividend without providing depreciation. However, as per the Companies Act, 1956, the Central Government, in the public interest, may allow any company to declare or pay dividend for any financial year out of the profits for that year or any previous financial year or years, without providing for depreciation.

Under the Companies Act, after the issuance of the Companies (Declaration and Payment of Dividend) Second Amendment Rules, 2015, the requirement that 'no company shall declare dividend unless carried over previous losses and depreciation not provided in previous year or years are set off against profit of the company of the current year' has been done away with. Under the Companies Act, 1956, Proviso (b) to the Section 205(1) provided that 'if the company has incurred any loss in any previous financial year or years, which falls or fall after the commencement of the Companies (Amendment) Act, 1960, then, the amount of the loss or an amount which is equal to the amount provided for depreciation for that year or those years whichever is less, shall be set off against the profits of the company for the year for which dividend is proposed to be declared or paid or against the profits of the company for any previous financial year or years, arrived at in both cases after providing for depreciation in accordance with the provisions of sub-section (2) or against both'.

Further, the Companies Act, 2013 also provides that for the purposes of this section, depreciation should be provided in accordance with the provisions of Schedule II.

The Companies Act, 1956 provides that for section 205, depreciation should be provided either:

(a) to the extent specified in Section 350; or

(b) in respect of each item of depreciable asset, for such an amount as is arrived at by dividing 95% of the original cost thereof to the company by the specified period in respect of such asset; or

(c) on any other basis approved by the Central Government which has the effect of writing off by way of depreciation 95% of the original cost to the company of each such depreciable asset on the expiry of the specified period; or

(d) as regards any other depreciable asset for which no rate of depreciation has been laid down, on such basis as may be approved by the Central Government by any general order published in the Official Gazette or by any special order in any particular case.

'Specified period' means the number of years at the end of which at least 95% of the original cost of that asset to the company would have been provided for by way of depreciation if depreciation were to be calculated according to Section 350.

Note: Section 350 of the Companies Act, 1956 provides that the amount of depreciation to be deducted for determination of net profits should be the amount of depreciation on assets as shown by the books of the company at the end of the financial year expiring at the commencement of Companies Act, 1956 or immediately thereafter and at the end of each subsequent financial year at the rate specified in Schedule XIV.

Chapter 12

Practical Issues

In this chapter, we have discussed the practical issues that may arise in the implementation of depreciation related requirements in the Companies Act, 2013. The discussion is based on interpretation of the Companies Act, 2013, discussion in various workshops and seminars and the practical experience of the authors. It may be noted that 'Schedule II to the Companies Act, 2013' is, hereinafter, referred as 'Schedule II' in this Chapter for the purposes of brevity.

12.1 APPLICABILITY

Issue 1

What is the date from which Schedule II of the Companies Act, 2013 is applicable?

Response

Schedule II of the Companies Act, 2013 is applicable in respect of financial year commencing on or after April 1, 2014.

Issue 2

X Ltd. has a financial year ending Dec 31, 2014. Is it required to follow Schedule II to the Companies Act, 2013 for the purpose of depreciation?

Response

Reference is drawn to Circular No. 8/2014 dated April 4, 2014 issued by the Ministry of Corporate Affairs, which clarified that financial statements, board reports, reference to Schedule II, etc. which relate to financial years that commenced before April 1, 2014 would be governed by the relevant provisions of the Companies Act, 1956. Consequently, Schedule II would be applicable to a company having a financial year beginning on and after April 1, 2014. In view of this, a company having financial year ending June 30, 2014 or September 30, 2014 or December 31, 2014 should continue to charge depreciation as per its existing accounting policy as per the Companies Act, 1956.

Issue 3

Upto 31st March, 2014, a company was considering the minimum rates of depreciation mentioned in Schedule XIV of the Companies Act, 1956 for depreciating its fixed assets. The company used to derive the useful life of the assets from the rates given in Schedule XIV and was considering the same for

its assets. With effect from 1st April, 2014, Schedule II of the Companies Act, 2013 became applicable. Whether the company can continue to consider the derived useful lives considered till 31st March, 2014?

Response

Schedule II of the Companies Act, 2013 is applicable w.e.f. 1st April, 2014. Hence, the useful lives as prescribed the Schedule II should only be followed w.e.f. 1st April, 2014. The derived rates considered by the company upto 31st March, 2014 will not be relevant after the introduction of Companies Act, 2013.

12.2 USEFUL LIFE AND RESIDUAL VALUE

Issue 4

As per Schedule II Amendment notification by MCA dated 29th August, 2014, para 3(i) of Part-A states as under:

> ***"The useful life of an asset shall not ordinarily be different from the useful life specified in Part 'C' and the residual value of an asset shall not be more than five per cent of the original cost of the asset:***
>
> ***Provided that where a company adopts a useful life different from what is specified in Part C or uses a residual value different from the limit specified above, the financial statements shall disclose such difference and provide justification in this behalf duly supported by technical advice."***

Can it be inferred that:

(a) **Useful life of an asset can be higher than the life indicated in Schedule II of the Companies Act, 2013?**

(b) **Residual value of an asset can be higher than 5% of the original cost of the asset?**

(c) **The useful life of an asset can be lower than the life indicated in Schedule II of the Companies Act, 2013?**

(d) **Residual value of an asset can be lower than 5% of the original cost of the asset?**

Response

(a) ***Yes,*** it can be inferred that the useful life of an asset can be higher than the life indicated in Schedule II of the Companies Act, 2013. This is evident from the fact that Schedule II provides that "where a company adopts a useful life different from what is specified in Part C, the financial statements shall disclose such difference and provide justification in this behalf duly supported by technical advice". Thus a company can adopt useful life of an asset higher than the life specified in Schedule II. However, it will be required to give a note justifying the basis of higher useful life.

(b) ***Yes,*** it can be inferred that the residual value of an asset can be higher than 5% of the original cost of the asset. This is evident from the fact that Schedule II provides that "where a company uses a residual value different from the limit specified, the financial statements shall disclose such difference and provide justification in this behalf duly supported by technical advice". Thus a company can adopt residual value of an asset higher than 5% of the original cost of the asset. However, it will be required to give a note justifying the basis of higher residual value.

(c) Yes, it can be inferred that the useful life of an asset can be lower than the life indicated in Schedule II of the Companies Act, 2013 for reasons similar to what has been discussed in part (a) above. It will be required to give a note justifying the basis of lower useful life.

(d) Yes, it can be inferred that the residual value of an asset can be lower than 5% of the original cost of the asset.

Issue 5

Is useful life of special plant and machinery determined based on nature of the asset or its usage?

Response

Schedule II specifies the useful life of special plant and machinery based on usage and not on the nature of the asset, e.g., an Earth-moving Equipment used in an entity that is engaged in open cast mining has been specified a useful life of 8 years (without extra shift depreciation), whereas similar Earth-moving Equipment used in the construction industry has been specified a single shift useful life of 9 years. Thus, one can infer that the useful life of special plant and machinery is based on usage and not the nature of an asset.

Issue 6

X Ltd. is incorporated in India and is a holding company of Y Ltd. (incorporated in India) and Z Inc. (incorporated in US). From April 1st 2014, onwards, the provisions of Schedule II of the Companies Act, 2013 are mandatory and accordingly, X Ltd. and Y Ltd. are required to compute depreciation as per the useful lives given in Schedule II. Z Inc. is required to compute depreciation as per the laws of its country of incorporation, i.e., Belgium, and the useful lives as per Belgium laws is significantly different from those specified in Schedule II. While consolidating, whether X Ltd. is required to align the depreciation computed in the books of Z Inc. in accordance with IGAAP (Schedule II of the Companies Act, 2013) or whether useful life as per Belgium GAAP can be continued to be followed in Z. Inc. while consolidating

along with a note stating that 'the useful lives of assets of subsidiary Z Inc. are considered in accordance with Belgium GAAP for the purpose of consolidation'?

Response

In our view, alignment of depreciation computed in the books of Z Inc. in accordance with IGAAP (Schedule II of the Companies Act, 2013) is not required because:

- Z Inc. is not required to comply with the Indian Companies Act, 2013.
- Depreciation has been computed on the basis of useful lives of the assets; and
- Dividends are always paid based on the standalone financial statements and not consolidated financial statements.

Hence, only a note stating that 'the useful lives of assets of subsidiary Z Inc. is in accordance with Belgium GAAP for the purpose of consolidation' should be sufficient.

Issue 7

Can a company adopt for some class of assets Schedule II useful lives and residual values and for some other class of assets a different useful life and residual value?

Response

Yes, a company can determine category wise useful life and residual value. Hence, it is permissible for companies to consider useful life and residual value as per Schedule II for some categories of assets and different life / residual value for the other categories of assets. However, the rationale is to be technically evaluated and disclosed in the financial statements where useful life as per Schedule II is not being followed.

Issue 8

How frequently do the companies need to review the useful life and residual value?

Response

As per Ind AS 16 and AS 10 (Revised), the companies will need to review the useful life and residual value at least at each financial year-end.

Issue 9

How should the useful life or residual value of a specified asset as notified for accounting purposes by a regulatory authority be considered- Whether Schedule II will prevail even in case of a specified asset notified for accounting purposes by a regulatory authority?

Response

No, the requirement of Schedule II will not be applicable in case the useful life or the residual value of any asset as notified for accounting purposes by a regulatory authority constituted under an act of Parliament or by the Central Government has been prescribed in calculating the depreciation to be provided for such asset.

Issue 10

A Ltd., a special purpose vehicle, entered into a service concession agreement signed with the grantor. The agreement is for 25 years and the option of renewal for additional period of 25 years is available with the company. The assets created by the company are capitalised as 'tangible assets'. How should the useful life of various assets be assessed by the company while applying Schedule II?

Response

Likelihood of renewal should be assessed by A Ltd. If there is a reasonable certainty at the inception of the service concession period that the agreement will be renewed for further period of 25 years, the same needs to be considered for the assessment of useful life of various assets.

The useful life would be lower of the life prescribed by Schedule II (or different useful life assessed by the management based on the technical justification) or service concession period of 25 years or 50 years.

Issue 10A

A Ltd. acquired a second hand plant for INR 10 crores from B Ltd. As per the estimate of B Lt5d., the useful life of the asset when it was newly acquired by it was 20 years out of which 14 years have already passed for which B Ltd. has used the asset. A Ltd. has estimated that it will be able to use the asset for 8 years from the date it has purchased the plant from B Ltd. What should be the useful life to be considered by A Ltd. for the purpose of depreciation?

Response

In this case, A Ltd. should provide depreciation on the plant on the basis of useful life of 8 years and not 6 years remaining as per the estimate of B Ltd. The expression 'available for use by an entity' in the definition of 'useful life' of assets as given in Para 1 of Part A of Schedule II clarifies that the useful life of an asset is estimated on the basis of the expectation of the company that purchased the asset. It does not make any difference whether the purchased asset is a new asset or an old asset.

12.3 METHODS OF DEPRECIATION

Issue 11

What are the methods permitted under Schedule II for charging depreciation?

Response

Schedule II provides indicative useful lives as against the depreciation rates for SLM and WDV given under Schedule XIV to the Companies Act, 1956. An entity can derive the rates for SLM as well as WDV based on the useful life. Further, it can also depreciate the assets on the basis of number of units of production or other similar units expected to be obtained from the use of the asset by the entity.

Issue 12

How should an entity compute the SLM rates based on the useful life given in Schedule II to the Companies Act, 2013?

Response

In SLM, the amount of annual depreciation is calculated as:

$$\frac{\text{Capitalised Cost} - \text{Estimated Residual Value}}{\text{Estimated Useful Life}}$$

SLM rate of depreciation can be computed as under:

Amount of annual depreciation*100/Capitalised Cost

Example

The useful life of towers used in telecommunications is specified to be 18 years in Schedule II of the Companies Act, 2013.

In case the residual value is assumed to be Nil, the SLM rate of depreciation p.a. will be computed as under:

$$\text{Amount of Annual Depreciation} = \frac{\text{Capitalised Cost} - \text{Estimated Residual Value}}{\text{Estimated Useful Life}}$$

Since residual value is assumed to be Nil, amount of annual depreciation = Capitalised Cost/18

SLM rate of depreciation can be computed as under:

Amount of annual depreciation*100/Capitalised Cost

= (Capitalised Cost/18)*100/Capitalised Cost

= 100/18

= 5.56% p.a.

In case the residual value is assumed to be 5% of capitalized cost, the SLM rate of depreciation p.a. will be computed as under:

$$\text{Amount of Annual Depreciation} = \frac{\text{Capitalised Cost} - \text{Estimated Residual Value}}{\text{Estimated Useful Life}}$$

= (Capitalised Cost - 5% of Capitalised Cost)/18

= 95% of Capitalised Cost/18

SLM rate of depreciation can be computed as under:

Amount of annual depreciation*100/Capitalised Cost

= (95% of Capitalised Cost/18)*100/Capitalised Cost

= 95/18

=5.28% p.a.

Issue 13

How should an entity compute the WDV rates based on the useful life given in Schedule II to the Companies Act, 2013?

Response

In WDV method, the rate of depreciation is calculated as:

$$1 - \sqrt[n]{\frac{\text{Estimated Residual Value}}{\text{Capitalised Cost}}}$$

Where n = useful life (in years)

Example

The useful life of towers used in telecommunications is specified to be 18 years in Schedule II of the Companies Act, 2013.

In case the residual value is assumed to be 5% of capitalized cost, the WDV rate of depreciation p.a. will be computed as under:

$$1 - \sqrt[n]{\frac{\text{Estimated Residual Value}}{\text{Capitalised Cost}}}$$

= [1-{(5% of Capitalised Cost/Capitalised Cost) ^ (1/18)}]*100

= [1-{(5%) ^ (1/18)}]*100

= [1-{(0.05) ^ (1/18)}]*100

= 15.33%

Issue 13A

Can a company apply different methods of depreciation for similar assets at different locations?

Response

Selection of a method of depreciation is a matter of judgement by the management considering various factors such as type of assets, the nature of the use of such assets and circumstances prevailing in the business, to allocate the depreciable amount of an asset over its useful life so that the depreciation method best reflects the way the asset is consumed. Different methods for similar assets at different geographical locations can only be used if the said methods are selected based on the factors discussed above. Otherwise, the use of different methods for similar assets at different geographical location is not justified.

Issue 14

How should a change in the method of depreciation be applied?

Response

Under Ind AS 16 as well as AS 10 (Revised), change in the method of deprecation is to be treated as a change in an accounting estimate. Such change should be applied prospectively.

12.4 DEPRECIATION RATES

Issue 15

Whether the Schedule II gives the minimum rates of depreciation?

Response

Firstly, Schedule II does not provide the rates of deprecation. What it gives is the indicative useful lives of various depreciable assets. An entity is required to compute the depreciation rates based on the useful lives. Earlier, under the Companies Act, 1956, it was not possible for an entity to charge depreciation at the rates lower than the ones prescribed in Schedule XIV to the Companies Act, 1956. In other words, there is no problem if an enterprise wants to charge depreciation at rates that are higher than the prescribed rates. However, depreciation rates cannot be lower than that prescribed under the Schedule XIV of the Companies Act, 1956.

Under Schedule II to the Companies Act, 2013, the useful lives are only indicative and not the maximum useful lives (maximum useful life translates to minimum rates of depreciation). Hence, an entity would be subject to the justification, to adopt higher or lower useful lives than what is prescribed in Schedule II to the Companies Act, 2013.

12.5 EXTRA SHIFT DEPRECIATION

Issue 16

What are the items of plant and machinery in respect of which no extra shift depreciation (NESD) is permitted under Schedule II?

Response

For the following items of plant and machinery, no extra shift depreciation is permitted under Schedule II.

Plant and Machinery
(i) General rate applicable to plant and machinery not covered under special plant and machinery
(a) continuous process plant for which no special rate has been prescribed under (ii) below
(ii) Special Plant and Machinery
(a) Plant and Machinery used in glass manufacturing
1. Plant and Machinery except direct fire glass melting furnaces Moulds
2. Float Glass Melting Furnaces
(b) Plant and Machinery used in mines and quarries—Portable underground machinery and earth moving machinery used in open cast mining
(c) Plant and Machinery used in Telecommunications
1. Towers
2. Telecom transceivers, switching centres, transmission and other network equipment
3. Telecom—Ducts, Cables and optical fibre
4. Satellites
(d) Plant and Machinery used in exploration, production and refining oil and gas
1. Refineries
2. Oil and gas assets (including wells), processing plant and facilities
3. Petrochemical Plant
4. Storage tanks and related equipment
5. Pipelines
6. Drilling Rig
7. Field operations (above ground) Portable boilers, drilling tools, well-head tanks, etc.
8. Loggers
(e) Plant and Machinery used in generation, transmission and distribution of power

	1. Thermal/ Gas/ Combined Cycle Power Generation Plant
	2. Hydro Power Generation Plant
	3. Nuclear Power Generation Plant
	4. Transmission lines, cables and other network assets
	5. Wind Power Generation Plant
	6. Electric Distribution Plant
	7. Gas Storage and Distribution Plant
	8. Water Distribution Plant including pipelines
(f)	Plant and Machinery used in manufacture of non-ferrous metals
	1. Metal pot line
	2. Bauxite crushing and grinding section
	3. Digester Section
	4. Turbine
	5. Equipments for Calcination
	6. Copper Smelter
	7. Equipments for Scalping, Slitting , etc.
	8. Copper refining plant
(g)	Plant and Machinery used in medical and surgical operations
	1. Electrical Machinery, X-ray and electrotherapeutic apparatus and accessories thereto, medical, diagnostic equipments, namely, Cat-scan, Ultrasound Machines, ECG Monitors, etc.
	2. Other Equipments.
(h)	Plant and Machinery used in manufacture of pharmaceuticals and chemicals
	1. Reactors
	2. Distillation Columns
	3. Drying equipments/Centrifuges and Decanters
	4. Vessel/storage tanks
(i)	Plant and Machinery used in civil construction
	1. Transmission line, Tunneling Equipments
	2. Others including Material Handling /Pipeline/Welding Equipments
(j)	Plant and Machinery used in salt works

Issue 17

Whether Schedule II provides separate useful life in case an asset is used for double or triple shift?

Response

The useful lives of assets working on shift basis have been specified in the Schedule II of the Companies Act, 2013, based on their single shift working only. Except for assets in respect of which no extra shift depreciation is permitted (indicated by NESD in Part C), if an asset is used for any time during the year for double shift, the depreciation should be increased by 50% for that period and, in case of the triple shift, the depreciation should be increased by100% for that period.

Issue 18

Has the term 'Shift' been defined in Schedule II?

Response

The term 'shift' has not been defined in the Companies Act, 1956 or Companies Act, 2013. So, it is understood in the common commercial parlance. Section 2(r) of the Factories Act, 1948, defines the term 'shift' as follows:

> *"Where work of the same kind is carried out by two or more sets of workers working during different periods of the day, each of such sets is called 'group' or 'relay' and each of such periods is called a 'shift'".*

Issue 19

How should a shift be calculated- Whether with reference to working days or the entire year?

Response

Calculation of a shift has to be with reference to working days and not with reference to the entire year. The calculation of the extra depreciation for double shift working and for triple shift working should be made separately in the proportion with the number of days for which the concern worked double shift or triple shift, as the case may be, bears to the normal number of working days during the year.

Issue 20

X Ltd. has a plant and machinery which has been used for 150 days in single shift and 150 days in double shift. The normal number of working days are 300 for this particular industry. The indicative useful life given in Schedule II for this plant and machinery is 10 years. Compute the single shift and double shift depreciation for this year for the plant and machinery assuming the cost of plant and machinery to be INR 10.50 crores and residual value INR 0.50 crores?

Response

Extra depreciation for double shift working should be the difference between the depreciation for double shift working and the depreciation for single shift working, adjusted in the proportion which the number of days for which the concern worked double shift bears to the normal working days during the year. The extra depreciation for double shift working, so calculated, has to be added to the depreciation for single shift working to arrive at the total depreciation for double shift working.

Depreciation for single shift working is 100/10= 10% based on SLM.

As per Schedule II, if an asset is used for any time during the year for double shift, the depreciation will increase by 50% for that period.

Extra Depreciation for double shift working is (10%*0.5)*(150/300), i.e., 2.5%.

Thus, the depreciation for the year would be computed as under:

Single Shift = INR 10.00 crores*10/100 = INR 1 crores

Extra Depreciation for double shift = INR 10.00 crores*2.5/100 = INR 0.25 crores

Total Depreciation = INR 1.25 crores

12.6 COMPONENT ACCOUNTING

Issue 21

What is the concept of component accounting? Is it mandatory under the Companies Act, 2013?

Response

Useful life specified in Part C of the Schedule II of the Companies Act, 2013, is for whole of the asset. Where cost of a part of the asset is significant to total cost of the asset and useful life of that part is different from the useful life of the remaining asset, useful life of that significant part should be determined separately. Thus, the Companies Act, 2013 has introduced the concept of component accounting which was not the case in the Companies Act, 1956.

Schedule II provides that the component accounting is mandatory. However, as per the Notification dated 29th August, 2014, a relaxation for one year has been given so that the companies can prepare themselves for the above. Accordingly, component accounting will be voluntary in respect of the financial year commencing on or after the 1st April, 2014 and mandatory for financial statements in respect of financial years commencing on or after the 1st April, 2015.

Issue 22

How should an entity identify the components for the purpose of component accounting?

Response

Companies may refer to AS 10 (Revised) and Ind AS 16 on 'Property, Plant and Equipment' which provides as under:

> *"Each part of an item of property, plant and equipment with a cost that*

is significant in relation to the total cost of the item should be depreciated separately.

An entity allocates the amount initially recognised in respect of an item of property, plant and equipment to its significant parts and depreciates separately each such part, e.g., it may be appropriate to depreciate separately the airframe and engines of an aircraft, whether owned or subject to a finance lease. Similarly, if an entity acquires property, plant and equipment subject to an operating lease in which it is the lessor, it may be appropriate to depreciate separately amounts reflected in the cost of that item that are attributable to favourable or unfavourable lease terms relative to market terms.

A significant part of an item of property, plant and equipment may have a useful life and a depreciation method that are the same as the useful life and the depreciation method of another significant part of that same item. Such parts may be grouped in determining the depreciation charge.

To the extent that an entity depreciates separately some parts of an item of property, plant and equipment, it also depreciates separately the remainder of the item. The remainder consists of the parts of the item that are individually not significant. If an entity has varying expectations for these parts, approximation techniques may be necessary to depreciate the remainder in a manner that faithfully represents the consumption pattern and/or useful life of its parts.

An entity may choose to depreciate separately the parts of an item that do not have a cost that is significant in relation to the total cost of the item."

Component approach requires more detailed record-keeping; fixed assets register will need to separately record (i) component and (ii) the rest of the asset. For this purpose, the total cost of the asset will need to be split into aforesaid two parts. In this regard, it may be noted that in many cases, an entity acquires an asset for a fixed sum without knowing the cost of the individual components. Thus, the cost of individual components should be estimated either with reference to current market prices (if possible), in consultation with the seller or contractor, or using some other reasonable method of approximation (e.g. relative values).

Even for an asset for which component accounting is applied for depreciation purposes, the financial statements may disclose a single asset, e.g., an airline may disclose aircraft as a class of assets, rather than disclosing separate information in respect of each of the components of the aircraft.

Issue 23

Suggest the significant components that can be identified for the following items of fixed assets:

(a) Ships

(b) Pharmaceuticals and Chemicals Plant

(c) Buildings

Response

(a) A ship can be segregated into the following components:

- Life raft
- Decks
- Boiler
- Bulkhead
- Propulsion system
- Others, etc.

(b) A pharmaceutical and chemical plant can be segregated into the following components:

- Reactors
- Distillation columns
- Drying equipments/centrifuges and decanters
- Vessel/storage tanks, etc.

(c) A building can be segregated into the following components:

- Structural design
- Elevators
- Heating system
- Water system
- Electrical system, etc.

Issue 24

Is componentisation of assets to be done retrospectively or prospectively?

Response

Note 4 of Part C to Schedule II states that "Useful life specified in Part C of the Schedule is for whole of the asset. Where cost of a part of the asset is significant to total cost of the asset and useful life of that part is different from the useful life of the remaining asset, useful life of that significant part shall be determined separately".

As per the notification dated 29th August, 2014, the requirement will be voluntary in respect of the financial year commencing on or after the 1st April, 2014 and mandatory for financial statements in respect of financial years commencing on or after the 1st April, 2015.

Hence, componentisation of all assets as on April 1, 2015 would have to be done, i.e., retrospectively, however, it will be required with respect to only those assets that have a carrying value greater than the residual value.

It may be noted that paragraph 8.3 of pre-revised AS 10 – Accounting for Fixed Assets states that "In certain circumstances, the accounting for an item of fixed asset may be improved if the total expenditure thereon is allocated to its component parts, provided they are in practice separable, and estimates are made of the useful lives of these components." This requirement is, however, optional.

Thus, in case, a company is already following component accounting, it may not be required to do any additional exercise for the same. However, if a company is not following component accounting, then it will be required to do the component accounting exercise for the assets existing on April 1, 2015 (April 1, 2014 in case the company voluntary adopts component accounting for the financial year 2014-15) .

Issue 25

How will the carrying values as on 31.03.2015 be bifurcated into various components for the purpose of component accounting?

Response

The bifurcation should be done based on either a technical estimate (internal or external) or on the basis of the current value of the fixed assets.

Issue 26

X Ltd. is incorporated in India and is a holding company of Y Ltd. (incorporated in India) and Z Inc. (incorporated in US). Z Inc. is required to compute depreciation as per the laws of its country of incorporation, i.e., Belgium. X Ltd. and Y Ltd. are required to follow component accounting as per Companies Act, 2013, whereas as per local laws of its country of incorporation, Z Inc. is not required to mandatorily adopt component accounting. While consolidating, whether X Ltd. is required to align the books of Z Inc. in accordance with IGAAP (Schedule II of the Companies Act, 2013) by adopting component accounting or whether justification note in the consolidated financials stating that 'Subsidiary Z Inc. is not following component accounting as per the requirements of Belgium GAAP' would suffice?

Response

Para 20 of Accounting Standard 21 on '*Consolidated Financial Statements*' requires that 'consolidated financial statements should be prepared using uniform accounting policies for like transactions and other events in similar circumstances. If it is not practicable to use uniform accounting policies in preparing the consolidated financial statements, that fact should be disclosed together with the proportions of the items in the consolidated financial statements to which the different accounting policies have been applied.'

In our view, considering the above requirement of AS 21, the accounting policy of component accounting should be uniform while preparing consolidated financial statements and accordingly, alignment of books of Z Inc. in accordance with IGAAP (Schedule II of the Companies Act, 2013) by adopting component accounting is necessary. Justification note in the consolidated financials stating that 'Subsidiary Z Inc. is not following component accounting as per the requirements of Belgium GAAP' will not suffice.

Issue 27

Are companies required to comply with the requirements of component accounting for the quarterly filings as well or is it required for annual financial statements only?

Response

A company will be required to comply with the requirement of component accounting for the quarterly filings as well in addition to the annual financial statements.

Issue 28

Whether component accounting is required only to the assets acquired on or after April 1, 2015 (the date when the component accounting becomes mandatory under the Companies Act, 2013?

Response

Component accounting requirement applies to all assets and is not limited to the assets acquired on or after April 1, 2015.

Issue 29

Whether component accounting will bring any change in the accounting for replacements? If yes, what is the change due to component accounting?

Response

Yes, component accounting will entail significant change in accounting of replacement costs. Earlier, the replacement costs were expensed as and when incurred. However, pursuant to component accounting being made mandatory, the replacement costs would be capitalised. The net carrying value, if any, of replaced part should be derecognized.

Issue 30

If a company has capitalized foreign exchange as part of the cost of fixed assets, does a proportionate amount need to be allocated to components as well?

Response

Yes, if a company has capitalized foreign exchange as part of the cost of fixed assets, a proportionate amount should be allocated to the relevant components.

12.7 DEPRECIATION ON ASSETS WITH VALUE LESS THAN RUPEES FIVE THOUSAND

Issue 31

In the absence of any provision regarding depreciation on assets with value less than Rupees five thousand in the Schedule II of the Companies Act, 2013, can it be construed that the earlier requirement of providing 100% depreciation on assets with value less than Rupees five thousand has now been dispensed off?

Response

Schedule XIV of the Companies Act, 1956 required that

> *"Notwithstanding anything mentioned in this Schedule depreciation on assets, whose actual cost does not exceed five thousand rupees, shall be provided depreciation at the rate of hundred per cent.*
>
> *Provided that where the aggregate actual cost of individual items of plant and machinery costing INR 5,000 or less constitutes more than 10 per cent of the total actual cost of plant and machinery, rates of depreciation applicable to such items shall be the rates as specified in Item II of the Schedule."*

However, Schedule II of the Companies Act, 2013 is silent in this respect. Thus, in our view, the requirement of fully depreciating the assets upto INR 5,000 does not exist in the Companies Act, 2013.

It may be noted that the provision under Schedule XIV to the Companies Act, 1956 to allow 100% depreciation in case of assets costing INR 5,000 or less was based on practices followed by the companies based on the materiality of the financial impact of such charge. Materiality of the financial impact of such charge should be considered with reference to the cost of the asset and size of the company. Accordingly, even after the introduction of Companies Act, 2013, a company may have the policy of 100% depreciation of assets upto certain threshold limits considering the aspect of materiality in the year of acquisition of the asset.

12.8 AMORTISATION IN CASE OF INTANGIBLE ASSETS

Issue 32

Whether the amendment regarding BOT assets allows revenue based amortization only for toll roads? Or can a company apply revenue based amortization to other type of intangible assets created under the BOT model?

Response

The amendment in Schedule II reads as follows: "For intangible assets, the provisions of the Accounting Standards applicable for the time being in force shall apply except in case of intangible assets (Toll roads) created under BOT, BOOT or any other form of Public Private Partnership route in case of road projects." The amendment clearly suggests that revenue based amortization applies to toll roads. The same method cannot be used for other intangible assets even if they are created under PPP schemes, such as airport infrastructure.

Issue 33

Schedule XIV of the Companies Act, 1956 contained a special treatment for amortisation of intangible assets in the form of toll roads. Is there a similar treatment given for the same in the Companies Act, 2013 as well?

Response

Depreciation rates for intangible assets under the Schedule II of the Companies Act, 2013 will be governed by the notified Accounting Standard (i.e., Accounting Standard 26 on *'Intangible Assets'*).

However, in case of intangible assets (Toll Roads) created under 'Build, Operate and Transfer', 'Build, Own, Operate and Transfer' or any other form of public private partnership route in case of road projects, amortization basis will be same as what was applicable under the Companies Act, 1956. *(Amendment to Schedule II vide notification by MCA dated 31st March, 2014)*

Amortisation in case of toll roads will be computed as under:

$$\text{Amortisation rate} = \frac{\text{Amortisation amount} \times 100}{\text{Cost of Intangible assets (A)}}$$

Amortisation Amount

$$\text{Cost of Intangible Asset} \times \frac{\text{Actual revenue for the year (B)}}{\text{Projected revenue from intangible Asset (till the end of the concession period)}}$$

Cost of Intangible Asset (A) = Cost incurred by the company in accordance with the accounting standard.

Actual revenue for the year (B) = Actual revenue (Toll Charges) received during the accounting year.

Projected revenue from Intangible asset (c) = Total Projected revenue from the intangible asset as provided to the project leader at the time of financial closure/agreement.

The amortisation amount or rate should ensure that the whole of the cost of the intangible asset is amortised over the concession period.

Total revenue would be reviewed at the end of each financial year end and the projected revenue will be adjusted to reflect any change in the estimate which will lead to the actual collection at the concession period.

Issue 34

What is the normal useful life of an intangible asset as per AS 26?

Response

The useful life of an intangible asset depends on various factors such as expected usage, product life cycle, technical factors, etc. However, AS 26 provides that normally the useful life of an intangible asset should not be taken as more than **10 years**. However, **this presumption is rebuttable**. If there is a persuasive evidence that the useful life of an intangible asset will be longer than 10 years then the asset should be amortised over that period.

Issue 35

Which method of amortisation should be applied by an entity for amortisation of intangible assets?

Response

The amortisation method used should reflect the pattern in which the asset's economic benefits are consumed by the enterprise. These methods include the straight-line method, the diminishing balance method and the unit of production method. If a pattern cannot be determined reliably, the straight-line method should be used.

Issue 36

How should the residual value of an intangible asset be ascertained?

Response

The residual value of an intangible asset should normally be taken as zero. However, in the following cases there could be a residual value:

(*i*) when there is a commitment by a third party to purchase the asset at the end of its useful life; or

(*ii*) when there is an active market for the asset and

(*a*) residual value can be determined by reference to that market; and (*b*) it is probable that such a market will exist at the end of the asset's useful life.

Issue 37

Is an entity required to review the amortisation period and method?

Response

The amortisation period and the amortisation method should be reviewed at least at each financial year-end. If the expected useful life of the asset is significantly different from previous estimates, the amortisation period should be changed accordingly. If there has been a significant change in the expected pattern of economic benefits from the asset, the amortisation method should be changed to reflect the changed pattern. Such changes should be accounted for in accordance with AS 5, *'Net Profit or Loss for the Period, Prior Period Items and Changes in Accounting Policies'.*

12.9 TRANSITIONAL PROVISIONS

Issue 38

Schedule II of the Companies Act, 2013 provides as follows:

From the date this Schedule comes into effect, the carrying amount of the asset as on that date–

(a) shall be depreciated over the remaining useful life of the asset as per this Schedule;

(b) after retaining the residual value, may be recognised in the opening balance of retained earnings where the remaining useful life of an asset is nil.

Whether adjustment against the retained earnings should be net of deferred tax impact?

Response

As per an ICAI notification on 'Tax effect of expenses/income adjusted directly against the reserves and/or Securities Premium Account':

Not recognising the tax benefit, arising from admissibility of expense charged to the reserves and/or Securities Premium Account, in the reserves and/or Securities Premium Account is contrary to the generally accepted accounting principles because it results in recognition and presentation of tax effect of an expense in a manner which is different from the manner in which the expense itself has been recognised and presented. Similarly, recognising and presenting the tax effect of an income in a manner which is different from the manner in which income itself has been recognised and presented is contrary to the generally accepted accounting principles. Accordingly, any expense charged directly to reserves and/or Securities

Premium Account should be net of tax benefits expected to arise from the admissibility of such expenses for tax purposes. Similarly, any income credited directly to a reserve account or a similar account should be net of its tax effect.

In view of the above, any item of income or expense adjusted directly to reserves and/or Securities Premium Account should be net of its tax effect

The ICAI announcement requires that adjustment of expense/ income to reserve should be net of its tax effect. Thus, if the carrying value of the asset is Nil after evaluating its useful life under the Companies Act, 2013, the company should adjust the opening carrying value of the asset to opening retained earnings net of the tax effect.

Issue 39

If the useful life of an asset is already over (as per Schedule II), however, it still has a carrying value on the date of transition, is it mandatory for an entity to recognise the carrying amount in the opening balance of retained earnings?

Response

Prior to the amendment notification dated 29th August, 2014, the carrying amount of the asset as on the date Schedule II comes into effect was, after retaining the residual value was compulsorily required to be recognised in the opening balance of retained earnings where the remaining useful life of an asset is Nil.

However, after the amendment, the carrying value (after retaining the residual value) may be recognised in the opening balance of retained earnings where the remaining useful life of an asset is Nil, i.e., carrying value can be recognised in the statement of profit and loss. Hence, the companies can avail the MAT benefits by reducing the book profits (if the same is permitted under the Income Tax Act, 1961).

Issue 40

In case the useful life is lower than the useful life as per Schedule II, will the transitional benefit still be available.

Response

Considering that the Schedule II itself permits to follow a useful life different from the indicative rates subject to justification and disclosure, the useful life so determined (whether indicative life or a different life) will be considered as Schedule II life and, hence, the transitional provisions should be available.

Issue 41

X Ltd. was following WDV method of depreciation under the Companies Act, 1956 till 31st March, 2014. The company decided to shift to SLM method w.e.f. 1st April, 2014, the date on which Schedule II of the Companies Act, 2013 became effective. Whether the same will be covered under the transitional provisions given in Schedule II?

Response

Change in the method of depreciation is a change in an accounting policy as per AS 5. It will not be covered in the transition provisions prescribed by Schedule II.

EXAMPLE 1

On April 1, 2008, A Ltd. installed a rolling mill at a cost of INR 20 lakh with prescribed useful life of 30 years under Schedule II. The company was depreciating the same on written down value method.

Under Schedule XIV to the Companies Act, 1956, the WDV rate for rolling mills was 13.91%.

Depreciation as per WDV till the time Schedule II became effective was as under:

(Amount in INR)

	Book value b/f	Depreciation@ 13.91%	Book value c/f
2008-09	2,000,000	278,200	1,721,800
2009-10	1,721,800	239,502	1,482,298
2010-11	1,482,298	206,188	1,276,110
2011-12	1,276,110	177,507	1,098,603
2012-13	1,098,603	152,816	945,787
2013-14	945,787	131,559	**814,228**
Total		**11,85,772**	

As on 31st March, 2014, the WDV of rolling mills was INR 8,14,228.

Now, on 1st April, 2014, Schedule II became effective. The useful life specified in Schedule II is 30 years.

As per the transition provisions, the carrying value on 1st April, 2014 needs to be depreciated over the remaining useful life which is 24 years (30 years -6 years).

Scenario 1: Company continues with WDV Method

In this case, revised WDV rate should be computed to depreciate the carrying value as on 31stMarch, 2014 over a period of 24 years assuming a residual value of 5%. The revised WDV rate would be 8.37 % and, hence, depreciation for FY 2014-15 till FY 2037-38 is as under:

(Amount in INR)

	Book value b/f	Depreciation@ 8.37%	Book value c/f
2014-15	814,228	68,151	746,077
2015-16	746,077	62,447	683,630
2016-17	683,630	57,220	626,411
2017-18	626,411	52,431	573,980
2018-19	573,980	48,042	525,938
2019-20	525,938	44,021	481,917
2020-21	481,917	40,336	441,580
2021-22	441,580	36,960	404,620
2022-23	404,620	33,867	370,753
2023-24	370,753	31,032	339,721
2024-25	339,721	28,435	311,287
2025-26	311,287	26,055	285,232
2026-27	285,232	23,874	261,358
2027-28	261,358	21,876	239,482
2028-29	239,482	20,045	219,438
2029-30	219,438	18,367	201,071
2030-31	201,071	16,830	184,241
2031-32	184,241	15,421	168,820
2032-33	168,820	14,130	154,690
2033-34	154,690	12,948	141,742
2034-35	141,742	11,864	129,879
2035-36	129,879	10,871	119,008
2036-37	119,008	9,961	109,047
2037-38	109,047	9,127	99,920*

*The difference of INR 80 in residual value is due to rounding off

Scenario 2: Company shifts to SLM Method

In this case, deficit/surplus arising due to change in method should be debited/credited to the statement of profit and loss.

Under Schedule XIV to the Companies Act, 1956, the SLM rate for rolling mills was 4.75%.

Depreciation that should have been charged using SLM Method = INR 20,00,000*4.75%*6 = INR 5,70,000.

Difference between the depreciation that should have been charged using SLM Method and the depreciation charged under WDV basis = INR 5,70,000 – INR 11,85,772 = INR 6,15,772.

The surplus of INR 6,15,772 arising due change in the method of depreciation should be credited to the statement of profit and loss.

Further, by applying transitional provisions of Schedule II, the carrying value as on 1st April, 2014 should be depreciated over a period of 24 years assuming a residual value of 5%.

Carrying value as on 1st April, 2014 = INR 20,00,000 – INR 5,70,000 = INR 14,30,000.

Carrying value remaining after 5% residual value = INR 14,30,000 – (INR 20,00,000*5%) = INR 13,30,000

Hence, depreciation for the FY 2014-15 to FY 2037-28 would be INR 13,30,000/ 24 years, i.e., INR 55,417 p.a.

SLM Depreciation Rate (on INR 14,30,000) = INR 55,417/ INR 14,30,000 = 3.88% p.a.

SLM Depreciation Rate (on INR 20,00,000) = INR 55,417/ INR 20,00,000 = 2.77% p.a.

Depreciation for FY 2014-15 till FY 2037-38 is as under:

(Amount in INR)

	Book value b/f	SLM Depreciation	Book value c/f
2014-15	1,430,000	55,417	1,374,583
2015-16	1,374,583	55,417	1,319,167
2016-17	1,319,167	55,417	1,263,750
2017-18	1,263,750	55,417	1,208,333
2018-19	1,208,333	55,417	1,152,917
2019-20	1,152,917	55,417	1,097,500
2020-21	1,097,500	55,417	1,042,083
2021-22	1,042,083	55,417	986,667
2022-23	986,667	55,417	931,250
2023-24	931,250	55,417	875,833

	Book value b/f	SLM Depreciation	Book value c/f
2024-25	875,833	55,417	820,417
2025-26	820,417	55,417	765,000
2026-27	765,000	55,417	709,583
2027-28	709,583	55,417	654,167
2028-29	654,167	55,417	598,750
2029-30	598,750	55,417	543,333
2030-31	543,333	55,417	487,917
2031-32	487,917	55,417	432,500
2032-33	432,500	55,417	377,083
2033-34	377,083	55,417	321,667
2034-35	321,667	55,417	266,250
2035-36	266,250	55,417	210,833
2036-37	210,833	55,417	155,417
2037-38	155,417	55,417	100,000

Note: **It may be noted with effect from 1 April 2016, the change in the method of depreciation would be considered as a change in an accounting estimate (in accordance with AS 10 (Revised) on 'Property, Plant and Equipment') to be accounted for prospectively.**

12.10 REVALUATION

Issue 42

In case of a revalued asset, should the depreciation charge to the Statement of Profit and Loss be based on the revalued amount or the original cost? How should the revaluation reserve be treated?

Response

As per ICAI's guidance note on treatment of reserve created on revaluation of fixed asset

> *"A question may arise, as to whether the additional depreciation provision required in consequence of revaluation can be adjusted against "Revaluation Reserve". As stated earlier, depreciation is required to be provided with reference to the total value of the fixed assets as appearing in the account after revaluation.* ***However, for certain statutory purposes e.g., dividends, managerial remuneration***

> ***etc., only depreciation relatable to the historical cost of the fixed assets is to be provided out of the current profits of the company. In the circumstance, the additional depreciation relatable to revaluation may be adjusted against Revaluation Reserve" by transfer to Profit and Loss Account.*** *In other words, as per the requirements of Part II of Schedule VI to the Companies Act, the company will have to provide the depreciation on the total book value of the fixed assets (including the increased amount as a result of revaluation) in the Profit and Loss Account of the relevant period, and thereafter the company can transfer an amount equivalent to the additional depreciation from the Revaluation Reserve. Such transfer from Revaluation Reserve should be shown in the Profit and Loss Account separately and an appropriate note by way of disclosure would be desirable. Such a disclosure would appear to be in consonance with the requirement of Part I of Schedule VI to the Companies Act, prescribing disclosure of write-up in the value of fixed asset for the first five years after revaluation*

Companies Act, 1956 required depreciation to be calculated on the historical cost of the asset for the purpose of dividend declaration. Accordingly, the ICAI guidance note allowed an amount equivalent to additional depreciation due to upward revaluation of the fixed asset to be transferred from Revaluation Reserve to the Profit and Loss Account. However, the Schedule II permits depreciation to be provided on the historical cost or amount substituted for the historical cost (i.e. revalued amount). Thus, as per the Act, in case a company has revalued its assets, depreciation should be provided on the revalued amount. Accordingly, it would no longer be permissible for the company to transfer an amount equivalent to additional depreciation due to upward revaluation of the fixed asset from Revaluation Reserve to the Profit and Loss Account.

AS 10 (Revised) permits the amount carried in Revaluation Reserve to be transferred directly to the General Reserve on retirement or disposal of revalued asset. Hence, as and when the asset is sold or disposed of, the related amount in the Revaluation Reserve can be transferred directly to General Reserve.

12.11 CONTINUOUS PROCESS PLANT

Issue 43

What is a continuous process plant? Is there any change in the meaning or depreciation rate for a continuous process plant under Schedule II as compared to Schedule XIV to the Companies Act, 1956?

Response

Continuous process plant is a plant which is required and designed to operate 24 hours a day.

There is no change in the meaning of a continuous process plant between Schedule XIV of the Companies Act, 1956 and Schedule II of the Companies Act, 2013.

However, there is a change in the depreciation rate for continuous process plant. Under the Schedule XIV to the Companies Act, 1956, the depreciation rate for continuous process plant for which no special rate has been prescribed was 5.28% for SLM and 15.33% for WDV.

However, under Schedule II to the Companies Act, 2013, the depreciation rate for continuous process plant for which no special rate has been prescribed is 3.80% for SLM and 11.29% for WDV (assuming residual value to be 5% of original cost).

Issue 44

Whether an existing asset as on 31 March, 2014 which was not identified and considered as continuous process plant under Schedule XIV of the Companies Act, 1956 in the financial statements can be retagged or re-determined as CPP under Schedule II of the Companies Act, 2013?

Response

Note 7 of Part C to Schedule II, which specifies the transition provision on the date when the Schedule comes into effect, states the manner of dealing with (only) the carrying value of the assets as on the date of transition. It does not provide for reversing or recalculating depreciation charged in periods prior to the effective date of the Schedule. Further, it may be noted that the definition of CPP has not changed under the 2013 Act as compared to the Companies Act, 1956. Hence, an existing asset as on 31 March, 2014 which was not identified and considered as continuous process plant under Schedule XIV of the Companies Act, 1956 in the financial statements cannot be retagged or re-determined as CPP under Schedule II of the Companies Act, 2013.

Annexure I

Schedule XIV under the Companies Act, 1956

RATES OF DEPRECIATION

Nature of assets	Single Shift		Double Shift		Triple Shift	
	W.D.V.	S.L.M.	W.D.V.	S.L.M.	W.D.V.	S.L.M.
1	2	3	4	5	6	7
I. (a) Buildings (other than factory buildings) (NESD)	5%	1.63%	..	..	..	..
(b) Factory Buildings	**10%**	**3.34%**	**..**	**..**	**..**	**..**
(c) Purely temporary erections such as wooden structures	100%	100%	..	..	..	..
II. Plant and Machinery						
(i) General rate applicable to						
(a) plant and machinery (not being a ship) other than continuous process plant for which no special rate has been prescribed under (ii) below:	**13.91%**	**4.75%**	**20.87%**	**7.42%**	**27.82%**	**10.34%**
(b) continuous process plant, for which no special rate has been prescribes under (ii) below (NSED)	15.33%	5.28%	..	..	..	..
(ii) Special rates						
A. 1. Cinematograph films-Machinery used in the production and exhibition of cinematograph films (NESD)	20%	7.07%	..	..	..	..
(a) Recording equipment, reproducing equipment, developing machines, printing machines, editing machines, synchronisers and studio lights except bulbs.	20%	7.07%	..	..	..	..
(b) Projecting equipment of film exhibiting concerns.	-do-	-do-	..	..	..	..
2. Cycles (NESD)	**20%**	**7.07%**	**..**	**..**	**..**	**..**

1	2	3	4	5	6	7
3. Electrical machinery, X-Ray and electro-therapeutic apparatus and accessories thereto, medical, diagnostic equipments, namely, Cat-scan, Ultrasound Machines, ECG Monitors etc. (NESD)	20%	7.07%	..	..	..	..
4. Juice boiling pairs (karhais) (NESD)	20%	7.07%	..	..	..	..
5. Motor-cars, motor cycles, scooters and other mopeds (NESD)	**25.89%**	**9.5%**	..	..	..	..
6. Electrically operated vehicles including battery powered or fuel call powered vehicles (NESD)	20%	7.07%	..	..	..	..
7. Sugarcane crushers (indigenous kolus and belans) (N.E.S.D.)	20%	7.07%	..	..	..	..
8. Glass manufacturing concerns except direct fire glass melting furnaces - Recuperative and regenerative glass melting furnaces	20%	7.07%	30%	11.31%	40%	16.21%
9. Machinery used in the manufacture of electronic goods or components.	15.62%	5.38%	23.42%	8.46%	31.23%	11.87%
B.1. Aeroplanes, Aero Engines, Simulators, Visual System and Quick Engine Change Equipment. (NESD)	16.2%	5.6%				
2. Concrete pipes manufacture Moulds (NESD)	30%	11.31%	..	..	..	..
3. Drum container manufacture dies (NESD)	-do-	-do-	..	..	..	..
4. Earth-moving machinery employed in heavy construction works, such as dams, tunnels, canals, etc. (NESD).	-do-	-do-	..	..	..	..
5. Glass manufacturing concerns except direct fire glass melting furnaces Moulds (NESD)	-do-	-do-	..	..	..	..
6. Moulds in iron foundaries (NESD)	-do-	-do-	..	..	..	..
7. Mineral oil concerns - Field operations (above ground) Portable boilers, drilling tools, well-head tanks, rigs, etc. (NESD)	-do-	-do-	..	..	..	..
8. Mines and quarries - Portable underground machinery and earth moving machinery used in open cast mining (NESD)	-do-	-do-	..	..	..	..

1	2	3	4	5	6	7
9. Motor buses and motor lorries other than those used in a business of running them on hire (NESD)	**30%**	**11.31%**	**..**	**..**	**..**	**..**
9A. Motor tractors, harvesting combines (NESD)	-do-	-do-	..	..	..	..
10. Patterns, dies and templates (NESD)	-do-	-do-	..	..	..	..
11. Ropeway structures - Ropeways, ropes and trestle sheaves and connected parts (NESD)	-do-	-do-	..	..	..	..
12. Shoe and other leather goods factories - Wooden lasts used in the manufacture of shoes	30%	11.31%	45%	18.96%	60%	29.05%
C. [Omitted]						
2. Motor buses, motor lorries and motor taxies used in a business of running them on hire (NESD)	40%	16.21%	..	..	..	..
3. Rubber and plastic goods factories Moulds (NESD)	-do-	-do-	..	..	..	..
4. Data processing machines including computers (NESD)	**-do-**	**-do-**	**..**	**..**	**..**	**..**
5. Gas cylinders including valves and regulators (NESD)	-do-	-do-	..	..	..	..
D.1. Artificial silk manufacturing machinery wooden parts	100	100%	..	..	..	..
2. Cinematograph films Bulbs of studio lights	-do-	-do-	..	..	..	..
3. Floor mills Rollers	-do-	-do-	..	..	..	..
4. Glass manufacturing concerns Direct fire glass melting furnaces	100	100%	..	..	..	..
4A. Float Glass Melting furnaces (NESD)	27%	10%	..	..	..	..
5. Iron and Steel industries Rolling mill rolls	100%	100%	..	..	..	..
6. Match factories Wooden match frames	-do-	-do-	..	..	..	..
7. Mineral oil concerns (a) Plant used in field operations (below ground) – Distribution – returnable packages (b) Plant used in field operations (below ground) but not including assets used in field operations (distribution) – Kerbside pumps including underground tanks and fittings	100%	100%	..	..	..	..

1	2	3	4	5	6	7
8. Mines and quarries – (a) Tubs, winding ropes, haulage ropes and sand stowing pipes	-do-	-do-	..	..	..	..
(b) Safety lamps			..	..	..	..
9. Salt works – Salt pans, reservoirs and condensers, etc., made of earthy, sandy or clay material or any other similar material	-do-	-do-	..	..	..	..
10. Sugar works—Rollers	-do-	-do-	..	..	..	..
III. Furniture and Fittings						
1. General rates (NESD)	**18.1**	**6.33**	..	..	..	..
2. Rate for furniture and fittings used in hotels, restaurants and boarding houses; schools, colleges and other educational institutions, libraries; welfare centres; meeting halls, cinema houses; theatres and circuses; and for furniture and fittings let out on hire for use on the occasion of marriages and similar functions (NESD)	25.88%	9.5%	..	..	..	..
IV. Ships						
1. Ocean-going ships-						
(i) Fishing vessels with wooden hull (NESD)	27.05%	10%	..	..	..	..
(ii) Dredgers, tugs, barges, survey launches and other similar ships used mainly for dredging purposes (NESD)	19.8%	7%	..	..	..	..
(iii) Other ships (NESD)	14.6%	5%	..	..	..	..
2. Vessels ordinarily operating on inland waters-						
(i) Speed boats (NESD)	20%	7.07%	..	..	..	..
(ii) Other vessels (NESD)	10%	3.34%	..	..	..	..

Notes

1. "Buildings" include roads, bridges, culverts, wells & tube-wells.
2. "Factory buildings" does not include offices, godowns, officers & employees' quarters, roads, bridges, culverts, wells & tube-wells.
3. "Speed boat" means a motor boat driven by a high speed internal combustion engine capable of propelling the boat at a speed exceeding 24 kilometres per hour in still water & so designed that when running at a speed it will plane, i.e., its bow will rise from the water.
4. Where, during any financial year, any addition has been made to any asset, or where any asset has been sold, discarded, demolished or destroyed, the depreciation on

such assets shall be calculated on a pro rata basis from the date of such addition or, as the case may be, up to the date on which such asset has been sold, discarded, demolished or destroyed.

5. The following information should also be disclosed in the accounts
   (i) Depreciation methods used; &
   (ii) Depreciation rates or the useful lives of the assets, if they are different from the principal rates specified in the Schedule.
6. The calculations of the extra depreciation for double shift working & for triple shift working shall be made separately in the proportion which the number of days for which the concern worked double shift or triple shift, as the case may be, bears to the normal number of working days during the year. For this purpose, the normal number of working days during the year shall be deemed to be
   (a) In the case of a seasonal factory or concern, the number of days on which the factory or concern actually worked during the year or 180 days, whichever is greater;
   (b) In any other case, the number of days on which the factory or concern actually worked during the year or 240 days, whichever is greater.

The extra shift depreciation shall not be charged in respect of any item of machinery or plant which has been specifically, excepted by inscription of the letters "N.E.S.D." (Meaning "No Extra Shift Depreciation") against it in sub-items above & also in respect of the following items of machinery & plant to which the general rate of depreciation of 13.91 per cent applies-

(1) Accounting machines.
(2) Air-conditioning machinery including room air-conditioners.
(3) Building contractor's machinery.
(4) Calculating machines.
(5) Electrical machinery - switchgear & instruments, transformers & other stationary plant & wiring & fitting of electric light & fan installations.
(6) Hydraulic works, pipelines & sluices.
(7) Locomotives, rolling stocks, tramways & railways used by concerns, excluding railway concerns.
(8) Mineral oil concerns - field operations- (b) Prime movers. (d) Storage tanks (above ground). (e) Pipelines (above ground). (f) Jetties & dry docks.
(9) Mineral oil concerns - field operations (distribution) - kerbside pumps, including underground tanks & fittings.
(10) Mineral oil concerns – refineries- (b) Prime movers. (d) LPG Plant
(11) Mines & quarries- (a) Surface & underground machinery (other than electrical machinery & portable underground machinery). (b) Head-gears. (c) Rails. (e) Shafts & inclines. (f) Tramways on the surface.
(12) Neo-post franking machines.
(13) Office machinery
(14) Overhead cables & wires.
(15) Railway sidings.
(16) Refrigeration plant containers, etc. (other than racks).
(17) Ropeway structures- (a) Trestle & station steel work. (b) Driving & tension gearing.

(18) Salt works - Reservoirs, condensers, salt pans, delivery channels & piers if constructed of masonry, concrete, cement, asphalt or similar materials; barges & floating plant; piers, quays & jetties; & pipelines for conveying brine if constructed of masonry, concrete, cement, asphalt or similar materials.

(19) Surgical instruments.

(20) Tramways electric & tramways run by internal combustion engines - permanent way: cars - car trucks, car bodies, electrical equipment & motors; tram cars including engines & gears.

(21) Typewriters.

(22) Weighing machines.

(23) Wireless apparatus & gear, wireless appliances & accessories.

7. "Continuous process plant" means a plant which is required & designed to operate 24 hours a day.

8. Notwithstanding anything mentioned in this Schedule depreciation on assets, whose actual cost does not exceed five thousand rupees, shall be provided depreciation at the rate of hundred per cent.

Provided that where the aggregate actual cost of individual items of plant & machinery costing Rs. 5,000 or less constitutes more than 10 per cent of the total actual cost of plant & machinery, rates of depreciation applicable to such items shall be the rates as specified in Item II of the Schedule.

Annexure II

Amendment to Schedule XIV

MINISTRY OF CORPORATE AFFAIRS NOTIFICATION

New Delhi, the 17th April, 2012

G.S.R. 298(E).-In exercise of the powers conferred by sub-section (1) of section 641 of the Companies Act, 1956 (1 of 1956), the Central Government hereby makes the following further alterations in the Schedule XIV of the said Act, namely:-

In schedule XIV of the Companies Act, 1956, after serial number IV relating to ship and the entries relating thereto, the following serial number and entries shall be inserted, namely:

"V-Intangible Assets

1. Intangible Assets (Toll Road) created under Build, Operate and Transfer, Build, Own, Operate and Transfer or any other form of Public Private Partnership Route.

$$\text{Amortization Rate} \quad \frac{\text{Amortization Amount} \times 100}{\text{Cost of Intangible Asset (A)}}$$

Amortization Amount

$$\text{Cost of Intangible Asset} \times \frac{\text{Actual Revenue for the year (B)}}{\text{Projected Revenue from Intangible Asset (till the end of the concession period)}}$$

2. Meaning of particulars are as follows:-

Cost of Intangible Asset (A)	=	Cost incurred by the Company in accordance with the Accounting Standards.
Actual Revenue for the year (B)	=	Actual Revenue (Toll Charges) received during the accounting year.
Projected Revenue from Intangible Asset (C)	=	Total Projected Revenue from the Intangible Asset as provided to the Project Lender at the time of financial closure/agreement.

The amortization amount or rate should ensure that the whole of the cost of the intangible asset is amortized over the concession period.
Total Revenue shall be reviewed at the end of each financial year and the projected revenue shall be adjusted to reflect any changes in the estimate which will lead to the actual collection at the end of the concession period.

3. For Example:-

Cost of creation of Intangible Assets	:	Rs. 500 crores
Total period of Agreement	:	20 years

Time use for creation of Intangible Assets : 2 years

Intangible Assets to be amortized in : 18 years

Let us assume that the Total revenue to be generated out of Intangible Assets over the Period would be Rs. 600 crores, in the following manner:

Year No.	Revenue (In Rs. crores)	Remarks
Year 1	5	Estimate*
Year 2	7.5	Estimate*
Year 3	10	Estimate*
Year 4	12.5	Estimate*
Year 5	17.5	Estimate*
Year 6	20	Estimate*
Year 7	23	Estimate*
Year 8	27	Estimate*
Year 9	31	Estimate*
Year 10	34	Estimate*
Year 11	38	Estimate*
Year 12	41	Estimate*
Year 13	46	Estimate*
Year 14	50	Estimate*
Year 15	53	Estimate*
Year 16	57	Estimate*
Year 17	60	Estimate*
Year 18	67.5	Estimate*
Total	**600**	

'*' will be actual at the end of financial year.

Based on this the charge for first year would be Rs. 4.16 crore (approximately) (*i.e.* Rs. 5/ Rs. 600 × Rs. 500 crores) which would be charged to profit and loss and 0.83% (i.e. Rs. 4.16 crore/Rs. 500 crore × 100) is the amortization rate for the first year."

Annexure III

Schedule II under Companies Act, 2013

(Incorporating the amendment at relevant places in the Schedule II itself)

SCHEDULE II

(*See* section 123)

USEFUL LIVES TO COMPUTE DEPRECIATION

PART 'A'

1. Depreciation is the systematic allocation of the depreciable amount of an asset over its useful life. The depreciable amount of an asset is the cost of an asset or other amount substituted for cost, less its residual value. The useful life of an asset is the period over which an asset is expected to be available for use by an entity, or the number of production or similar units expected to be obtained from the asset by the entity.

2. For the purpose of this Schedule, the term depreciation includes amortisation.

3. Without prejudice to the foregoing provisions of paragraph 1,

"(i) The useful life of an asset shall not ordinarily be different from the useful life specified in Part 'C' and the residual value of an asset shall not be more than five per cent of the original cost of the asset.

Provided that where a company adopts a useful life different from what is specified in Part C or uses a residual value different from the limit specified above, the financial statements shall disclose such difference and provide justification in this behalf duly supported by technical advice.

"(ii) For intangible assets, the provisions of the accounting standards applicable for the time being in force shall apply, except in case of intangible assets (Toll Roads) created under 'Build, Operate and Transfer', 'Build, Own, Operate and Transfer'

or any other form of public private partnership route in case of road projects. Amortisation in such cases may be done as follows:

(a) Mode of amortization

$$\textit{Amortization Rate} \quad \frac{\text{Amortization Amount} \times 100}{\text{Cost of Intangible Asset (A)}}$$

Amortization Amount

$$\text{Cost of Intangible Asset} \quad \times \quad \frac{\text{Actual Revenue for the year (B)}}{}$$

Projected Revenue from Intangible Asset
(till the end of the concession period)

Meaning of particulars are as follows:-

Cost of Intangible Asset (A)	=	Cost incurred by the Company in accordance with the Accounting Standards.
Actual Revenue for the year (B)	=	Actual Revenue (Toll Charges) received during the accounting year.
Projected Revenue from Intangible Asset (C)	=	Total Projected Revenue from the Intangible Asset as provided to the Project Lender at the time of financial closure/agreement.

The amortization amount or rate should ensure that the whole of the cost of the intangible asset is amortized over the concession period.

Total Revenue shall be reviewed at the end of each financial year and the projected revenue shall be adjusted to reflect any changes in the estimate which will lead to the actual collection at the end of the concession period.

For Example:-

Cost of creation of Intangible Assets	Rs. 500 crores
Total period of Agreement	20 years
Time use for creation of Intangible Assets	2 years
Intangible Assets to be amortized in	18 years

Assuming that the Total revenue to be generated out of Intangible Assets over the Period would be Rs. 600 crores, in the following manner:

Year No.	Revenue (In Rs. crores)	Remarks
Year 1	5	Actual
Year 2	7.5	Estimate*
Year 3	10	Estimate*
Year 4	12.5	Estimate*
Year 5	17.5	Estimate*
Year 6	20	Estimate*
Year 7	23	Estimate*
Year 8	27	Estimate*
Year 9	31	Estimate*
Year 10	34	Estimate*
Year 11	38	Estimate*
Year 12	41	Estimate*
Year 13	46	Estimate*
Year 14	50	Estimate*
Year 15	53	Estimate*
Year 16	57	Estimate*

Year No.	Revenue (In Rs. crores)	Remarks
Year 17	60	Estimate*
Year 18	67.5	Estimate*
Total	**600**	

'*' will be actual at the end of financial year.

Based on this the charge for first year would be Rs. 4.16 crore (approximately) (*i.e.* Rs. 5/ Rs. 600 × Rs. 500 crores) which would be charged to profit and loss and 0.83% (*i.e.* Rs. 4.16 crore/Rs. 500 crore × 100) is the amortization rate for the first year."

Where a company arrives at the amortisation amount in respect of the said Intangible Assets in accordance with any method as per the applicable Accounting Standards, it shall disclose the same

PART 'B'

4. The useful life or residual value of any specific asset, as notified for accounting purposes by a Regulatory Authority constituted under an Act of Parliament or by the Central Government shall be applied in calculating the depreciation to be provided for such asset irrespective of the requirements of this Schedule.

PART 'C'

5. Subject to Parts A and B above, the following are the useful lives of various tangible assets:

Nature of assets	Useful Life
I. Buildings [NESD]	
(*a*) Buildings (other than factory buildings) RCC Frame Structure	60 Years
(*b*) Buildings (other than factory buildings) other than RCC Frame Structure	30 Years
(*c*) Factory buildings	-do-
(*d*) Fences, wells, tube wells	5 Years
(*e*) Others (including temporary structure, etc.)	3 Years
II. Bridges, culverts, bunders, etc. [NESD]	30 Years
III. Roads [NESD]	
(*a*) Carpeted roads	
(*i*) Carpeted Roads-RCC	10 Years
(*ii*) Carpeted Roads-other than RCC	5 Years
(*b*) Non-carpeted roads	3 Years
IV. Plant and Machinery	
(*i*) **General rate applicable to plant and machinery not covered under special plant and machinery**	
(*a*) Plant and Machinery other than continuous process plant not covered under specific industries	15 Years

Nature of assets	Useful Life
(*b*) continuous process plant for which no special rate has been prescribed under (*ii*) below [NESD]	25 Years
(*ii*) **Special Plant and Machinery**	
(*a*) Plant and Machinery related to production and exhibition of Motion Picture Films	
1. Cinematograph films—Machinery used in the production and exhibition of cinematograph films, recording and reproducing equipments, developing machines, printing machines, editing machines, synchronizers and studio lights except bulbs	13 Years
2. Projecting equipment for exhibition of films	-do-
(*b*) Plant and Machinery used in glass manufacturing	
1. Plant and Machinery except direct fire glass melting furnaces — Recuperative and regenerative glass melting furnaces	13 Years
2. Plant and Machinery except direct fire glass melting furnaces — Moulds [NESD]	8 Years
3. Float Glass Melting Furnaces [NESD]	10 Years
(*c*) Plant and Machinery used in mines and quarries—Portable underground machinery and earth moving machinery used in open cast mining [NESD]	8 Years
(*d*) Plant and Machinery used in Telecommunications [NESD]	
1. Towers	18 Years
2. Telecom transceivers, switching centres, transmission and other network equipment	13 Years
3. Telecom—Ducts, Cables and optical fibre	18 Years
4. Satellites	-do-
(*e*) Plant and Machinery used in exploration, production and refining oil and gas [NESD]	
1. Refineries	25 Years
2. Oil and gas assets (including wells), processing plant and facilities	-do-
3. Petrochemical Plant	-do-
4. Storage tanks and related equipment	-do-
5. Pipelines	30 Years
6. Drilling Rig	-do-
7. Field operations (above ground) Portable boilers, drilling tools, well-head tanks, etc.	8 Years
8. Loggers	-do-
(*f*) Plant and Machinery used in generation, transmission and distribution of power [NESD]	
1. Thermal/ Gas/ Combined Cycle Power Generation Plant	40 Years
2. Hydro Power Generation Plant	-do-

Nature of assets	Useful Life
3. Nuclear Power Generation Plant	-do-
4. Transmission lines, cables and other network assets	-do-
5. Wind Power Generation Plant	22 Years
6. Electric Distribution Plant	35 Years
7. Gas Storage and Distribution Plant	30 Years
8. Water Distribution Plant including pipelines	-do-
(*g*) Plant and Machinery used in manufacture of steel	
1. Sinter Plant	20 Years
2. Blast Furnace	-do-
3. Coke ovens	-do-
4. Rolling mill in steel plant	-do-
5. Basic oxygen Furnace Converter	25 Years
(*h*) Plant and Machinery used in manufacture of non-ferrous metals	
1. Metal pot line [NESD]	40 Years
2. Bauxite crushing and grinding section [NESD]	-do-
3. Digester Section [NESD]	-do-
4. Turbine [NESD]	-do-
5. Equipments for Calcination [NESD]	-do-
6. Copper Smelter [NESD]	-do-
7. Roll Grinder	40 Years
8. Soaking Pit	30 Years
9. Annealing Furnace	-do-
10. Rolling Mills	-do-
11. Equipments for Scalping, Slitting, etc. [NESD]	-do-
12. Surface Miner, Ripper Dozer, etc., used in mines	25 Years
13. Copper refining plant [NESD]	-do-
(*i*) Plant and Machinery used in medical and surgical operations [NESD]	
1. Electrical Machinery, X-ray and electrotherapeutic apparatus and accessories thereto, medical, diagnostic equipments, namely, Cat-scan, Ultrasound Machines, ECG Monitors, etc.	13 Years
2. Other Equipments.	15 Years
(*j*) Plant and Machinery used in manufacture of pharmaceuticals and chemicals [NESD]	
1. Reactors	20 Years
2. Distillation Columns	-do-
3. Drying equipments/Centrifuges and Decanters	-do-
4. Vessel/storage tanks	–do-

Nature of assets	Useful Life
(*k*) Plant and Machinery used in civil construction	
1. Concreting, Crushing, Piling Equipments and Road Making Equipments	12 Years
2. Heavy Lift Equipments—	
Cranes with capacity of more than 100 tons	20 Years
Cranes with capacity of less than 100 tons	15 Years
3. Transmission line, Tunneling Equipments [NESD]	10 Years
4. Earth-moving equipments	9 Years
5. Others including Material Handling /Pipeline/Welding Equipments [NESD]	12 Years
(*l*) Plant and Machinery used in salt works [NESD]	15 Years
V. Furniture and fittings [NESD]	
(*i*) General furniture and fittings	10 Years
(*ii*) Furniture and fittings used in hotels, restaurants and boarding houses, schools, colleges and other educational institutions, libraries; welfare centres; meeting halls, cinema houses; theatres and circuses; and furniture and fittings let out on hire for use on the occasion of marriages and similar functions.	8 Years
VI. Motor Vehicles [NESD]	
1. Motor cycles, scooters and other mopeds	10 Years
2. Motor buses, motor lorries, motor cars and motor taxies used in a business of running them on hire	6 Years
3. Motor buses, motor lorries and motor cars other than those used in a business of running them on hire	8 Years
4. Motor tractors, harvesting combines and heavy vehicles	-do-
5. Electrically operated vehicles including battery powered or fuel cell powered vehicles	8 Years
VII. Ships [NESD]	
1. Ocean-going ships	
(*i*) Bulk Carriers and liner vessels	25 Years
(*ii*) Crude tankers, product carriers and easy chemical carriers with or without conventional tank coatings.	20 Years
(*iii*) Chemicals and Acid Carriers:	
(*a*) With Stainless steel tanks	25 Years
(*b*) With other tanks	20 Years
(*iv*) Liquified gas carriers	30 Years
(*v*) Conventional large passenger vessels which are used for cruise purpose also	-do-
(*vi*) Coastal service ships of all categories	-do-

Nature of assets	Useful Life
(*vii*) Offshore supply and support vessels	20 Years
(viii) Catamarans and other high speed passenger for ships or boats	–do-
(*ix*) Drill ships	25 Years
(*x*) Hovercrafts	15 Years
(*xi*) Fishing vessels with wooden hull	10 Years
(*xii*) Dredgers, tugs, barges, survey launches and other similar ships used mainly for dredging purposes	14 Years
2. Vessels ordinarily operating on inland waters—	
(*i*) Speed boats	13 Years
(*ii*) Other vessels	28 Years
VIII. Aircrafts or Helicopters [NESD]	20 Years
IX. Railways sidings, locomotives, rolling stocks, tramways and railways used by concerns, excluding railway concerns [NESD]	15 Years
X. Ropeway structures [NESD]	15 Years
XI. Office equipment [NESD]	5 Years
XII. Computers and data processing units [NESD]	
(*i*) Servers and networks	6 Years
(*ii*) End user devices, such as, desktops, laptops, etc.	3 Years
XIII. Laboratory equipment [NESD]	
(*i*) General laboratory equipment	10 Years
(*ii*) Laboratory equipments used in educational institutions	5 Years
XIV. Electrical Installations and Equipment [NESD]	10 years
XV. Hydraulic works, pipelines and sluices [NESD]	15 Years

Notes:

1. "Factory buildings" does not include offices, godowns, staff quarters.

2. Where, during any financial year, any addition has been made to any asset, or where any asset has been sold, discarded, demolished or destroyed, the depreciation on such assets shall be calculated on a *pro rata* basis from the date of such addition or, as the case may be, up to the date on which such asset has been sold, discarded, demolished or destroyed.

3. The following information shall also be disclosed in the accounts, namely:
   (*i*) depreciation methods used; and
   (*ii*) the useful lives of the assets for computing depreciation, if they are different from the life specified in the Schedule.

4. (a) Useful life specified in Part C of the Schedule is for whole of the asset. Where cost of a part of the asset is significant to total cost of the asset and useful life of that part is different from the useful life of the remaining asset, useful life of that significant part shall be determined separately.

(b) The requirement under sub-paragraph (a) shall be voluntary in respect of the financial year commencing on or after the 1st April, 2014 and mandatory for financial statements in respect of financial years commencing on or after the 1st April, 2015.

5. The useful lives of assets working on shift basis have been specified in the Schedule based on their single shift working. Except for assets in respect of which no extra shift depreciation is permitted (indicated by NESD in Part C above), if an asset is used for any time during the year for double shift, the depreciation will increase by 50% for that period and in case of the triple shift the depreciation shall be calculated on the basis of 100% for that period.

6. From the date this Schedule comes into effect, the carrying amount of the asset as on that date—

(*a*) shall be depreciated over the remaining useful life of the asset as per this Schedule;

(*b*) after retaining the residual value, may be recognised in the opening balance of retained earnings where the remaining useful life of an asset is nil.

7. ''Continuous process plant'' means a plant which is required and designed to operate for twenty-four hours a day.

Annexure IV

Amendment to Schedule II

New Delhi, the 31st March, 2014

G.S.R. 237 (E).—In exercise of the powers conferred by sub-section (2) of Section 123 read with sub-sections (1) of Section 467 of the Companies Act, 2013 (18 of 2013), the Central Government hereby makes the following alterations to Schedule II to the said Act, namely:— 1. In Schedule II,—

(1) in Part 'A', in para 3, for sub-paragraphs (i) to (iii), the following sub-paragraphs shall be substituted, namely:—

"(i) The useful life of an asset shall not be longer than the useful life specified in Part 'C' and the residual value of an asset shall not be more than five per cent of the original cost of the asset:

Provided that where a company uses a useful life or residual value of the asset which is different from the above limits, justification for the difference shall be disclosed in its financial statement.

"(ii) For intangible assets, the provisions of the accounting standards applicable for the time being in force shall apply, except in case of intangible assets (Toll Roads) created under 'Build, Operate and Transfer', 'Build, Own, Operate and Transfer' or any other form of public private partnership route in case of road projects. Amortisation in such cases may be done as follows:

(a) Mode of amortization

$$\text{Amortisation Amount} = \frac{\text{Amortisation Rate} \times 100}{\text{Cost of Intangible Assets (A)}}$$

Amortisation Amount

$$= \text{Cost of Intangible Assets (A)} \times \frac{\text{Actual Revenue for the year (B)}}{\text{Projected Revenue from Intangible Asset (till the end of the concession period) (C)}}$$

(b) Meaning of particulars arc as follows :—

Cost of Intangible Assets (A)	=	Cost incurred by the company in accordance with the accounting standards.
Actual Revenue for the year (B)	=	Actual revenue (Toll Charges) received during the accounting year.
Projected Revenue from Intangible Asset (C)	=	Total projected revenue from the Intangible Assets as provided to the project lender at the time of financial closure /agreement.

The amortisation amount or rate should ensure that the whole of the cost of the intangible asset is amortised over the concession period.

Revenue shall be reviewed at the end of each financial year and projected revenue shall be adjusted to reflect such changes, if any, in the estimates as will lead to the actual collection at the end of the concession period.

(c) Example:—

Cost of creation of Intangible Assets	:	Rs. 500 Crores
Total period of Agreement	:	20 Years
Time used for creation of Intangible Assets	:	2 Years
Intangible Assets to be amortised in	:	18 Years

Assuming that the Total revenue to be generated out of Intangible Assets over the period would be

Rs. 600 Crores, in the following manner:—

Year No.	Revenue (In Rs. Crores)	Remarks
Year 1	5	Actual
Year 2	7.5	Estimate *
Year 3	10	Estimate *
Year 4	12.5	Estimate *
Year 5	17.5	Estimate *
Year 6	20	Estimate *
Year 7	23	Estimate *
Year 8	27	Estimate *
Year 9	31	Estimate *
Year 10	34-	Estimate *
Year 1 1	38	Estimate *
Year 12	41	Estimate *
Year 13	46	Estimate *
Year 14	50	Estimate *
Year 15	53	Estimate *
Year 16	57	Estimate *
Year 17	60	Estimate *
Year 18	67.5	Estimate *
Total	600	

'*' will be actual at the end of financial year.

Based on this the charge for first year would be Rs. 4.16 Crore (approximately) (i.e. Rs. 5/Rs. 600 × Rs. 500 Crores) which would be charged to profit and loss and 0.83% (i.e. Rs. 4.16 Crore/ Rs. 500 Crore × 100) is the amortisation rate for the first year.

Where a company arrives at the amortisation amount in respect of the said Intangible Assets in accordance with any method as per the applicable Accounting Standards, it shall disclose the same.".

(2) in Part 'C', in para 5, in item IV, in sub-item (i), for clause (b), the following clause shall be substituted, namely:—

"(b) continuous process plant for which no special rate has been prescribed, under (ii) below [NESD] 25 years"

(3) under the heading 'Notes', appearing after Part 'C', paragraph 5 shall be omitted.

2. This notification shall come into force with effect from 01 April, 2014.

Annexure V

Further amendment to Schedule II

New Delhi, the 29th August, 2014

G.S.R. 627(E).—In exercise of the powers conferred by sub section (1) of Section 467 of the Companies Act, 2013 (18 of 2013), the Central Government hereby makes the following amendments farther to amend Schedule II of the said Act with effect from the date of publication of this notification in the Official Gazette, namely:—

1. In Schedule II of the Companies Act, 2013,—

(a) in Part 'A', in paragraph 3, for sub-paragraph (i), the following sub-paragraph shall be substituted, namely:—

"(i) The useful life of an asset shall not ordinarily be different from the useful life specified in Part C and the residual value of an asset shall not be more than five per cent, of the original cost of the asset:

Provided that where a company adopts a useful life different from what is specified in Part C or uses a residual value different from the limit specified above, the financial statements shall disclose such difference and provide justification in this behalf duly supported by technical advice",.

(b) after Part 'C', under the heading Notes,—

(i) for paragraph 4 the following paragraph shall be substituted namely:—

"4(a) Useful life specified in Part C of the Schedule is for whole of the asset and where cost of a part of the asset is significant to total cost of the asset and useful life of that part is different from the useful life of the remaining asset, useful life of that significant part shall be determined separately.

(b) The requirement under sub-paragraph (a) shall be voluntary in respect of the financial year commencing on or after the 1st April, 2014 and mandatory for financial statements in respect of financial years commencing on or after the 1st April, 2015."

(c) in paragraph 7, in sub-paragraph (b) for the words "shall be recognized", the words "may be recognized" shall be substituted.

Note: Schedule II of the Companies Act, 2013 came into force with effect from the 1st April, 2014 and was amended (with effect from 1st April, 2014) *vide* notification number S. O. 237(E), dated the 31st March, 2014.

Annexure VI

Important provisions under the Companies Act, 2013 pertaining to depreciation

Section 2(57) of the Companies Act, 2013

"Net worth" means the aggregate value of the paid-up share capital and all reserves created out of the profits and securities premium account, after deducting the aggregate value of the accumulated losses, deferred expenditure and miscellaneous expenditure not written off, as per the audited balance sheet, but does not include reserves created out of revaluation of assets, write-back of depreciation and amalgamation.

Section 123 of the Companies Act, 2013

(*1*) No dividend shall be declared or paid by a company for any financial year except

(*a*) out of the profits of the company for that year arrived at after providing for depreciation in accordance with the provisions of sub-section (*2*), or out of the profits of the company for any previous financial year or years arrived at after providing for depreciation in accordance with the provisions of that sub-section and remaining undistributed, or out of both; or

(*b*) out of money provided by the Central Government or a State Government for the payment of dividend by the company in pursuance of a guarantee given by that Government:

Provided that a company may, before the declaration of any dividend in any financial year, transfer such percentage of its profits for that financial year as it may consider appropriate to the reserves of the company:

Provided further that where, owing to inadequacy or absence of profits in any financial year, any company proposes to declare dividend out of the accumulated profits earned by it in previous years and transferred by the company to the reserves, such declaration of dividend shall not be made except in accordance with such rules as may be prescribed in this behalf: Provided also that no dividend shall be declared or paid by a company from its reserves other than free reserves.

(*2*) For the purposes of clause (*a*) of sub-section (*1*), depreciation shall be provided in accordance with the provisions of Schedule II.

(*3*) The Board of Directors of a company may declare interim dividend during any financial year out of the surplus in the profit and loss account and out of profits of the financial year in which such interim dividend is sought to be declared:

Provided that in case the company has incurred loss during the current financial year up to the end of the quarter immediately preceding the date of declaration of interim dividend, such interim dividend shall not be declared at a rate higher than the average dividends declared by the company during the immediately preceding three financial years.

(*4*) The amount of the dividend, including interim dividend, shall be deposited in a scheduled bank in a separate account within five days from the date of declaration of such dividend.

(*5*) No dividend shall be paid by a company in respect of any share therein except to the registered shareholder of such share or to his order or to his banker and shall not be payable except in cash:

Provided that nothing in this sub-section shall be deemed to prohibit the capitalisation of profits or reserves of a company for the purpose of issuing fully paid-up bonus shares or paying up any amount for the time being unpaid on any shares held by the members of the company:

Provided further that any dividend payable in cash may be paid by cheque or warrant or in any electronic mode to the shareholder entitled to the payment of the dividend.

(*6*) A company which fails to comply with the provisions of sections 73 and 74 shall not, so long as such failure continues, declare any dividend on its equity shares.

Rule 3 of Companies (Declaration and Payment of Dividend) Rules, 2014 read with Companies (Declaration and Payment of Dividend) Amendment Rules, 2014

Declaration of dividend out of reserves

In the event of inadequacy or absence of profits in any year, a company may declare dividend out of surplus subject to the fulfillment of the following conditions, namely:

(1) The rate of dividend declared shall not exceed the average of the rates at which dividend was declared by it in the three years immediately preceding that year;

However, this will not apply to a company, which has not declared any dividend in each of the three preceding financial year.

(2) The total amount to be drawn from such accumulated profits should not exceed an amount equal to one-tenth of the sum of its paid-up share capital and free reserves as appearing in the latest audited financial statement;

(3) The amount so drawn should first be utilised to set off the losses incurred in the financial year in which dividend is declared before any dividend in respect of equity shares is declared.

(4) The balance of reserves after such withdrawal should not fall below fifteen per cent of its paid up share capital as appearing in the latest audited financial statement.

(5) No company can declare dividend unless carried over previous losses and depreciation not provided in previous year or years are set off against profit of the company of the current year.

Annexure VII

Indian Accounting Standard (Ind AS) 16 on Property, Plant and Equipment

(*This Indian Accounting Standard includes paragraphs set in* **bold** *type and plain type, which have equal authority. Paragraphs in bold type indicate the main principles.*)

Objective

1 The objective of this Standard is to prescribe the accounting treatment for property, plant and equipment so that users of the financial statements can discern information about an entity's investment in its property, plant and equipment and the changes in such investment. The principal issues in accounting for property, plant and equipment are the recognition of the assets, the determination of their carrying amounts and the depreciation charges and impairment losses to be recognised in relation to them.

Scope

2 This Standard shall be applied in accounting for property, plant and equipment except when another Standard requires or permits a different accounting treatment.

3 This Standard does not apply to:

(a) property, plant and equipment classified as held for sale in accordance with Ind AS 105, *Non-current Assets Held for Sale and Discontinued Operations*.

(b) biological assets related to agricultural activity other than bearer plants (See Ind AS 41, *Agriculture*). This Standard applies to bearer plants but it does not apply to the produce on bearer plants.

(c) the recognition and measurement of exploration and evaluation assets (see Ind AS 106, *Exploration for and Evaluation of Mineral Resources*).

(d) mineral rights and mineral reserves such as oil, natural gas and similar non-regenerative resources.

However, this Standard applies to property, plant and equipment used to develop or maintain the assets described in (b)–(d).

4 Other Indian Accounting Standards may require recognition of an item of property, plant and equipment based on an approach different from that in this Standard. For example, Ind AS 17, *Leases,* requires an entity to evaluate its recognition of an item of leased property, plant and equipment on the basis of the transfer of risks and rewards. However, in such cases other aspects of the accounting treatment for these assets, including depreciation, are prescribed by this Standard.

5 An entity accounting for investment property in accordance with Ind AS 40, *Investment Property,* shall use the cost model in this Standard.

Definitions

6 The following terms are used in this Standard with the meanings specified:

A *bearer plant* is a living plant that:

(a) is used in the production or supply of agricultural produce;

(b) is expected to bear produce for more than one period; and

(c) has a remote likelihood of being sold as agricultural produce, except for incidental scrap sales.

***Carrying amount* is the amount at which an asset is recognised after deducting any accumulated depreciation and accumulated impairment losses.**

Cost* is the amount of cash or cash equivalents paid or the fair value of the other consideration given to acquire an asset at the time of its acquisition or construction or, where applicable, the amount attributed to that asset when initially recognised in accordance with the specific requirements of other Indian Accounting Standards, eg Ind AS 102, *Share-based Payment.

***Depreciable amount* is the cost of an asset, or other amount substituted for cost, less its residual value.**

***Depreciation* is the systematic allocation of the depreciable amount of an asset over its useful life.**

***Entity-specific value* is the present value of the cash flows an entity expects to arise from the continuing use of an asset and from its disposal at the end of its useful life or expects to incur when settling a liability.**

***Fair value* is the price that would be received to sell an asset or paid to transfer a liability in an orderly transaction between market participants at the measurement date. (See Ind AS 113, *Fair Value Measurement.*)**

An *impairment loss* is the amount by which the carrying amount of an asset exceeds its recoverable amount.

***Property, plant and equipment* are tangible items that:**

(a) are held for use in the production or supply of goods or services, for rental to others, or for administrative purposes; and

(b) are expected to be used during more than one period.

***Recoverable amount* is the higher of an asset's fair value less costs to sell and its value in use.**

The *residual value* of an asset is the estimated amount that an entity would currently obtain from disposal of the asset, after deducting the estimated costs of disposal, if the asset were already of the age and in the condition expected at the end of its useful life.

Useful life is:

(a) the period over which an asset is expected to be available for use by an entity; or

(b) the number of production or similar units expected to be obtained from the asset by an entity.

Recognition

7 The cost of an item of property, plant and equipment shall be recognised as an asset if, and only if:

(a) it is probable that future economic benefits associated with the item will flow to the entity; and

(b) the cost of the item can be measured reliably.

8 Items such as spare parts, stand-by equipment and servicing equipment are recognised in accordance with this Ind AS when they meet the definition of property, plant and equipment. Otherwise, such items are classified as inventory.

9 This Standard does not prescribe the unit of measure for recognition, ie what constitutes an item of property, plant and equipment. Thus, judgement is required in applying the recognition criteria to an entity's specific circumstances. It may be appropriate to aggregate individually insignificant items, such as moulds, tools and dies, and to apply the criteria to the aggregate value.

10 An entity evaluates under this recognition principle all its property, plant and equipment costs at the time they are incurred. These costs include costs incurred initially to acquire or construct an item of property, plant and equipment and costs incurred subsequently to add to, replace part of, or service it.

Initial costs

11 Items of property, plant and equipment may be acquired for safety or environmental reasons. The acquisition of such property, plant and equipment, although not directly increasing the future economic benefits of any particular existing item of property, plant and equipment, may be necessary for an entity to obtain the future economic benefits from its other assets. Such items of property, plant and equipment qualify for recognition as assets because they enable an entity to derive future economic benefits from related assets in excess of what could be derived had those items not been acquired. For example, a chemical manufacturer may install new chemical handling processes to comply with environmental requirements for the production and storage of dangerous chemicals; related plant enhancements are recognised as an asset because without them the entity is unable to manufacture and sell chemicals. However, the resulting carrying amount of such an asset and related assets is reviewed for impairment in accordance with Ind AS 36, *Impairment of Assets*.

Subsequent costs

12 Under the recognition principle in paragraph 7, an entity does not recognise in the carrying amount of an item of property, plant and equipment the costs of the day-to-day servicing of the item. Rather, these costs are recognised in profit or loss as incurred. Costs of day-to-day servicing are primarily the costs of labour and consumables, and may include the cost of small parts. The purpose of these expenditures is often described as for the 'repairs and maintenance' of the item of property, plant and equipment.

13 Parts of some items of property, plant and equipment may require replacement at regular intervals. For example, a furnace may require relining after a specified number of hours of use, or aircraft interiors such as seats and galleys may require replacement several times during the life of the airframe. Items of property, plant and equipment may also be acquired to make a less frequently recurring replacement, such as replacing the interior walls of a building, or to make a nonrecurring replacement. Under the recognition principle in

paragraph 7, an entity recognises in the carrying amount of an item of property, plant and equipment the cost of replacing part of such an item when that cost is incurred if the recognition criteria are met. The carrying amount of those parts that are replaced is derecognised in accordance with the derecognition provisions of this Standard (see paragraphs 67–72).

14 A condition of continuing to operate an item of property, plant and equipment (for example, an aircraft) may be performing regular major inspections for faults regardless of whether parts of the item are replaced. When each major inspection is performed, its cost is recognised in the carrying amount of the item of property, plant and equipment as a replacement if the recognition criteria are satisfied. Any remaining carrying amount of the cost of the previous inspection (as distinct from physical parts) is derecognised. This occurs regardless of whether the cost of the previous inspection was identified in the transaction in which the item was acquired or constructed. If necessary, the estimated cost of a future similar inspection may be used as an indication of what the cost of the existing inspection component was when the item was acquired or constructed.

Measurement at recognition

15 An item of property, plant and equipment that qualifies for recognition as an asset shall be measured at its cost.

Elements of cost

16 The cost of an item of property, plant and equipment comprises:

(a) its purchase price, including import duties and non-refundable purchase taxes, after deducting trade discounts and rebates.

(b) any costs directly attributable to bringing the asset to the location and condition necessary for it to be capable of operating in the manner intended by management.

(c) the initial estimate of the costs of dismantling and removing the item and restoring the site on which it is located, the obligation for which an entity incurs either when the item is acquired or as a consequence of having used the item during a particular period for purposes other than to produce inventories during that period.

17 Examples of directly attributable costs are:

(a) costs of employee benefits (as defined in Ind AS 19, *Employee Benefits*) arising directly from the construction or acquisition of the item of property, plant and equipment;

(b) costs of site preparation;

(c) initial delivery and handling costs;

(d) installation and assembly costs;

(e) costs of testing whether the asset is functioning properly, after deducting the net proceeds from selling any items produced while bringing the asset to that location and condition (such as samples produced when testing equipment); and

(f) professional fees.

18 An entity applies Ind AS 2, *Inventories,* to the costs of obligations for dismantling, removing and restoring the site on which an item is located that are incurred during a particular period as a consequence of having used the item to produce inventories during that period. The obligations for costs accounted for in accordance with Ind AS 2 or Ind AS 16 are recognised and measured in accordance with Ind AS 37, *Provisions, Contingent Liabilities and Contingent Assets*.

19 Examples of costs that are not costs of an item of property, plant and equipment are:

(a) costs of opening a new facility;

(b) costs of introducing a new product or service (including costs of advertising and promotional activities);

(c) costs of conducting business in a new location or with a new class of customer (including costs of staff training); and

(d) administration and other general overhead costs.

20 Recognition of costs in the carrying amount of an item of property, plant and equipment ceases when the item is in the location and condition necessary for it to be capable of operating in the manner intended by management. Therefore, costs incurred in using or redeploying an item are not included in the carrying amount of that item. For example, the following costs are not included in the carrying amount of an item of property, plant and equipment:

(a) costs incurred while an item capable of operating in the manner intended by management has yet to be brought into use or is operated at less than full capacity;

(b) initial operating losses, such as those incurred while demand for the item's output builds up; and

(c) costs of relocating or reorganising part or all of an entity's operations.

21 Some operations occur in connection with the construction or development of an item of property, plant and equipment, but are not necessary to bring the item to the location and condition necessary for it to be capable of operating in the manner intended by management. These incidental operations may occur before or during the construction or development activities. For example, income may be earned through using a building site as a car park until construction starts. Because incidental operations are not necessary to bring an item to the location and condition necessary for it to be capable of operating in the manner intended by management, the income and related expenses of incidental operations are recognised in profit or loss and included in their respective classifications of income and expense.

22 The cost of a self-constructed asset is determined using the same principles as for an acquired asset. If an entity makes similar assets for sale in the normal course of business, the cost of the asset is usually the same as the cost of constructing an asset for sale (see Ind AS 2). Therefore, any internal profits are eliminated in arriving at such costs. Similarly, the cost of abnormal amounts of wasted material, labour, or other resources incurred in self-constructing an asset is not included in the cost of the asset. Ind AS 23, *Borrowing Costs,* establishes criteria for the recognition of interest as a component of the carrying amount of a selfconstructed item of property, plant and equipment.

22A Bearer plants are accounted for in the same way as self-constructed items of property, plant and equipment before they are in the location and condition necessary to be capable of operating in the manner intended by management. Consequently, references to 'construction' in this Standard should be read as covering activities that are necessary to cultivate the bearer plants before they are in the location and condition necessary to be capable of operating in the manner intended by management.

Measurement of cost

23 The cost of an item of property, plant and equipment is the cash price equivalent at the recognition date. If payment is deferred beyond normal credit terms, the difference between

the cash price equivalent and the total payment is recognized as interest over the period of credit unless such interest is capitalised in accordance with Ind AS 23.

24 One or more items of property, plant and equipment may be acquired in exchange for a non-monetary asset or assets, or a combination of monetary and nonmonetary assets. The following discussion refers simply to an exchange of one non-monetary asset for another, but it also applies to all exchanges described in the preceding sentence. The cost of such an item of property, plant and equipment is measured at fair value unless (a) the exchange transaction lacks commercial substance or (b) the fair value of neither the asset received nor the asset given up is reliably measurable. The acquired item is measured in this way even if an entity cannot immediately derecognise the asset given up. If the acquired item is not measured at fair value, its cost is measured at the carrying amount of the asset given up.

25 An entity determines whether an exchange transaction has commercial substance by considering the extent to which its future cash flows are expected to change as a result of the transaction. An exchange transaction has commercial substance if:

(a) the configuration (risk, timing and amount) of the cash flows of the asset received differs from the configuration of the cash flows of the asset transferred; or

(b) the entity-specific value of the portion of the entity's operations affected by the transaction changes as a result of the exchange; and

(c) the difference in (a) or (b) is significant relative to the fair value of the assets exchanged.

For the purpose of determining whether an exchange transaction has commercial substance, the entity-specific value of the portion of the entity's operations affected by the transaction shall reflect post-tax cash flows. The result of these analyses may be clear without an entity having to perform detailed calculations.

26 The fair value of an asset is reliably measurable if (a) the variability in the range of reasonable fair value measurements is not significant for that asset or (b) the probabilities of the various estimates within the range can be reasonably assessed and used when measuring fair value. If an entity is able to measure reliably the fair value of either the asset received or the asset given up, then the fair value of the asset given up is used to measure the cost of the asset received unless the fair value of the asset received is more clearly evident.

27 The cost of an item of property, plant and equipment held by a lessee under a finance lease is determined in accordance with Ind AS 17.

Measurement after recognition

29 An entity shall choose either the cost model in paragraph 30 or the revaluation model in paragraph 31 as its accounting policy and shall apply that policy to an entire class of property, plant and equipment.

Cost model

30 After recognition as an asset, an item of property, plant and equipment shall be carried at its cost less any accumulated depreciation and any accumulated impairment losses.

Revaluation model

31 After recognition as an asset, an item of property, plant and equipment whose fair value can be measured reliably shall be carried at a revalued amount, being its fair value at the date of the revaluation less any subsequent accumulated depreciation and

subsequent accumulated impairment losses. Revaluations shall be made with sufficient regularity to ensure that the carrying amount does not differ materially from that which would be determined using fair value at the end of the reporting period.

32 [Refer Appendix 1].

33 [Refer Appendix 1].

34 The frequency of revaluations depends upon the changes in fair values of the items of property, plant and equipment being revalued. When the fair value of a revalued asset differs materially from its carrying amount, a further revaluation is required. Some items of property, plant and equipment experience significant and volatile changes in fair value, thus necessitating annual revaluation. Such frequent revaluations are unnecessary for items of property, plant and equipment with only insignificant changes in fair value. Instead, it may be necessary to revalue the item only every three or five years.

35 When an item of property, plant and equipment is revalued, the carrying amount of that asset is adjusted to the revalued amount. At the date of the revaluation, the asset is treated in one of the following ways:

(a) the gross carrying amount is adjusted in a manner that is consistent with the revaluation of the carrying amount of the asset. For example, the gross carrying amount may be restated by reference to observable market data or it may be restated proportionately to the change in the carrying amount. The accumulated depreciation at the date of the revaluation is adjusted to equal the difference between the gross carrying amount and the carrying amount of the asset after taking into account accumulated impairment losses; or

(b) the accumulated depreciation is eliminated against the gross carrying amount of the asset.

The amount of the adjustment of accumulated depreciation forms part of the increase or decrease in carrying amount that is accounted for in accordance with paragraphs 39 and 40.

36 If an item of property, plant and equipment is revalued, the entire class of property, plant and equipment to which that asset belongs shall be revalued.

37 A class of property, plant and equipment is a grouping of assets of a similar nature and use in an entity's operations. The following are examples of separate classes:

(a) land;

(b) land and buildings;

(c) machinery;

(d) ships;

(e) aircraft;

(f) motor vehicles;

(g) furniture and fixtures;

(h) office equipment; and

(i) bearer plants.

38 The items within a class of property, plant and equipment are revalued simultaneously to avoid selective revaluation of assets and the reporting of amounts in the financial statements that are a mixture of costs and values as at different dates. However, a class of assets may be revalued on a rolling basis provided revaluation of the class of assets is completed within a short period and provided the revaluations are kept up to date.

39 If an asset's carrying amount is increased as a result of a revaluation, the increase shall be recognised in other comprehensive income and accumulated in equity under the heading of revaluation surplus. However, the increase shall be recognised in profit or loss to the extent that it reverses a revaluation decrease of the same asset previously recognised in profit or loss.

40 If an asset's carrying amount is decreased as a result of a revaluation, the decrease shall be recognised in profit or loss. However, the decrease shall be recognised in other comprehensive income to the extent of any credit balance existing in the revaluation surplus in respect of that asset. The decrease recognised in other comprehensive income reduces the amount accumulated in equity under the heading of revaluation surplus.

41 The revaluation surplus included in equity in respect of an item of property, plant and equipment may be transferred directly to retained earnings when the asset is derecognised. This may involve transferring the whole of the surplus when the asset is retired or disposed of. However, some of the surplus may be transferred as the asset is used by an entity. In such a case, the amount of the surplus transferred would be the difference between depreciation based on the revalued carrying amount of the asset and depreciation based on the asset's original cost. Transfers from revaluation surplus to retained earnings are not made through profit or loss.

42 The effects of taxes on income, if any, resulting from the revaluation of property, plant and equipment are recognised and disclosed in accordance with Ind AS 12, *Income Taxes*.

Depreciation

43 Each part of an item of property, plant and equipment with a cost that is significant in relation to the total cost of the item shall be depreciated separately.

44 An entity allocates the amount initially recognised in respect of an item of property, plant and equipment to its significant parts and depreciates separately each such part. For example, it may be appropriate to depreciate separately the airframe and engines of an aircraft, whether owned or subject to a finance lease. Similarly, if an entity acquires property, plant and equipment subject to an operating lease in which it is the lessor, it may be appropriate to depreciate separately amounts reflected in the cost of that item that are attributable to favourable or unfavourable lease terms relative to market terms.

45 A significant part of an item of property, plant and equipment may have a useful life and a depreciation method that are the same as the useful life and the depreciation method of another significant part of that same item. Such parts may be grouped in determining the depreciation charge.

46 To the extent that an entity depreciates separately some parts of an item of property, plant and equipment, it also depreciates separately the remainder of the item. The remainder consists of the parts of the item that are individually not significant. If an entity has varying expectations for these parts, approximation techniques may be necessary to depreciate the remainder in a manner that faithfully represents the consumption pattern and/or useful life of its parts.

47 An entity may choose to depreciate separately the parts of an item that do not have a cost that is significant in relation to the total cost of the item.

48 The depreciation charge for each period shall be recognised in profit or loss unless it is included in the carrying amount of another asset.

49 The depreciation charge for a period is usually recognised in profit or loss. However, sometimes, the future economic benefits embodied in an asset are absorbed in producing other assets. In this case, the depreciation charge constitutes part of the cost of the other asset and is included in its carrying amount. For example, the depreciation of manufacturing plant and equipment is included in the costs of conversion of inventories (see Ind AS 2). Similarly, depreciation of property, plant and equipment used for development activities may be included in the cost of an intangible asset recognised in accordance with Ind AS 38, *Intangible Assets*.

Depreciable amount and depreciation period

50 The depreciable amount of an asset shall be allocated on a systematic basis over its useful life.

51 The residual value and the useful life of an asset shall be reviewed at least at each financial year-end and, if expectations differ from previous estimates, the change(s) shall be accounted for as a change in an accounting estimate in accordance with Ind AS 8, *Accounting Policies, Changes in Accounting Estimates and Errors*.

52 Depreciation is recognised even if the fair value of the asset exceeds its carrying amount, as long as the asset's residual value does not exceed its carrying amount. Repair and maintenance of an asset do not negate the need to depreciate it.

53 The depreciable amount of an asset is determined after deducting its residual value. In practice, the residual value of an asset is often insignificant and therefore immaterial in the calculation of the depreciable amount.

54 The residual value of an asset may increase to an amount equal to or greater than the asset's carrying amount. If it does, the asset's depreciation charge is zero unless and until its residual value subsequently decreases to an amount below the asset's carrying amount.

55 Depreciation of an asset begins when it is available for use, ie when it is in the location and condition necessary for it to be capable of operating in the manner intended by management. Depreciation of an asset ceases at the earlier of the date that the asset is classified as held for sale (or included in a disposal group that is classified as held for sale) in accordance with Ind AS 105 and the date that the asset is derecognised. Therefore, depreciation does not cease when the asset becomes idle or is retired from active use unless the asset is fully depreciated. However, under usage methods of depreciation the depreciation charge can be zero while there is no production.

56 The future economic benefits embodied in an asset are consumed by an entity principally through its use. However, other factors, such as technical or commercial obsolescence and wear and tear while an asset remains idle, often result in the diminution of the economic benefits that might have been obtained from the asset. Consequently, all the following factors are considered in determining the useful life of an asset:

(a) expected usage of the asset. Usage is assessed by reference to the asset's expected capacity or physical output.

(b) expected physical wear and tear, which depends on operational factors such as the number of shifts for which the asset is to be used and the repair and maintenance programme, and the care and maintenance of the asset while idle.

(c) technical or commercial obsolescence arising from changes or improvements in production, or from a change in the market demand for the product or service output of the asset. Expected future reductions in the selling price of an item that was produced using an asset could indicate the expectation of technical or commercial obsolescence of the asset, which, in turn, might reflect a reduction of the future economic benefits embodied in the asset.

(d) legal or similar limits on the use of the asset, such as the expiry dates of related leases.

57 The useful life of an asset is defined in terms of the asset's expected utility to the entity. The asset management policy of the entity may involve the disposal of assets after a specified time or after consumption of a specified proportion of the future economic benefits embodied in the asset. Therefore, the useful life of an asset may be shorter than its economic life. The estimation of the useful life of the asset is a matter of judgement based on the experience of the entity with similar assets.

58 Land and buildings are separable assets and are accounted for separately, even when they are acquired together. With some exceptions, such as quarries and sites used for landfill, land has an unlimited useful life and therefore is not depreciated. Buildings have a limited useful life and therefore are depreciable assets. An increase in the value of the land on which a building stands does not affect the determination of the depreciable amount of the building.

59 If the cost of land includes the costs of site dismantlement, removal and restoration, that portion of the land asset is depreciated over the period of benefits obtained by incurring those costs. In some cases, the land itself may have a limited useful life, in which case it is depreciated in a manner that reflects the benefits to be derived from it.

Depreciation method

60 The depreciation method used shall reflect the pattern in which the asset's future economic benefits are expected to be consumed by the entity.

61 The depreciation method applied to an asset shall be reviewed at least at each financial year-end and, if there has been a significant change in the expected pattern of consumption of the future economic benefits embodied in the asset, the method shall be changed to reflect the changed pattern. Such a change shall be accounted for as a change in an accounting estimate in accordance with Ind AS 8.

62 A variety of depreciation methods can be used to allocate the depreciable amount of an asset on a systematic basis over its useful life. These methods include the straight-line method, the diminishing balance method and the units of production method. Straight-line depreciation results in a constant charge over the useful life if the asset's residual value does not change. The diminishing balance method results in a decreasing charge over the useful life. The units of production method results in a charge based on the expected use or output. The entity selects the method that most closely reflects the expected pattern of consumption of the future economic benefits embodied in the asset. That method is applied consistently from period to period unless there is a change in the expected pattern of consumption of those future economic benefits.

62A A depreciation method that is based on revenue that is generated by an activity that includes the use of an asset is not appropriate. The revenue generated by an activity that includes the use of an asset generally reflects factors other than the consumption of the economic benefits of the asset. For example, revenue is affected by other inputs and processes, selling activities and changes in sales volumes and prices. The price component of revenue may be affected by inflation, which has no bearing upon the way in which an asset is consumed.

Impairment

63 To determine whether an item of property, plant and equipment is impaired, an entity applies Ind AS 36, *Impairment of Assets*. That Standard explains how an entity reviews the carrying amount of its assets, how it determines the recoverable amount of an asset, and when it recognises, or reverses the recognition of, an impairment loss.

64 [Refer Appendix 1]

Compensation for impairment

65 Compensation from third parties for items of property, plant and equipment that were impaired, lost or given up shall be included in profit or loss when the compensation becomes receivable.

66 Impairments or losses of items of property, plant and equipment, related claims for or payments of compensation from third parties and any subsequent purchase or construction of replacement assets are separate economic events and are accounted for separately as follows:

(a) impairments of items of property, plant and equipment are recognised in accordance with Ind AS 36;

(b) derecognition of items of property, plant and equipment retired or disposed of is determined in accordance with this Standard;

(c) compensation from third parties for items of property, plant and equipment that were impaired, lost or given up is included in determining profit or loss when it becomes receivable; and

(d) the cost of items of property, plant and equipment restored, purchased or constructed as replacements is determined in accordance with this Standard.

Derecognition

67 The carrying amount of an item of property, plant and equipment shall be derecognised:

(a) on disposal; or

(b) when no future economic benefits are expected from its use or disposal.

68 The gain or loss arising from the derecognition of an item of property, plant and equipment shall be included in profit or loss when the item is derecognised (unless Ind AS 17 requires otherwise on a sale and leaseback). Gains shall not be classified as revenue.

68A However, an entity that, in the course of its ordinary activities, routinely sells items of property, plant and equipment that it has held for rental to others shall transfer such assets to inventories at their carrying amount when they cease to be rented and become held for sale. The proceeds from the sale of such assets shall be recognised as revenue in accordance with Ind AS 115, *Revenue from Contracts with Customers*. Ind AS 105 does not apply when assets that are held for sale in the ordinary course of business are transferred to inventories.

69 The disposal of an item of property, plant and equipment may occur in a variety of ways (eg by sale, by entering into a finance lease or by donation). The date of disposal of an item of property, plant and equipment is the date the recipient obtains control of that item in accordance with the requirements for determining when a performance obligation is satisfied in Ind AS 115. Ind AS 17 applies to disposal by a sale and leaseback.

70 If, under the recognition principle in paragraph 7, an entity recognises in the carrying amount of an item of property, plant and equipment the cost of a replacement for part of the

item, then it derecognises the carrying amount of the replaced part regardless of whether the replaced part had been depreciated separately. If it is not practicable for an entity to determine the carrying amount of the replaced part, it may use the cost of the replacement as an indication of what the cost of the replaced part was at the time it was acquired or constructed.

71 The gain or loss arising from the derecognition of an item of property, plant and equipment shall be determined as the difference between the net disposal proceeds, if any, and the carrying amount of the item.

72 The amount of consideration to be included in the gain or loss arising from the derecognition of an item of property, plant and equipment is determined in accordance with the requirements for determining the transaction price in paragraphs 47–72 of Ind AS 115. Subsequent changes to the estimated amount of the consideration included in the gain or loss shall be accounted for in accordance with the requirements for changes in the transaction price in Ind AS 115.

Disclosure

73 The financial statements shall disclose, for each class of property, plant and equipment:

- **(a) the measurement bases used for determining the gross carrying amount;**
- **(b) the depreciation methods used;**
- **(c) the useful lives or the depreciation rates used;**
- **(d) the gross carrying amount and the accumulated depreciation (aggregated with accumulated impairment losses) at the beginning and end of the period; and**
- **(e) a reconciliation of the carrying amount at the beginning and end of the period showing:**
  - **(i) additions;**
  - **(ii) assets classified as held for sale or included in a disposal group classified as held for sale in accordance with Ind AS 105 and other disposals;**
  - **(iii) acquisitions through business combinations;**
  - **(iv) increases or decreases resulting from revaluations under paragraphs 31, 39 and 40 and from impairment losses recognised or reversed in other comprehensive income in accordance with Ind AS 36;**
  - **(v) impairment losses recognised in profit or loss in accordance with Ind AS 36;**
  - **(vi) impairment losses reversed in profit or loss in accordance with Ind AS 36;**
  - **(vii) depreciation;**
  - **(viii) the net exchange differences arising on the translation of the financial statements from the functional currency into a different presentation currency, including the translation of a foreign operation into the presentation currency of the reporting entity; and**
  - **(ix) other changes.**

74 The financial statements shall also disclose:

- **(a) the existence and amounts of restrictions on title, and property, plant and equipment pledged as security for liabilities;**
- **(b) the amount of expenditures recognised in the carrying amount of an item of property, plant and equipment in the course of its construction;**

(c) the amount of contractual commitments for the acquisition of property, plant and equipment; and

(d) if it is not disclosed separately in the statement of profit and loss, the amount of compensation from third parties for items of property, plant and equipment that were impaired, lost or given up that is included in profit or loss.

75 Selection of the depreciation method and estimation of the useful life of assets are matters of judgement. Therefore, disclosure of the methods adopted and the estimated useful lives or depreciation rates provides users of financial statements with information that allows them to review the policies selected by management and enables comparisons to be made with other entities. For similar reasons, it is necessary to disclose:

(a) depreciation, whether recognised in profit or loss or as a part of the cost of other assets, during a period; and

(b) accumulated depreciation at the end of the period.

76 In accordance with Ind AS 8 an entity discloses the nature and effect of a change in an accounting estimate that has an effect in the current period or is expected to have an effect in subsequent periods. For property, plant and equipment, such disclosure may arise from changes in estimates with respect to:

(a) residual values;

(b) the estimated costs of dismantling, removing or restoring items of property, plant and equipment;

(c) useful lives; and

(d) depreciation methods.

77 If items of property, plant and equipment are stated at revalued amounts, the following shall be disclosed in addition to the disclosures required by Ind AS 113:

(a) the effective date of the revaluation;

(b) whether an independent valuer was involved;

(c) [Refer Appendix 1]

(d) [Refer Appendix 1]

(e) for each revalued class of property, plant and equipment, the carrying amount that would have been recognised had the assets been carried under the cost model; and

(f) the revaluation surplus, indicating the change for the period and any restrictions on the distribution of the balance to shareholders.

78 In accordance with Ind AS 36 an entity discloses information on impaired property, plant and equipment in addition to the information required by paragraph 73(e)(iv)–(vi).

79 Users of financial statements may also find the following information relevant to their needs:

(a) the carrying amount of temporarily idle property, plant and equipment;

(b) the gross carrying amount of any fully depreciated property, plant and equipment that is still in use;

(c) the carrying amount of property, plant and equipment retired from active use and not classified as held for sale in accordance with Ind AS 105; and

(d) when the cost model is used, the fair value of property, plant and equipment when this is materially different from the carrying amount.

Therefore, entities are encouraged to disclose these amounts.

Appendix A

Changes in Existing Decommissioning, Restoration and Similar Liabilities

This Appendix is an integral part of the Ind AS.

Background

1 Many entities have obligations to dismantle, remove and restore items of property, plant and equipment. In this Appendix such obligations are referred to as 'decommissioning, restoration and similar liabilities'. Under Ind AS 16, the cost of an item of property, plant and equipment includes the initial estimate of the costs of dismantling and removing the item and restoring the site on which it is located, the obligation for which an entity incurs either when the item is acquired or as a consequence of having used the item during a particular period for purposes other than to produce inventories during that period. Ind AS 37 contains requirements on how to measure decommissioning, restoration and similar liabilities. This Appendix provides guidance on how to account for the effect of changes in the measurement of existing decommissioning, restoration and similar liabilities.

Scope

2 This Appendix applies to changes in the measurement of any existing decommissioning, restoration or similar liability that is both:

(a) recognised as part of the cost of an item of property, plant and equipment in accordance with Ind AS 16; and

(b) recognised as a liability in accordance with Ind AS 37.

For example, a decommissioning, restoration or similar liability may exist for decommissioning a plant, rehabilitating environmental damage in extractive industries, or removing equipment.

Issue

3 This Appendix addresses how the effect of the following events that change the measurement of an existing decommissioning, restoration or similar liability should be accounted for:

(a) a change in the estimated outflow of resources embodying economic benefits (eg cash flows) required to settle the obligation;

(b) a change in the current market-based discount rate as defined in paragraph 47 of Ind AS 37 (this includes changes in the time value of money and the risks specific to the liability); and

(c) an increase that reflects the passage of time (also referred to as the unwinding of the discount).

Accounting Principles

4 Changes in the measurement of an existing decommissioning, restoration and similar liability that result from changes in the estimated timing or amount of the outflow of resources embodying economic benefits required to settle the obligation, or a change in the discount rate, shall be accounted for in accordance with paragraphs 5–7 below.

5 If the related asset is measured using the cost model:

(a) subject to (b), changes in the liability shall be added to, or deducted from, the cost of the related asset in the current period.

(b) the amount deducted from the cost of the asset shall not exceed its carrying amount. If a decrease in the liability exceeds the carrying amount of the asset, the excess shall be recognised immediately in profit or loss.

(c) if the adjustment results in an addition to the cost of an asset, the entity shall consider whether this is an indication that the new carrying amount of the asset may not be fully recoverable. If it is such an indication, the entity shall test the asset for impairment by estimating its recoverable amount, and shall account for any impairment loss, in accordance with Ind AS 36.

6 If the related asset is measured using the revaluation model:

(a) changes in the liability alter the revaluation surplus or deficit previously recognised on that asset, so that:

(i) a decrease in the liability shall (subject to (b)) be recognised in other comprehensive income and increase the revaluation surplus within equity, except that it shall be recognised in profit or loss to the extent that it reverses a revaluation deficit on the asset that was previously recognised in profit or loss;

(ii) an increase in the liability shall be recognised in profit or loss, except that it shall be recognised in other comprehensive income and reduce the revaluation surplus within equity to the extent of any credit balance existing in the revaluation surplus in respect of that asset.

(b) in the event that a decrease in the liability exceeds the carrying amount that would have been recognised had the asset been carried under the cost model, the excess shall be recognised immediately in profit or loss.

(c) a change in the liability is an indication that the asset may have to be revalued in order to ensure that the carrying amount does not differ materially from that which would be determined using fair value at the end of the reporting period. Any such revaluation shall be taken into account in determining the amounts to be recognised in profit or loss or in other comprehensive income under (a). If a revaluation is necessary, all assets of that class shall be revalued.

(d) Ind AS 1 requires disclosure in the statement of profit and loss of each component of other comprehensive income or expense. In complying with this requirement, the change in the revaluation surplus arising from a change in the liability shall be separately identified and disclosed as such.

7 The adjusted depreciable amount of the asset is depreciated over its useful life. Therefore, once the related asset has reached the end of its useful life, all subsequent changes in the liability shall be recognised in profit or loss as they occur. This applies under both the cost model and the revaluation model.

8 The periodic unwinding of the discount shall be recognised in profit or loss as a finance cost as it occurs. Capitalisation under Ind AS 23 is not permitted.

Appendix B

This appendix is an integral part of the Ind AS.

Stripping Costs in the Production Phase of a Surface Mine

Background

1. In surface mining operations, entities may find it necessary to remove mine waste materials ('overburden') to gain access to mineral ore deposits. This waste removal activity is known as 'stripping'.

2. During the development phase of the mine (before production begins), stripping costs are usually capitalised as part of the depreciable cost of building, developing and constructing the mine. Those capitalised costs are depreciated or amortised on a systematic basis, usually by using the units of production method, once production begins.

3. A mining entity may continue to remove overburden and to incur stripping costs during the production phase of the mine.

4. The material removed when stripping in the production phase will not necessarily be a total waste; often it will be a combination of ore and waste. The ratio of ore to waste can range from uneconomic low grade to profitable high grade. Removal of material with a low ratio of ore to waste may produce some usable material, which can be used to produce inventory. This removal might also provide access to deeper levels of material that have a higher ratio of ore to waste. There can therefore be two benefits accruing to the entity from the stripping activity: usable ore that can be used to produce inventory and improved access to further quantities of material that will be mined in future periods.

5. This Appendix considers when and how to account separately for these two benefits arising from the stripping activity, as well as how to measure these benefits both initially and subsequently.

Scope

6. This Appendix applies to waste removal costs that are incurred in surface mining activity during the production phase of the mine ('production stripping costs').

Issues

7. This Appendix addresses the following issues:

(a) recognition of production stripping costs as an asset;

(b) initial measurement of the stripping activity asset; and

(c) subsequent measurement of the stripping activity asset.

Accounting Principles

Recognition of production stripping costs as an asset

8. To the extent that the benefit from the stripping activity is realised in the form of inventory produced, the entity shall account for the costs of that stripping overburden removal activity in accordance with the principles of Ind AS 2, *Inventories*. To the extent the benefit is improved access to ore, the entity shall recognise these costs as a non-current asset, say, Stripping Activity Asset, if the criteria in paragraph 9 below are met.

9. An entity shall recognise a stripping activity asset if, and only if, all of the following are met:

(a) it is probable that the future economic benefit (improved access to the ore body) associated with the stripping activity will flow to the entity;

(b) the entity can identify the component of the ore body for which access has been improved; and

(c) the costs relating to the stripping activity associated with that component can be measured reliably.

10. The stripping activity asset shall be accounted for as an addition to, or as an enhancement of, an existing asset. In other words, the stripping activity asset will be accounted for as *part* of an existing asset.

11. The stripping activity asset's classification as a tangible or intangible asset is the same as the existing asset. In other words, the nature of this existing asset will determine whether the entity shall classify the stripping activity asset as tangible or intangible.

Initial measurement of the stripping activity asset

12. The entity shall initially measure the stripping activity asset at cost, this being the accumulation of costs directly incurred to perform the stripping activity that improves access to the identified component of ore, plus an allocation of directly attributable overhead costs. Examples of the types of costs that would be included as directly attributable overhead costs include an allocation of salary costs of the mine supervisor overseeing that component of the mine, and the rental costs of any equipment that was hired specifically to perform the stripping activity. Some incidental operations may take place at the same time as the production stripping activity, but which are not necessary for the production stripping activity to continue as planned. The costs associated with these incidental operations shall not be included in the cost of the stripping activity asset. An example of such type of incidental operations would be building an access road in the area in which the stripping campaign is taking place.

13. When the costs of the stripping activity asset and the inventory produced are not separately identifiable, the entity shall allocate the production stripping costs between the inventory produced and the stripping activity asset by using an allocation basis that is based on a relevant production measure. This production measure shall be calculated for the identified component of the ore body, and shall be used as a benchmark to identify the extent to which the additional activity of creating a future benefit has taken place. Examples of such measures include:

(a) cost of inventory produced compared with expected cost;

(b) volume of waste extracted compared with expected volume, for a given volume of ore production; and

(c) mineral content of the ore extracted compared with expected mineral content to be extracted, for a given quantity of ore produced.

13A The production measure shall not be calculated using a basis that is based on sales values. A basis that is based on sales values, in the context of stripping costs, is inappropriate because it is not closely linked to the activity taking place. Furthermore, if the current sales price of the relevant material is used in determining the allocation basis, the same current sales price will be applied to the volume of the mineral in both the extracted ore and the identified component. Hence, the relevant variable will be the volume of mineral in both the extracted ore and the identified component, i.e., the current sales price will not change the allocation basis. Applying a future sales price basis involves practical difficulties. Identifying a future sales price for ore that will be mined in the future can be difficult, given the volatility of market prices for many minerals. Further complexities may arise when more than one mineral is present (whether byproducts or joint products) when the ore is extracted.

Subsequent measurement of the stripping activity asset

14. After initial recognition, the stripping activity asset shall be carried at either its cost or its revalued amount less depreciation or amortisation and less impairment losses, in the same way as the existing asset of which it is a part.

15. The stripping activity asset shall be depreciated or amortised on a systematic basis, over the expected useful life of the identified component of the ore body that becomes more

accessible as a result of the stripping activity. The units of production method shall be applied unless another method is more appropriate.

16. The expected useful life of the identified component of the ore body that is used to depreciate or amortise the stripping activity asset will differ from the expected useful life that is used to depreciate or amortise the mine itself and the related life-of-mine assets. The exception to this are those limited circumstances when the stripping activity provides improved access to the whole of the remaining ore body. For example, this might occur towards the end of a mine's useful life when the identified component represents the final part of the ore body to be extracted.

Appendix C

References to matters contained in other Indian Accounting Standards

This Appendix is an integral part of the Ind AS.

This appendix lists the appendices which are part of other Indian Accounting Standards and make reference to Ind AS 16, *Property, Plant and Equipment.*

1 Appendix C, *Service Concession Arrangements* contained in Ind AS 115, *Revenue from Contracts with Customers*.

2 Appendix D, *Service Concession Arrangements: Disclosures* contained inInd AS 115, *Revenue from Contracts with Customers*.

3 Appendix C, *Determining whether an Arrangement contains a Lease* contained in Ind AS 17, *Leases*.

4 Appendix A, *Intangible Assets—Web Site Costs* contained in Ind AS 38, *Intangible Assets*.

Appendix 1

Note: This Appendix is not a part of the Indian Accounting Standard. The purpose of this Appendix is only to bring out the major differences, if any, between Indian Accounting Standard (Ind AS) 16 and the corresponding International Accounting Standard (IAS) 16, Property, Plant and Equipment, and IFRIC 1, Changes in Existing Decommissioning, Restoration and Similar Liabilities and IFRIC 20, Stripping Costs in the Production Phase of a Surface Mine issued by the International Accounting Standards Board.

Comparison with IAS 16, *Property, Plant and Equipment,* IFRIC 1 and IFRIC 20

1 The transitional provisions given in IAS 16 and IFRIC 1 and IFRIC 20 have not been given in Ind AS 16, since all transitional provisions related to Ind ASs, wherever considered appropriate have been included in Ind AS 101, *First-time Adoption of Indian Accounting Standards* corresponding to IFRS 1, *First-time Adoption of International Financial Reporting Standards.*

2 Different terminology is used in this standard, eg, the term 'balance sheet' is used instead of 'Statement of financial position' and 'Statement of profit' and loss is used instead of 'Statement of comprehensive income'.

3 Paragraph 28 has been deleted since Ind AS 20, Accounting for Government Grants *and Disclosure of Government Assistance,* does not permit the option of reducing the carrying amount of an item of property, plant and equipment by the amount of government grant received in respect of such an item, which is permitted in IAS 20. However, to maintain consistency with paragraph numbers of IAS 16, this paragraph number is retained in Ind AS 16.

4 The following paragraph numbers appear as 'Deleted' in IAS 16. In order to maintain consistency with paragraph numbers of IAS 16, the paragraph numbers are retained in Ind AS 16:

(i) paragraphs 32-33

(ii) paragraph 64

(iii) paragraph 77(c)-(d)

5 Paragraphs 5 of Ind AS 16 has been modified, since Ind AS 40, *Investment Property*, prohibits the use of fair value model.

6 Paragraph 12 of Appendix B has been modified and paragraph 13A of Appendix B has been added to provide guidance with regard to the requirements contained in the paragraphs 12 and 13.

Annexure VIII

Accounting Standard (AS) 10 Property, Plant and Equipment

(This Accounting Standard includes paragraphs set in ***bold italic*** *type and plain type, which have equal authority. Paragraphs in bold italic type indicate the main principles. This Accounting Standard should be read in the context of the General Instructions contained in part A of the Annexure to the Notification.)*

Objective

1. The objective of this Standard is to prescribe the accounting treatment for property, plant and equipment so that users of the financial statements can discern information about investment made by an enterprise in its property, plant and equipment and the changes in such investment. The principal issues in accounting for property, plant and equipment are the recognition of the assets, the determination of their carrying amounts and the depreciation charges and impairment losses to be recognised in relation to them.

Scope

2. ***This Standard should be applied in accounting for property, plant and equipment except when another Accounting Standard requires or permits a different accounting treatment.***

3. This Standard does not apply to:

   (a) biological assets related to agricultural activity other than bearer plants. This Standard applies to bearer plants but it does not apply to the produce on bearer plants; and

   (b) wasting assets including mineral rights, expenditure on the exploration for and extraction of minerals, oil, natural gas and similar non-regenerative resources.

   However, this Standard applies to property, plant and equipment used to develop or maintain the assets described in

   (a) and (b) above.

4. Other Accounting Standards may require recognition of an item of property, plant and equipment based on an approach different from that in this Standard. For example, AS 19, Leases, requires an enterprise to evaluate its recognition of an item of leased property, plant and equipment on the basis of the transfer of risks and rewards. However, in such cases other aspects of the accounting treatment for these assets, including depreciation, are prescribed by this Standard.

5. Investment property, as defined in AS 13, Accounting for Investments, should be accounted for only in accordance with the cost model prescribed in this standard.

Definitions

6. ***The following terms are used in this Standard with the meanings specified:***

Agricultural Activity is the management by an enterprise of the biological transformation and harvest of biological assets for sale or for conversion into agricultural produce or into additional biological assets.

Agricultural Produce is the harvested product of biological assets of the enterprise.

Bearer plant is a plant that

(a) is used in the production or supply of agricultural produce;

(b) is expected to bear produce for more than a period of twelve months; and

(c) has a remote likelihood of being sold as agricultural produce, except for incidental scrap sales.

The following are not bearer plants:

(i) plants cultivated to be harvested as agricultural produce (for example, trees grown for use as lumber);

(ii) plants cultivated to produce agricultural produce when there is more than a remote likelihood that the entity will also harvest and sell the plant as agricultural produce, other than as incidental scrap sales (for example, trees that are cultivated both for their fruit and their lumber); and

(iii) annual crops (for example, maize and wheat).

When bearer plants are no longer used to bear produce they might be cut down and sold as scrap, for example, for use as firewood. Such incidental scrap sales would not prevent the plant from satisfying the definition of a bearer plant.

Biological Asset is a living animal[1] or plant.

Carrying amount is the amount at which an asset is recognised after deducting any accumulated depreciation and accumulated impairment losses.

Cost is the amount of cash or cash equivalents paid or the fair value of the other consideration given to acquire an asset at the time of its acquisition or construction or, where applicable, the amount attributed to that asset when initially recognised in accordance with the specific requirements of other Accounting Standards.

Depreciable amount is the cost of an asset, or other amount substituted for cost, less its residual value. Depreciation is the systematic allocation of the depreciable amount of an asset over its useful life.

---

[1] An Accounting Standard on Agriculture is under formulation, which will, inter alia, cover accounting for livestock. Till the time, the Accounting Standard on Agriculture is issued, accounting for livestock meeting the definition of Property, Plant and Equipment, will be covered as per AS 10 (Revised), Property, Plant and Equipment.

Enterprise -specific value ***is the present value of the cash flows an enterprise expects to arise from the continuing use of an asset and from its disposal at the end of its useful life or expects to incur when settling a liability.***

Fair value ***is the amount for which an asset could be exchanged between knowledgeable, willing parties in an arm's length transaction.***

Gross carrying amount ***of an asset is its cost or other amount substituted for the cost in the books of account, without making any deduction for accumulated depreciation and accumulated impairment losses.***

An impairment loss is the amount by which the carrying amount of an asset exceeds its recoverable amount. Property, plant and equipment are tangible items that:

(a) ***are held for use in the production or supply of goods or services, for rental to others, or for administrative purposes; and***

(b) ***are expected to be used during more than a period of twelve months. Recoverable amount is the higher of an asset's net selling price and its value in use.***

The residual value of an asset is the estimated amount that an enterprise would currently obtain from disposal of the asset, after deducting the estimated costs of disposal, if the asset were already of the age and in the condition expected at the end of its useful life.

Useful life is:

(a) ***the period over which an asset is expected to be available for use by an enterprise ; or***

(b) ***the number of production or similar units expected to be obtained from the asset by an enterprise.***

Recognition

7. ***The cost of an item of property, plant and equipment should be recognised as an asset if, and only if:***

(a) ***it is probable that future economic benefits associated with the item will flow to the enterprise; and***

(b) ***the cost of the item can be measured reliably.***

8. Items such as spare parts, stand-by equipment and servicing equipment are recognised in accordance with this Standard when they meet the definition of property, plant and equipment. Otherwise, such items are classified as inventory.

9. This Standard does not prescribe the unit of measure for recognition, i.e., what constitutes an item of property, plant and equipment. Thus, judgement is required in applying the recognition criteria to specific circumstances of an enterprise. An example of a 'unit of measure' can be a 'project' of construction of a manufacturing plant rather than individual assets comprising the project in appropriate cases for the purpose of capitalisation of expenditure incurred during construction period.

Similarly, it may be appropriate to aggregate individually insignificant items, such as moulds, tools and dies and to apply the criteria to the aggregate value. An enterprise may decide to expense an item which could otherwise have been included as property, plant and equipment, because the amount of the expenditure is not material.

10. An enterprise evaluates under this recognition principle all its costs on property, plant and equipment at the time they are incurred. These costs include costs incurred:

(a) initially to acquire or construct an item of property, plant and equipment; and

(b) subsequently to add to, replace part of, or service it.

Initial Costs

11. The definition of 'property, plant and equipment' covers tangible items which are held for use or for administrative purposes. The term 'administrative purposes' has been used in wider sense to include all business purposes other than production or supply of goods or services or for rental for others. Thus, property, plant and equipment would include assets used for selling and distribution, finance and accounting, personnel and other functions of an enterprise. Items of property, plant and equipment may also be acquired for safety or environmental reasons. The acquisition of such property, plant and equipment, although not directly increasing the future economic benefits of any particular existing item of property, plant and equipment, may be necessary for an enterprise to obtain the future economic benefits from its other assets. Such items of property, plant and equipment qualify for recognition as assets because they enable an enterprise to derive future economic benefits from related assets in excess of what could be derived had those items not been acquired. For example, a chemical manufacturer may install new chemical handling processes to comply with environmental requirements for the production and storage of dangerous chemicals; related plant enhancements are recognised as an asset because without them the enterprise is unable to manufacture and sell chemicals. The resulting carrying amount of such an asset and related assets is reviewed for impairment in accordance with AS 28, *Impairment of Assets*.

Subsequent Costs

12. Under the recognition principle in paragraph 7, an enterprise does not recognise in the carrying amount of an item of property, plant and equipment the costs of the day-to-day servicing of the item. Rather, these costs are recognised in the statement of profit and loss as incurred. Costs of day-to-day servicing are primarily the costs of labour and consumables, and may include the cost of small parts. The purpose of such expenditures is often described as for the 'repairs and maintenance' of the item of property, plant and equipment.

13. Parts of some items of property, plant and equipment may require replacement at regular intervals. For example, a furnace may require relining after a specified number of hours of use, or aircraft interiors such as seats and galleys may require replacement several times during the life of the airframe. Similarly, major parts of conveyor system, such as, conveyor belts, wire ropes, etc., may require replacement several times during the life of the conveyor system. Items of property, plant and equipment may also be acquired to make a less frequently recurring replacement, such as replacing the interior walls of a building, or to make a non-recurring

replacement. Under the recognition principle in paragraph 7, an enterprise recognises in the carrying amount of an item of property, plant and equipment the cost of replacing part of such an item when that cost is incurred if the recognition criteria are met. The carrying amount of those parts that are replaced is derecognised in accordance with the derecognition provisions of this Standard (see paragraphs 74-80).

14. A condition of continuing to operate an item of property, plant and equipment (for example, an aircraft) may be performing regular major inspections for faults regardless of whether parts of the item are replaced. When each major inspection is performed, its cost is recognised in the carrying amount of the item of property, plant and equipment as a replacement if the recognition criteria are satisfied. Any remaining carrying amount of the cost of the previous inspection (as distinct from physical parts) is derecognised.

15. The derecognition of the carrying amount as stated in paragraphs 13-14 occurs regardless of whether the cost of the previous part / inspection was identified in the transaction in which the item was acquired or constructed. If it is not practicable for an enterprise to determine the carrying amount of the replaced part/ inspection, it may use the cost of the replacement or the estimated cost of a future similar inspection as an indication of what the cost of the replaced part/ existing inspection component was when the item was acquired or constructed.

Measurement at Recognition

16. **An item of property, plant and equipment that qualifies for recognition as an asset should be measured at its cost.**

Elements of Cost

17. The cost of an item of property, plant and equipment comprises:

(a) its purchase price, including import duties and non –refundable purchase taxes,, after deducting trade discounts and rebates.

(b) any costs directly attributable to bringing the asset to the location and condition necessary for it to be capable of operating in the manner intended by management.

(c) the initial estimate of the costs of dismantling, removing the item and restoring the site on which it is located, referred to as 'decommissioning, restoration and similar liabilities', the obligation for which an enterprise incurs either when the item is acquired or as a consequence of having used the item during a particular period for purposes other than to produce inventories during that period.

18. Examples of directly attributable costs are:

(a) costs of employee benefits (as defined in AS 15, Employee Benefits) arising directly from the construction or acquisition of the item of property, plant and equipment;

(b) costs of site preparation;

(c) initial delivery and handling costs;

(d) installation and assembly costs;

(e) costs of testing whether the asset is functioning properly, after deducting the net proceeds from selling any items produced while bringing the asset to that location and condition (such as samples produced when testing equipment); and

(f) professional fees.

19. An enterprise applies AS 2, Valuation of Inventories, to the costs of obligations for dismantling, removing and restoring the site on which an item is located that are incurred during a particular period as a consequence of having used the item to produce inventories during that period. The obligations for costs accounted for in accordance with AS 2 or AS 10 are recognised and measured in accordance with AS 29, Provisions, Contingent Liabilities and Contingent Assets.

20. Examples of costs that are not costs of an item of property, plant and equipment are:

(a) costs of opening a new facility or business, such as, inauguration costs;

(b) costs of introducing a new product or service(including costs of advertising and promotional activities);

(c) costs of conducting business in a new location or with a new class of customer (including costs of staff training); and

(d) administration and other general overhead costs.

21. Recognition of costs in the carrying amount of an item of property, plant and equipment ceases when the item is in the location and condition necessary for it to be capable of operating in the manner intended by management. Therefore, costs incurred in using or redeploying an item are not included in the carrying amount of that item. For example, the following costs are not included in the carrying amount of an item of property, plant and equipment:

(a) costs incurred while an item capable of operating in the manner intended by management has yet to be brought into use or is operated at less than full capacity;

(b) initial operating losses, such as those incurred while demand for the output of an item builds up; and

(c) costs of relocating or reorganising part or all of the operations of an enterprise.

22. Some operations occur in connection with the construction or development of an item of property, plant and equipment, but are not necessary to bring the item to the location and condition necessary for it to be capable of operating in the manner intended by management. These incidental operations may occur before or during the construction or development activities. For example, income may be earned through using a building site as a car park until construction starts. Because incidental operations are not necessary to bring an item to the location and condition necessary for it to be capable of operating in the manner intended by management, the income and related expenses of incidental operations are recognised in the statement of profit and loss and included in their respective classifications of income and expense.

23. The cost of a self-constructed asset is determined using the same principles as for an acquired asset. If an enterprise makes similar assets for sale in the normal course of business, the cost of the asset is usually the same as the cost of constructing an asset for sale (see AS 2). Therefore, any internal profits are eliminated in arriving at such costs. Similarly, the cost of abnormal amounts of wasted material, labour, or other resources incurred in self- constructing an asset is not included in the cost of the asset. AS 16, Borrowing Costs, establishes criteria for the recognition of interest as a component of the carrying amount of a self-constructed item of property, plant and equipment.

24. Bearer plants are accounted for in the same way as self-constructed items of property, plant and equipment before they are in the location and condition necessary to be capable of operating in the manner intended by management. Consequently, references to 'construction' in this Standard should be read as covering activities that are necessary to cultivate the bearer plants before they are in the location and condition necessary to be capable of operating in the manner intended by management.

Measurement of Cost

25. The cost of an item of property, plant and equipment is the cash price equivalent at the recognition date. If payment is deferred beyond normal credit terms, the difference between the cash price equivalent and the total payment is recognised as interest over the period of credit unless such interest is capitalised in accordance with AS 16.

26. One or more items of property, plant and equipment may be acquired in exchange for a non-monetary asset or assets, or a combination of monetary and non-monetary assets. The following discussion refers simply to an exchange of one non-monetary asset for another, but it also applies to all exchanges described in the preceding sentence. The cost of such an item of property, plant and equipment is measured at fair value unless (a) the exchange transaction lacks commercial substance or (b) the fair value of neither the asset(s) received nor the asset(s) given up is reliably measurable. The acquired item(s) is/are measured in this manner even if an enterprise cannot immediately derecognise the asset given up. If the acquired item(s) is/are not measured at fair value, its/their cost is measured at the carrying amount of the asset(s) given up.

27. An enterprise determines whether an exchange transaction has commercial substance by considering the extent to which its future cash flows are expected to change as a result of the transaction. An exchange transaction has commercial substance if:

(a) the configuration (risk, timing and amount) of the cash flows of the asset received differs from the configuration of the cash flows of the asset transferred; or

(b) the enterprise-specific value of the portion of the operations of the enterprise affected by the transaction changes as a result of the exchange;

(c) and the difference in (a) or (b) is significant relative to the fair value of the assets exchanged.

For the purpose of determining whether an exchange transaction has commercial substance, the enterprise - specific value of the portion of operations of the enterprise affected by the transaction should reflect post-tax cash flows. In certain cases, the result of these analyses may be clear without an enterprise having to perform detailed calculations.

28. The fair value of an asset is reliably measurable if (a) the variability in the range of reasonable fair value measurements is not significant for that asset or (b) the probabilities of the various estimates within the range can be reasonably assessed and used when measuring fair value. If an enterprise is able to measure reliably the fair value of either the asset received or the asset given up, then the fair value of the asset given up is used to measure the cost of the asset received unless the fair value of the asset received is more clearly evident.

29. Where several items of property, plant and equipment are purchased for a consolidated price, the consideration is apportioned to the various items on the basis of their respective fair values at the date of acquisition. In case the fair values of the items acquired cannot be measured reliably, these values are estimated on a fair basis as determined by competent valuers.

30. The cost of an item of property, plant and equipment held by a lessee under a finance lease is determined in accordance with AS 19, Leases.

31. The carrying amount of an item of property, plant and equipment may be reduced by government grants in accordance with AS 12, Accounting for Government Grants.

Measurement after Recognition

32. An enterprise should choose either the cost model in paragraph 33 or the revaluation model in paragraph 34 as its accounting policy and should apply that policy to an entire class of property, plant and equipment.

Cost Model

33. After recognition as an asset, an item of property, plant and equipment should be carried at its cost less any accumulated depreciation and any accumulated impairment losses.

Revaluation Model

34. After recognition as an asset, an item of property, plant and equipment whose fair value can be measured reliably should be carried at a revalued amount, being its fair value at the date of the revaluation less any subsequent accumulated depreciation and subsequent accumulated impairment losses. Revaluations should be made with sufficient regularity to ensure that the carrying amount does not differ materially from that which would be determined using fair value at the balance sheet date.

35. The fair value of items of property, plant and equipment is usually determined from market-based evidence by appraisal that is normally undertaken by professionally qualified valuers.

36. If there is no market-based evidence of fair value because of the specialised nature of the item of property, plant and equipment and the item is rarely sold, except as part

of a continuing business, an enterprise may need to estimate fair value using an income approach (for example, based on discounted cash flow projections) or a depreciated replacement cost approach which aims at making a realistic estimate of the current cost of acquiring or constructing an item that has the same service potential as the existing item.

37. The frequency of revaluations depends upon the changes in fair values of the items of property, plant and equipment being revalued. When the fair value of a revalued asset differs materially from its carrying amount, a further revaluation is required. Some items of property, plant and equipment experience significant and volatile changes in fair value, thus necessitating annual revaluation. Such frequent revaluations are unnecessary for items of property, plant and equipment with only insignificant changes in fair value. Instead, it may be necessary to revalue the item only every three or five years.

38. When an item of property, plant and equipment is revalued, the carrying amount of that asset is adjusted to the revalued amount. At the date of the revaluation, the asset is treated in one of the following ways:

(a) the gross carrying amount is adjusted in a manner that is consistent with the revaluation of the carrying amount of the asset. For example, the gross carrying amount may be restated by reference to observable market data or it may be restated proportionately to the change in the carrying amount. The accumulated depreciation at the date of the revaluation is adjusted to equal the difference between the gross carrying amount and the carrying amount of the asset after taking into account accumulated impairment losses; or

(b) the accumulated depreciation is eliminated against the gross carrying amount of the asset.

The amount of the adjustment of accumulated depreciation forms part of the increase or decrease in carrying amount that is accounted for in accordance with paragraphs 42 and 43.

39. **If an item of property, plant and equipment is revalued, the entire class of property, plant and equipment to which that asset belongs should be revalued.**

40. A class of property, plant and equipment is a grouping of assets of a similar nature and use in operations of an enterprise. The following are examples of separate classes:

(a) land;

(b) land and buildings;

(c) machinery;

(d) ships;

(e) aircraft;

(f) motor vehicles;

(g) furniture and fixtures;

(h) office equipment;and

(i) bearer plants.

41. The items within a class of property, plant and equipment are revalued simultaneously to avoid selective revaluation of assets and the reporting of amounts in the financial statements that are a mixture of costs and values as at different dates. However, a class of assets may be revalued on a rolling basis provided revaluation of the class of assets is completed within a short period and provided the revaluations are kept up to date.

42. An increase in the carrying amount of an asset arising on revaluation should be credited directly to owners' interests under the heading of revaluation surplus However, the increase should be recognised in the statement of profit and loss to the extent that it reverses a revaluation decrease of the same asset previously recognised in the statement of profit and loss.

43. A decrease in the carrying amount of an asset arising on revaluation should be charged to the statement of profit and loss. However, the decrease should be debited directly to owners' interests under the heading of revaluation surplus to the extent of any credit balance existing in the revaluation surplus in respect of that asset.

44. The revaluation surplus included in owners' interests in respect of an item of property, plant and equipment may be transferred to the revenue reserves when the asset is derecognised. This may involve transferring the whole of the surplus when the asset is retired or disposed of. However, some of the surplus may be transferred as the asset is used by an enterprise. In such a case, the amount of the surplus transferred would be the difference between depreciation based on the revalued carrying amount of the asset and depreciation based on its original cost. Transfers from revaluation surplus to the revenue reserves are not made through the statement of profit and loss.

Depreciation

45. Each part of an item of property, plant and equipment with a cost that is significant in relation to the total cost of the item should be depreciated separately.

46. An enterprise allocates the amount initially recognised in respect of an item of property, plant and equipment to its significant parts and depreciates each such part separately. For example, it may be appropriate to depreciate separately the airframe and engines of an aircraft, whether owned or subject to a finance lease.

47. A significant part of an item of property, plant and equipment may have a useful life and a depreciation method that are the same as the useful life and the depreciation method of another significant part of that same item. Such parts may be grouped in determining the depreciation charge.

48. To the extent that an enterprise depreciates separately some parts of an item of property, plant and equipment, it also depreciates separately the remainder of the item. The remainder consists of the parts of the item that are individually not significant. If an enterprise has varying expectations for these parts, approximation techniques may be necessary to depreciate the remainder in a manner that faithfully represents the consumption pattern and/or useful life of its parts.

49. An enterprise may choose to depreciate separately the parts of an item that do not have a cost that is significant in relation to the total cost of the item.

50. **The depreciation charge for each period should be recognised in the statement of profit and loss unless it is included in the carrying amount of another asset.**

51. The depreciation charge for a period is usually recognised in the statement of profit and loss. However, sometimes, the future economic benefits embodied in an asset are absorbed in producing other assets. In this case, the depreciation charge constitutes part of the cost of the other asset and is included in its carrying amount. For example, the depreciation of manufacturing plant and equipment is included in the costs of conversion of inventories (see AS 2). Similarly, the depreciation of property, plant and equipment used for development activities may be included in the cost of an intangible asset recognised in accordance with AS 26, *Intangible Assets*.

Depreciable Amount and Depreciation Period

52. **The depreciable amount of an asset should be allocated on a systematic basis over its useful life.**

53. **The residual value and the useful life of an asset should be reviewed at least at each financial year-end and, if expectations differ from previous estimates, the change(s) should be accounted for as a change in an accounting estimate in accordance with AS 5, Net Profit or Loss for the Period, Prior Period Items and Changes in Accounting Policies.**

54. Depreciation is recognised even if the fair value of the asset exceeds its carrying amount, as long as the asset's residual value does not exceed its carrying amount. Repair and maintenance of an asset do not negate the need to depreciate it.

55. The depreciable amount of an asset is determined after deducting its residual value.

56. The residual value of an asset may increase to an amount equal to or greater than its carrying amount. If it does, depreciation charge of the asset is zero unless and until its residual value subsequently decreases to an amount below its carrying amount.

57. Depreciation of an asset begins when it is available for use, *i.e.*, when it is in the location and condition necessary for it to be capable of operating in the manner intended by management. Depreciation of an asset ceases at the earlier of the date that the asset is retired from active use and is held for disposal and the date that the asset is derecognised. Therefore, depreciation does not cease when the asset becomes idle or is retired from active use (but not held for disposal) unless the asset is fully depreciated. However, under usage methods of depreciation, the depreciation charge can be zero while there is no production.

58. The future economic benefits embodied in an asset are consumed by an enterprise principally through its use. However, other factors, such as technical or commercial obsolescence and wear and tear while an asset remains idle, often result in the diminution of the economic benefits that might have been obtained from the asset. Consequently, all the following factors are considered in determining the useful life of an asset:

(a) expected usage of the asset. Usage is assessed by reference to the expected capacity or physical output of the asset.

(b) expected physical wear and tear, which depends on operational factors such as the number of shifts for which the asset is to be used and the repair and maintenance programme, and the care and maintenance of the asset while idle.

(c) technical or commercial obsolescence arising from changes or improvements in production, or from a change in the market demand for the product or service output of the asset. Expected future reductions in the selling price of an item that was produced using an asset could indicate the expectation of technical or commercial obsolescence of the asset, which, in turn, might reflect a reduction of the future economic benefits embodied in the asset.

(d) legal or similar limits on the use of the asset, such as the expiry dates of related leases.

59. The useful life of an asset is defined in terms of its expected utility to the enterprise. The asset management policy of the enterprise may involve the disposal of assets after a specified time or after consumption of a specified proportion of the future economic benefits embodied in the asset. Therefore, the useful life of an asset may be shorter than its economic life. The estimation of the useful life of the asset is a matter of judgement based on the experience of the enterprise with similar assets.

60. Land and buildings are separable assets and are accounted for separately, even when they are acquired together. With some exceptions, such as quarries and sites used for landfill, land has an unlimited useful life and therefore is not depreciated. Buildings have a limited useful life and therefore are depreciable assets. An increase in the value of the land on which a building stands does not affect the determination of the depreciable amount of the building.

61. If the cost of land includes the costs of site dismantlement, removal and restoration, that portion of the land asset is depreciated over the period of benefits obtained by incurring those costs. In some cases, the land itself may have a limited useful life, in which case it is depreciated in a manner that reflects the benefits to be derived from it.

Depreciation Method

62. The depreciation method used should reflect the pattern in which the future economic benefits of the asset are expected to be consumed by the enterprise.

63. The depreciation method applied to an asset should be reviewed at least at each financial year-end and, if there has been a significant change in the expected pattern of consumption of the future economic benefits embodied in the asset, the method should be changed to reflect the changed pattern. Such a change should be accounted for as a change in an accounting estimate in accordance with AS 5.

64. A variety of depreciation methods can be used to allocate the depreciable amount of an asset on a systematic basis over its useful life. These methods include the straight-line method, the diminishing balance method and the units of production method. Straight-line depreciation results in a constant charge over the useful life if the residual value of the asset does not change. The diminishing balance method results in a decreasing charge over the useful life. The units of production method results in a charge based on the expected use or output. The enterprise selects the method that most closely reflects the expected pattern of consumption of the future economic benefits embodied in the asset. That method is applied consistently from period to period unless there is a change in the expected pattern of consumption of those future

economic benefits or that the method is changed in accordance with the statute to best reflect the way the asset is consumed.

65. A depreciation method that is based on revenue that is generated by an activity that includes the use of an asset is not appropriate. The revenue generated by an activity that includes the use of an asset generally reflects factors other than the consumption of the economic benefits of the asset. For example, revenue is affected by other inputs and processes, selling activities and changes in sales volumes and prices. The price component of revenue may be affected by inflation, which has no bearing upon the way in which an asset is consumed.

Changes in Existing Decommissioning, Restoration and Other Liabilities

66. The cost of property, plant and equipment may undergo changes subsequent to its acquisition or construction on account of changes in liabilities, price adjustments, changes in duties, changes in initial estimates of amounts provided for dismantling, removing, restoration and similar factors and included in the cost of the asset in accordance with paragraph 16. Such changes in cost should be accounted for in accordance with paragraphs 67–68 below.

67. If the related asset is measured using the cost model:

(a) subject to (b), changes in the liability should be added to, or deducted from, the cost of the related asset in the current period.

(b) the amount deducted from the cost of the asset should not exceed its carrying amount. If a decrease in the liability exceeds the carrying amount of the asset, the excess should be recognised immediately in the statement of profit and loss.

(c) if the adjustment results in an addition to the cost of an asset, the enterprise should consider whether this is an indication that the new carrying amount of the asset may not be fully recoverable. If it is such an indication, the enterprise should test the asset for impairment by estimating its recoverable amount, and should account for any impairment loss, in accordance with AS 28.

68. If the related asset is measured using the revaluation model:

(a) changes in the liability alter the revaluation surplus or deficit previously recognised on that asset, so that:

(i) a decrease in the liability should (subject to (b)) be credited directly to revaluation surplus in the owners' interest, except that it should be recognised in the statement of profit and loss to the extent that it reverses a revaluation deficit on the asset that was previously recognised in the statement of profit and loss;

(ii) an increase in the liability should be recognised in the statement of profit and loss, except that it should be debited directly to revaluation surplus in the owners' interest to the extent of any credit balance existing in the revaluation surplus in respect of that asset.

(b) in the event that a decrease in the liability exceeds the carrying amount that would have been recognised had the asset been carried under the cost

model, the excess should be recognised immediately in the statement of profit and loss.

(c) a change in the liability is an indication that the asset may have to be revalued in order to ensure that the carrying amount does not differ materially from that which would be determined using fair value at the balance sheet date. Any such revaluation should be taken into account in determining the amounts to be taken to the statement of profit and loss and the owners' interest under (a). If a revaluation is necessary, all assets of that class should be revalued.

69. The adjusted depreciable amount of the asset is depreciated over its useful life. Therefore, once the related asset has reached the end of its useful life, all subsequent changes in the liability should be recognised in the statement of profit and loss as they occur. This applies under both the cost model and the revaluation model.

Impairment

70. To determine whether an item of property, plant and equipment is impaired, an enterprise applies AS 28, Impairment of Assets. AS 28 explains how an enterprise reviews the carrying amount of its assets, how it determines the recoverable amount of an asset, and when it recognises, or reverses the recognition of, an impairment loss.

Compensation for Impairment

71. Compensation from third parties for items of property, plant and equipment that were impaired, lost or given up should be included in the statement of profit and loss when the compensation becomes receivable.

72. Impairments or losses of items of property, plant and equipment, related claims for or payments of compensation from third parties and any subsequent purchase or construction of replacement assets are separate economic events and are accounted for separately as follows:

(a) impairments of items of property, plant and equipment are recognised in accordance with AS 28;

(b) derecognition of items of property, plant and equipment retired or disposed of is determined in accordance with this Standard;

(c) compensation from third parties for items of property, plant and equipment that were impaired, lost or given up is included in determining profit or loss when it becomes receivable; and

(d) the cost of items of property, plant and equipment restored, purchased or constructed as replacements is determined in accordance with this Standard.

Retirements

73. Items of property, plant and equipment retired from active use and held for disposal should be stated at the lower of their carrying amount and net realisable value. Any write-down in this regard should be recognised immediately in the statement of profit and loss.

Derecognition

74. ***The carrying amount of an item of property, plant and equipment should be derecognised***

(a) on disposal; or

(b) when no future economic benefits are expected from its use or disposal.

75. ***The gain or loss arising from the derecognition of an item of property, plant and equipment should be included in the statement of profit and loss when the item is derecognised (unless AS 19, Leases, requires otherwise on a sale and leaseback). Gains should not be classified as revenue, as defined in AS 9, Revenue Recognition.***

76. ***However, an enterprise that in the course of its ordinary activities, routinely sells items of property, plant and equipment that it had held for rental to others should transfer such assets to inventories at their carrying amount when they cease to be rented and become held for sale. The proceeds from the sale of such assets should be recognised in revenue in accordance with AS 9, Revenue Recognition.***

77. The disposal of an item of property, plant and equipment may occur in a variety of ways (e.g. by sale, by entering into a finance lease or by donation). In determining the date of disposal of an item, an enterprise applies the criteria in AS 9 for recognising revenue from the sale of goods. AS 19, Leases, applies to disposal by a sale and leaseback.

78. If, under the recognition principle in paragraph 7, an enterprise recognises in the carrying amount of an item of property, plant and equipment the cost of a replacement for part of the item, then it derecognises the carrying amount of the replaced part regardless of whether the replaced part had been depreciated separately. If it is not practicable for an enterprise to determine the carrying amount of the replaced part, it may use the cost of the replacement as an indication of what the cost of the replaced part was at the time it was acquired or constructed.

79. The gain or loss arising from the derecognition of an item of property, plant and equipment should be determined as the difference between the net disposal proceeds, if any, and the carrying amount of the item.

80. The consideration receivable on disposal of an item of property, plant and equipment is recognised in accordance with the principles enunciated in AS 9.

Disclosure

81. ***The financial statements should disclose, for each class of property, plant and equipment:***

(a) the measurement bases (i.e., cost model or revaluation model) used for determining the gross carrying amount;

(b) the depreciation methods used;

(c) the useful lives or the depreciation rates used. In case the useful lives or the depreciation rates used are different from those specified in the statute governing the enterprise, it should make a specific mention of that fact;

(d) ***the gross carrying amount and the accumulated depreciation (aggregated with accumulated impairment losses) at the beginning and end of the period; and***

(e) ***a reconciliation of the carrying amount at the beginning and end of the period showing:***

(i) ***additions;***

(ii) ***assets retired from active use and held for disposal;***

(iii) ***acquisitions through business combinations ;***

(iv) ***increases or decreases resulting from revaluations under paragraphs 34, 42 and 43 and from impairment losses recognised or reversed directly in revaluation surplus in accordance with AS 28;***

(v) ***impairment losses recognised in the statement of profit and loss in accordance with AS 28;***

(vi) ***impairment losses reversed in the statement of profit and loss in accordance with AS 28;***

(vii) ***depreciation;***

(viii) ***the net exchange differences arising on the translation of the financial statements of a non-integral foreign operation in accordance with AS 11, The Effects of Changes in Foreign Exchange Rates; and***

(ix) ***other changes.***

82. The financial statements should also disclose:

(a) ***the existence and amounts of restrictions on title, and property, plant and equipment pledged as security for liabilities;***

(b) ***the amount of expenditure recognised in the carrying amount of an item of property, plant and equipment in the course of its construction;***

(c) ***the amount of contractual commitments for the acquisition of property, plant and equipment;***

(d) ***if it is not disclosed separately on the face of the statement of profit and loss, the amount of compensation from third parties for items of property, plant and equipment that were impaired, lost or given up that is included in the statement of profit and loss; and***

(e) ***the amount of assets retired from active use and held for disposal.***

83. Selection of the depreciation method and estimation of the useful life of assets are matters of judgement. Therefore, disclosure of the methods adopted and the estimated useful lives or depreciation rates provides users of financial statements with information that allows them to review the policies selected by management and enables comparisons to be made with other enterprises. For similar reasons, it is necessary to disclose:

(a) depreciation, whether recognised in the statement of profit and loss or as a part of the cost of other assets, during a period; and

(b) accumulated depreciation at the end of the period.

84. In accordance with AS 5, an enterprise discloses the nature and effect of a change in an accounting estimate that has an effect in the current period or is expected to have an effect in subsequent periods. For property, plant and equipment, such disclosure may arise from changes in estimates with respect to:

(a) residual values;

(b) the estimated costs of dismantling, removing or restoring items of property, plant and equipment;

(c) useful lives; and

(d) depreciation methods.

85. If items of property, plant and equipment are stated at revalued amounts, the following should be disclosed:

(a) the effective date of the revaluation;

(b) whether an independent valuer was involved;

(c) the methods and significant assumptions applied in estimating fair values of the items;

(d) the extent to which fair values of the items were determined directly by reference to observable prices in an active market or recent market transactions on arm's length terms or were estimated using other valuation techniques; and

(e) the revaluation surplus, indicating the change for the period and any restrictions on the distribution of the balance to shareholders.

86. In accordance with AS 28, an enterprise discloses information on impaired property, plant and equipment in addition to the information required by paragraph 81 (e), (iv), (v) and (vi).

87. An enterprise is encouraged to disclose the following:

(a) the carrying amount of temporarily idle property, plant and equipment;

(b) the gross carrying amount of any fully depreciated property, plant and equipment that is still in use;

(c) for each revalued class of property, plant and equipment, the carrying amount that would have been recognised had the assets been carried under the cost model;

(d) the carrying amount of property, plant and equipment retired from active use and not held for disposal.

Transitional Provisions

88. Where an entity has in past recognized an expenditure in the statement of profit and loss which is eligible to be included as a part of the cost of a project for construction of property, plant and equipment in accordance with the requirements of paragraph 9, it may do so retrospectively for such a project. The effect of such retrospective application of this requirement, should be recognised net-of-tax in revenue reserves.

89. The requirements of paragraphs 26-28 regarding the initial measurement of an item of property, plant and equipment acquired in an exchange of assets transaction should be applied prospectively only to transactions entered into after this Standard becomes mandatory.

90. On the date of this Standard becoming mandatory, the spare parts, which hitherto were being treated as inventory under AS 2, Valuation of Inventories, and are now required to be capitalised in accordance with the requirements of this Standard, should be capitalised at their respective carrying amounts. The spare parts so capitalised should be depreciated over their remaining useful lives prospectively as per the requirements of this Standard.

91. The requirements of paragraph 32 and paragraphs 34 – 44 regarding the revaluation model should be applied prospectively. In case, on the date of this Standard becoming mandatory, an enterprise does not adopt the revaluation model as its accounting policy but the carrying amount of item(s) of property, plant and equipment reflects any previous revaluation it should adjust the amount outstanding in the revaluation reserve against the carrying amount of that item. However, the carrying amount of that item should never be less than residual value. Any excess of the amount outstanding as revaluation reserve over the carrying amount of that item should be adjusted in revenue reserves".